The Making and Unmaking
of a Revolutionary Family

Jeffersonian America

Jan Ellen Lewis, Peter S. Onuf, and James Horn, Editors

The Making and Unmaking of a Revolutionary Family *The Tuckers of Virginia, 1752–1830*

PHILLIP HAMILTON

University of Virginia Press
Charlottesville and London

UNIVERSITY OF VIRGINIA PRESS
© 2003 by the Rector and Visitors of the University of Virginia
All rights reserved
Printed in the United States of America on acid-free paper

First published 2003

9 8 7 6 5 4 3 2 1

Library of Congress Cataloging-in-Publication Data
Hamilton, Phillip, 1961–
    The making and unmaking of a Revolutionary family : the Tuckers of Virginia,
1752–1830 / Phillip Hamilton.
        p.   cm.   —(Jeffersonian America)
Includes bibliographical references and index.
    ISBN 0-8139-2164-3 (acid-free paper)
    1. Tucker family.   2. Tucker, St. George, 1752–1827.   3. Gentry—Virginia—
Biography.   4. Plantation life—Virginia.   5. Gentry—Virginia—Social conditions.   6. Family—Virginia—History.   7. Virginia—Social conditions—18th
century.   8. Virginia—Social conditions—19th century.   9. Virginia—History—Revolution, 1775–1783—Social aspects.   10. United States—History—
Revolution, 1775–1783—Social aspects.   I. Title.   II. Series.
    F225 .H215 2003
    975.5′0086′21—dc21

                                                                    2002153277

For Chris

Contents

Illustrations

Acknowledgments

This study has benefited enormously from the help and advice of many people. I wish especially to thank David Thomas Konig, who brought the Tucker family to my attention more than a decade ago as a possible dissertation topic. Not only did David serve as a sterling graduate adviser, giving me the time and counsel needed to see the dissertation through to completion, but he also helped and encouraged me afterwards as I revised the work into a publishable book.

Daniel Blake Smith assisted me at various stages of my efforts. He provided me with valuable advice on the Tucker family's complex relationship with slavery and later read a significant portion of the nearly completed manuscript. Dan has at all times given me both intelligent guidance and strong support for my ideas. Iver Bernstein's keen understanding of the complexities of the early Republic and the antebellum era persuaded me to explore all the implications of what I found in the Tuckers' letters, journals, and other materials. Robert J. Brugger willingly and patiently answered my many questions about the Tuckers and their place in early national Virginia. Peter H. Griffin, my former colleague at Lindenwood University, generously read the entire manuscript and offered many useful suggestions and recommendations. I would also like to thank Richard Holway of the University of Virginia Press. Dick was interested in the story of the Tuckers from the start, and he remained supportive and patient as I completed the manuscript. I have greatly profited from the helpful comments and criticisms of a number of other scholars, including Rowland Berthoff, Douglas Egerton, Eugene Genovese, James Horn, Michael Jarvis, Richard L. John, Gary J. Kornblith, David Moltke-Hansen, Philip D. Morgan, Raymond Scupin, James Sidbury, Linda Sturtz, and Len Travers. And I cannot forget to thank my fellow members of the St. George Tucker Society for their insights.

The staffs of many research depositories have been gracious in providing both assistance in my work and congenial settings in which to pursue research. In particular, Margaret Cook and her staff at the Swem Library at the College of William and Mary were exceptionally helpful and cooperative. Margaret's knowledge of the Tucker family and its manuscripts is unparalleled. She always put up with my repeated queries and many requests for help with kindness and thoughtfulness. Her efforts and especially her friendship are deeply appreciated. Frances Pollard and her staff at the Virginia Historical Society, moreover, were most accommodating and courteous during several productive research trips to Richmond. The assistance given to me by these library staffs demonstrates that the "old Virginia spirit of hospitality" is alive and well. This project also would have never been completed had it not been for the steady assistance of the interlibrary loan staffs at Washington University in St. Louis and the College of William and Mary, particularly in obtaining the microfilmed copies of the Tucker-Coleman Papers. I wish to thank the Manuscripts and Rare Books Department of the Earl Gregg Swem Library at the College of William and Mary for permission to quote from the Tucker-Coleman Papers.

Surviving members of the Tucker family contributed in many ways to this study. Robert Dennard Tucker is a dedicated and talented genealogist who shared with me his book, *The Descendants of William Tucker*. My copy of this work is well-worn, indicating just how much I learned from it. Cynthia Barlowe, whose mother, Dr. Janet Kimbrough, was a Tucker descendant, gave me a long and informative tour of the St. George Tucker house in Williamsburg. Cynthia also provided me with many of the negatives of pictures that appear in this book. I would also like to thank Raymond D. Kimbrough Jr. and Erich Kimbrough for their kind permission in allowing me to reproduce several family portraits.

The Virginia Historical Society provided two Andrew W. Mellon Research Fellowships, which allowed me to commence and continue my research. In addition, Washington University provided me with a Research Fellowship, which permitted me to complete the project in a more timely fashion.

Portions of chapters 1 and 3 have appeared in "Education in the St. George Tucker Household: Change and Continuity in Jeffersonian Virginia," *Virginia Magazine of History and Biography* 102 (April 1994): 167–92, and are reprinted by permission of the Virginia Historical Society. Portions of chapters 5 and 6 were previously published in "Revolutionary Principles and Family Loyalties: Slavery's Transformation in the St. George

Tucker Household of Early National Virginia," *William and Mary Quarterly*, 3d ser., 55 (Oct. 1998): 531–56, and are reprinted by permission of the Omohundro Institute of Early American History and Culture.

Members of my own family, more than anyone else, know that this book has been a collective endeavor. Their help and encouragement have been truly invaluable, reminding me time and again how important families are, regardless of the century. My mother, Catherine Hamilton, has always provided me with enthusiastic support in all my endeavors. My two sons, Tommy and Jake, have greatly enriched my life. Indeed, I do not know how I could have fully described the Tuckers' feelings for their children without delving into my own emotions for these two wonderful boys. Finally, I owe the most to my wife, Chris. She not only read the entire manuscript and provided me with superb editorial feedback, but her ongoing love and confidence are what really made this study possible.

The Tuckers of Bermuda

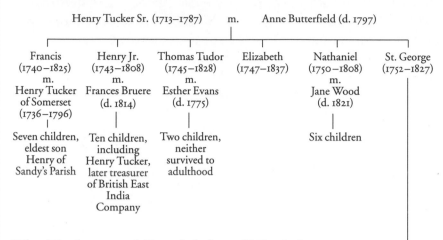

Henry Tucker Sr. (1713–1787) m. Anne Butterfield (d. 1797)

Francis
(1740–1825)
m.
Henry Tucker
of Somerset
(1736–1796)

Seven children,
eldest son
Henry of
Sandy's Parish

Henry Jr.
(1743–1808)
m.
Frances Bruere
(d. 1814)

Ten children,
including
Henry Tucker,
later treasurer
of British East
India
Company

Thomas Tudor
(1745–1828)
m.
Esther Evans
(d. 1775)

Two children,
neither
survived to
adulthood

Elizabeth
(1747–1837)

Nathaniel
(1750–1808)
m.
Jane Wood
(d. 1821)

Six children

St. George
(1752–1827)

The Tuckers and Randolphs of Virginia

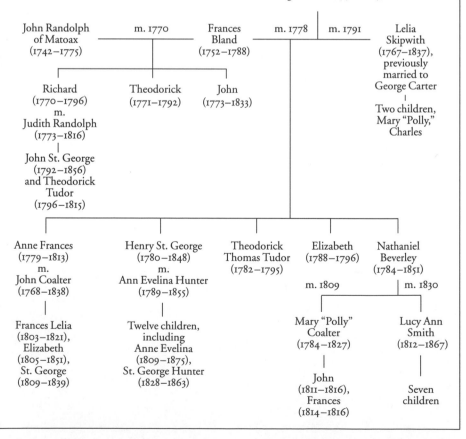

St. George Tucker (1752–1827)

John Randolph
of Matoax
(1742–1775)   m. 1770   Frances
Bland
(1752–1788)   m. 1778   m. 1791   Lelia
Skipwith
(1767–1837),
previously
married to
George Carter

Two children,
Mary "Polly,"
Charles

Richard
(1770–1796)
m.
Judith Randolph
(1773–1816)

John St. George
(1792–1856)
and Theodorick
Tudor
(1796–1815)

Theodorick
(1771–1792)

John
(1773–1833)

Anne Frances
(1779–1813)
m.
John Coalter
(1768–1838)

Frances Lelia
(1803–1821),
Elizabeth
(1805–1851),
St. George
(1809–1839)

Henry St. George
(1780–1848)
m.
Ann Evelina Hunter
(1789–1855)

Twelve children,
including
Anne Evelina
(1809–1875),
St. George Hunter
(1828–1863)

**Theodorick
Thomas Tudor**
(1782–1795)

Elizabeth
(1788–1796)

m. 1809

Mary "Polly"
Coalter
(1784–1827)

John
(1811–1816),
Frances
(1814–1816)

**Nathaniel
Beverley**
(1784–1851)

m. 1830

Lucy Ann
Smith
(1812–1867)

Seven
children

The Making and Unmaking
of a Revolutionary Family

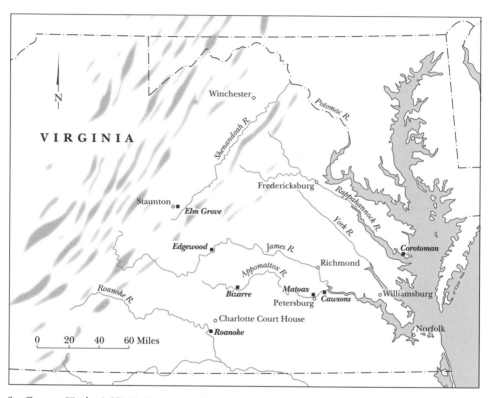

St. George Tucker's Virginia, 1771–1827

Introduction

In mid-April 1814 Virginia congressman John Randolph of Roanoke brooded over his family's decline since the Revolution. Staying with a friend in Richmond, the unmarried and childless politician remembered how his tobacco-growing ancestors had once dominated the state politically, socially, and economically. They had lived in sumptuous surroundings, Randolph recalled, owning great mansions, ornate carriages, and beautiful furnishings and being served by slaves imported from Africa. When his mind turned to the present, however, all was dark and depressing. Not only did his branch of the Randolph clan face extinction upon his death, but much of his family's land, wealth, and power had vanished since the war with Great Britain. Larger social concerns added to his anxieties. From Randolph's point of view, the deep bonds of kinship that had once united and strengthened the great planter class seemed to be crumbling. Democratic leveling at home and an overweening federal government in Washington, D.C., also appeared to be crushing the values and customs of old.

Three weeks before his Richmond visit, Randolph's gloom had deepened when he traveled to Cawsons, the once-magnificent estate of his maternal grandfather, Theodorick Bland Sr. (1708–1784). The visit to the mansion, prominently situated near the confluence of the James and Appomattox Rivers, initially had invigorated the forty-year-old Randolph. "The sight of the noble sheet of water in front of the house seemed to revive me," he wrote to a friend soon afterwards. "The scenes of my early youth were renewed."[1] Before the Revolution, Cawsons had been a "spacious," hospitable seat of "taste and elegance," its occupant a respected member of Virginia's glittering planter aristocracy, one of a race of gentlemen who were, according to Randolph, loyal, refined, and "well-educated."[2] During the trip Randolph may also have thought about Matoax, the great plantation of his father, John Randolph Sr., located upriver across from Petersburg. To the congressman his father had embodied the fundamental virtues of Virginia's old gentry: commitment to landed property, belief in personal independence, and passionate devotion to family.

Randolph's fond memories were short-lived. As if descending into a gothic novel, he explained that "when the boat struck the beach [at Cawsons], all was sad and desolate. The fires of ancient hospitality were long since extinguished, the hearthstone cold. Here was my mother given in marriage, and here was I born; once the seat of plenty and cheerfulness, associated with my earliest and tenderest recollections, now mute and deserted." As he strode across the mansion's yard, a single "old gray-headed domestic" appeared to see if the congressman wanted anything. The slave's presence, Randolph noted, rendered his own "solitude" even more stark. Like Matoax, Cawsons had passed out of the family's hands two decades before to men Randolph thought inferior in birth, rank, and manners. In addition to his own family's decline, he saw eastern Virginia itself, once the landed gentry's center of power, sinking into obscurity. "Nothing . . . can be more melancholy than the aspect of the whole country on Tidewater," he concluded, with "dismantled county seats, ruinous churches, fields forsaken and grown up with mournful evergreens, cedar, and pine."[3]

From his friend's lodgings, Randolph searched for the reasons behind his family's decline and the collapse of the state's Revolutionary gentry. Why had this noble world of planter gentlemen, familial loyalties, and elegant estates vanished? In his efforts to grasp the changes about him, Randolph fixated on his stepfather and onetime guardian, the well-known jurist St. George Tucker.

Tucker had married John Randolph's widowed mother, Frances Bland Randolph, during the Revolution. Born in Bermuda in 1752, he belonged to a wealthy, close-knit, and well-connected merchant-shipping family that did business throughout the Atlantic world. Tucker's father sent him to the Old Dominion in 1771 to study law at the College of William and Mary. Upon arriving, the youth found a confident and stable plantation society dominated by powerful gentry clans that cherished land, slaves, and close connections to one another. In Williamsburg, Tucker soon built close ties to some of the colony's most powerful families, and after the war with Great Britain erupted, he helped to smuggle arms and supplies into the new nation. Following his marriage, moreover, he joined the state militia and fought in several key campaigns.

After the conflict Tucker ardently wished to use the lands he controlled to become a great tobacco planter. With his wife's assistance and with the aid of nearby tidewater kin, he attempted to prosper by means of the economic practices and customs of the late colonial era. But Tucker soon found that the Revolution had unleashed a host of changes which significantly undermined the power of the state's gentry. Substantial debts incurred before the war came due, and overseas tobacco markets failed to regain the vitality they had possessed before 1775. Independence unleashed other forces that members of the elite found difficult to handle—political democratization, economic change, accelerated westward expansion—all of which steadily undermined their authority and influence. As the years passed, the utility of extended kinship ties and social connections dramatically eroded as individuals were forced more and more to fend for themselves, their spouses, and their children. The broad-based family alliances of the prewar era had become untenable.

Understanding the magnitude of these changes, St. George Tucker took steps to protect his family. In the post-Revolutionary period, he educated his children, stepsons, and other kin to abandon the old gentry's fundamental precepts—reliance on kinship connections, expected deference from the lower social ranks, and even land ownership—in order to survive. To preserve family wealth, power, and prestige in a rapidly changing world, Tucker sold off his own plantations and demanded a more individualistic course. He told family members that they must now rely on their own talents, education, and training in order to succeed. After seeing many families in the planter class "reduced to wretchedness," Tucker told one young cousin, "If there was a period in the History of Man which demonstrated the necessity of a Man's being able to place his reliance on *Himself,* the last thirty years may be considered as furnishing the most awful and instructive Lessons upon that Head."[4] Tucker particularly urged the rising generation to pursue careers in the learned professions—especially the law—to support families without depending on either extended kin or unprofitable plantations. In essence, he proposed a radically different strategy to cope with the winds of change that ensued after the War for Independence.

In the spring of 1814, however, with much of his patrimony gone and with the Randolph family's power a fading memory, John turned on his stepfather with a ferocious bitterness. Ignoring the substantial debts of his own father and the broader economic changes that had swept Virginia, Randolph blamed Tucker for almost everything that had gone wrong over the passing years. Writing a long, hostile letter from his friend's rooms, he declared, "I have been . . . treated [by you] with injustice." Randolph accused his stepfather of squandering and embezzling the land, property, and slaves that Tucker had managed during John's and his two, now-deceased, brothers' minority. John was sure that Tucker had illegally used this patrimony to benefit himself and his own biological children, leaving his stepsons out in the cold. Thus, Tucker had come to personify all the changes Randolph hated in early nineteenth-century Virginia: the decline of extended family loyalties, the abandonment of landed property, and the growth of excessive individuality and greed. Therefore, he announced his determination "to drop an intercourse which it is painful to keep up." [5] A devastated Tucker could only sputter that if Randolph felt himself ill-used, he could seek redress in the state's courts. Despite Tucker's proud front, he never understood the true reasons for his stepson's break. The split proved permanent, as the two men neither saw nor corresponded with one another again.

At first glance the break between St. George Tucker and John Randolph seems only a minor incident in the history of the early Republic. But the bitter parting of these two figures reveals a great deal about the Old Dominion after the Revolution. The War for Independence clearly left few aspects of public and private life unaltered. Like many Virginians, Tucker and Randolph struggled to come to grips with the events that spun out of the war, when the British-American society in which their families had once prospered died and when a new and more democratic nation emerged.

This book explores two generations of the Tucker family in order to examine important questions regarding the Revolution's paradoxical legacy in Virginia: Why did its leading planter families decline after their great victory over the British Empire? How did members of the gentry respond both privately and publicly to the evaporation of their power? In other words, how did they make sense of and cope with the momentous changes around them, both inside and outside their households? How did they alter their ways and outlook on life? Furthermore, why did Virginia's leading figures who were deeply influenced by the eighteenth-century Enlightenment turn so profoundly conservative and pessimistic in the early nineteenth century? Finally, what are the larger implications of these developments for Virginia's early national history? Indeed, what do the Tuckers' experiences and reactions tell us about the state's complex transition from the Revolutionary age to the antebellum era?

Like all works of history, this one is built upon a foundation of earlier scholarship which has deepened our understanding of the Revolution's impact on America's development. Over the past decade, for instance, a number of well-received studies have celebrated the "radical" changes that followed the conflict, changes that fundamentally altered the new United States in political, social, and geographic terms. Some histories have explored the metamorphosis that took place within middle-class culture, with average citizens gaining more affluent lifestyles, refined manners, and political assertiveness. One scholar even sees the extreme commercial-mindedness of ordinary Americans as a direct result of liberty from Great Britain. Common to these books, however, is their penchant to write Virginia and the South out of the American mainstream. Whenever the region is mentioned in the context of the post-Revolutionary period, southerners are portrayed as odd aberrations to the national norm, inexplicably conservative, driven by slavery, and not at all like their entrepreneurial countrymen to the north.[6]

Historians of the South, on the other hand, remind us that the region remained politically, economically, and intellectually dynamic in the years between the Revolution and Civil War. Old Dominion presidents long dominated the federal government's executive branch, and the state's congressional delegation was the nation's largest until 1820.[7] Several works have explored the antebellum South's political economy and its increasing divergence from the industrializing North. These studies describe a profoundly agrarian region which adhered to patriarchal norms after the Revolution with goals focused not on maximized profits within a market economy but on strong paternalistic relationships both inside the home and throughout society.[8] Others argue that the South's farmers and planters embraced capitalism and made economic decisions based on rational evaluations of the marketplace's demands.[9] Historians examining the South's intellectual patterns over time have discovered two differing systems of thought for two very different time periods. Whereas leaders of the Revolutionary South largely embraced the Enlightenment and the liberal ideals contained in the nation's founding documents, antebellum southerners later rejected such notions and instead adopted conservative values predicated on the inherent inequality of human beings and the superiority of the white race.[10] These varied works have considerably increased our understanding of the region, but overall they fail to explain the South's evolution through the Jeffersonian period. There remains little understanding of the process of change, about exactly how and why southerners abandoned one set of beliefs and took up another.

Social historians dealing with the family and gender relations have greatly expanded our understanding of southern households. Some scholars of the family view the early national age through the lens of continuity and argue that patriarchal ties born in the eighteenth century persisted in binding men and women together until the Civil War. Before and after the Revolution, wives and daughters found themselves dominated by their menfolk while occupying distinctly inferior positions in their homes.[11] On the other hand, a growing number of studies point to the rise of intimate affection between marriage partners and among parents and children based on love, equality, and mutual respect. This intensification of personal relationships is frequently linked to larger social developments that swept through the Western world during the early modern period.[12]

I have chosen to focus on a single family in order to elucidate the general trends that reshaped Virginia. Although no family can ever be regarded as truly typical, the Tuckers are a worthwhile group for study. Over the course of six decades, St. George Tucker meticulously saved nearly every piece of correspondence that came into his hands, and he taught other family members to do the same. These manuscripts form the Tucker-Coleman Papers at the College of William and Mary and comprise one of the richest archives in the nation for the study of the Revolutionary, Jeffersonian, and antebellum eras. In hundreds of letters to one another and in the many other documents they preserved, the Tuckers were remarkably articulate about their personal lives and about the larger events surrounding them.

The Tuckers also engaged in an extraordinarily wide range of activities over the years: they fought in wars, pursued professional careers, served in political office, raised and educated children, managed plantations and slaves, and pushed westward along with many others into lands beyond the Appalachians. Furthermore, they possessed a wide circle of important friends, acquaintances, and connections, including George Wythe, John Page, and James Monroe, with whom they shared their insights, ideas, and frustrations. Thus, the Tuckers' story has much to tell us about the great events of the age and how these developments profoundly reshaped individual lives.[13]

The Tuckers additionally provide a window into how early republican families operated. The family is an important prism through which to understand eighteenth- and nineteenth-century individuals. People during these decades often organized their identities and viewed their destinies as inherently linked to their membership in a larger familial unit. When nineteen-year-old St. George Tucker sailed for Virginia before the Revolution, he knew very well that he would be judged not simply as a well-mannered young gentleman but as an emissary of his large Bermuda clan. In the 1770s the family was hardly the intensely private emotional unit it would later become; at the outset of the War for Independence, the family was more a public than a private institution. Although kinship bonds provided people with love and comfort, such ties more importantly furnished essential jobs, connections, and economic assistance. In the Jeffersonian age, however, as the founders' generation gave way to the next, family life underwent a period of rapid and permanent change, with kinship networks declining and the nuclear family emerging as a sentimental haven from a bewildering public arena.[14] Therefore, examining this one clan helps us to understand how the large families of the era functioned and how the events of the late eighteenth and early nineteenth centuries changed them forever.

Finally, this book unapologetically focuses on the elites of these times. Compelling histories have recently been written revealing the complex and extraordinary contributions ordinary people have made to America's development, and the Tuckers' interactions with those they viewed as socially and racially beneath them are hardly ignored here. Nevertheless, the Old Dominion remained a hierarchical society throughout the early Republic, despite cries to the contrary by some contemporary Virginians. The members of the Tucker clan and those in their circle remained influential people who helped lead the state throughout the entire era and beyond. Therefore, their actions and unfolding beliefs reveal much about Virginia's and the South's overall development.

One

Family Ambitions within the Realm

On 3 December 1771 Henry Tucker Jr. wrote from his family's count-inghouse in Bermuda to his youngest brother, St. George Tucker. The younger Tucker had sailed from the island several months beforehand to pursue a legal education at the College of William and Mary in Virginia. Knowing his nineteen-year-old brother's good "Heart" and superior "intel-lectual Abilities," Henry had "not a doubt" that St. George would answer "the most sanguine Expectations of their Friends." But Henry pointedly re-minded his brother that upon leaving home and Bermuda, he had entered the "grand Theatre of the World." Through his activities abroad, Henry told St. George, he should not simply pursue "Credit and Reputation" for himself, but more importantly he must strive to bring "Honor to their Family." [1]

In the mid-eighteenth century the Tucker brothers belonged to a con-fident, ambitious, and prominent clan whose members lived at the very center of Great Britain's Atlantic empire. Led by their father, Henry Tucker Sr., a merchant-shipper and politician, the family had firmly established it-self on the island. The Tuckers' position had been gained over the decades not because of the efforts of any one individual but rather out of a collective determination to advance the entire family's fortunes. Like many elites in Britain's pre-Revolutionary empire, the Tuckers defined family in the broadest sense possible, believing that all kin members together formed a large corporate entity. In their minds family included not just members of the conjugal unit—parents and children—but extended and affinal relations as well, including uncles, aunts, cousins, nephews, nieces, and so on. Before the Revolution the Tuckers greatly depended on these extensive kin networks. Drawing few distinctions between their public and private lives, they derived love and affection as well as vital economic and political connections from a broadly conceived kin universe.

After the Seven Years' War ended in 1763, Henry Tucker Sr., often referred to as "the Colonel," his Bermuda militia rank, had great ambitions for his extended family. With business and social ties stretching across the Atlantic in both directions, he aimed to expand his family's influence well beyond the island, to London and the British Isles and west to the empire's increasingly prosperous North American colonies. To accomplish his goals, the Colonel vigorously cultivated his mercantile connections abroad, transmitted the importance of familial loyalty to the rising generation, and presented his family to the world as a model of cosmopolitan gentility and intellectual refinement. Mercantile profits, family attachments, and genteel behavior, he hoped, would earn the Tuckers respect, honor, and preferment in Britain's highest circles.

Despite Tucker Sr.'s plans, the post–Seven Years' War period proved difficult and tumultuous. During the 1760s and early 1770s, British rule throughout the Atlantic disintegrated, and the Tuckers confronted great challenges to their social standing at home and trading enterprises abroad. Family members nonetheless always remembered that their collective interests were inherently tied together. In the opening years of the Revolutionary crisis, the Tuckers repeatedly worked and cooperated together as a unit to maintain their economic position and social reputation. They emotionally supported one another, moreover, in efforts to cope with and adjust to their perplexing times.

The Tuckers' presence in Bermuda stretched back almost to the beginning of English colonization when a distant ancestor, Captain Daniel Tucker, served as the colony's second governor from 1616 to 1619. Following Daniel's tenure, two brothers named George and Daniel Tucker of Milton in Kent County purchased twenty shares of the Somers Island Company, the joint-stock corporation that organized settlement efforts in Bermuda during the first half of the seventeenth century. The first Tucker to settle permanently on Bermuda was a royalist named George Tucker, who arrived on the island in the late 1640s. Heir to the Somers Island shares, George wished to develop the family's investment in the New World while at the same time he escaped from Parliamentarians who had just triumphed over the king.[2] He was joined by a relative named Henry Tucker, and both men quickly won positions in the island's government: George became a member of the governor's council, while Henry served for many years as the colony's secretary. Throughout the seventeenth and eighteenth centuries, the family proliferated on the island and its wealth, power, and influence grew apace. Not only did Tuckers occupy key positions in the colonial government, but they also participated in the maritime commerce spawned by global wars and commercial development. By the mid-1700s this Bermuda clan was large, affluent, and politically powerful.[3]

Colonel Henry Tucker Sr., great-grandson of George Tucker, was born in 1713. Tucker matured at a propitious time in British history. During the first half century of his life, the royal government centered in London built "a new kind of empire" across the globe, one that was territorially large with extensive possessions in North America, the Caribbean, and India. Between 1655 and 1763 its size grew fivefold. Great Britain's population grew dramatically as well: England itself went from 5 million inhabitants in 1700 to 8.6 million by 1800, while its North American population jumped from 250,000 individuals at the eighteenth century's outset to over 2 million when St. George Tucker arrived on the continent in 1771. This empire flourished in large part on the backs of hundreds of thousands of African and African-American slaves, who labored incessantly in the Caribbean and North America to earn profits for their white masters. Because the disposable incomes of whites were generally rising throughout the Atlantic and because the Royal Navy increasingly dominated global sea-lanes, Britain's commercial trade ballooned during the eighteenth century. European demand for New World tobacco, rice, sugar, molasses, and other products led to a skyrocketing demand in the colonies for both the manufactured goods of the mother country and ever more slaves from Africa.[4]

Bermuda's mid-eighteenth-century population stood at between 10,000 and 12,000, half white and half black, and the island fully participated in Britain's "new empire." Although tiny—fourteen miles from east to west and one mile wide—the fish-hooked shaped isle was noted for its tall and much-in-demand cedar trees. The shortage of land meant that settlers could sustain themselves only with subsistence agriculture and fishing. By the mid-1700s they had also gained fame as first-rate shipbuilders as nearly one hundred Bermudian-owned ships plied the Atlantic, trading lumber, food, and molasses between Virginia, the Bahamas, and the Leeward Islands. Yet the small size of Bermuda ships, with most under one hundred tons, limited direct trade with England, and the majority of islanders felt themselves distinctly isolated from the mother country. Distance from the center led many to violate (often blatantly) the empire's mercantile laws, with smugglers frequently trading restricted goods with foreign colonies and landing commodities on the island at night to avoid imperial duties.[5]

Bermudians most actively smuggled goods at the island's West End, away from the capital of St. George's. Above the beaches where smugglers off-loaded goods stood an elegant and imposing mansion, Colonel Tucker's seat in Southampton Parish that he named The Grove. Although the home, its extensive gardens and outbuildings are no longer extant, the Colonel's third son, St. George's lyrical brother Nathaniel, wrote of the estate in his 1774 poem called *The Bermudian:*

> Beneath my bending eye, serenely neat,
> Appears my ever-blest paternal seat.
> Far in front the level lawn extends,
> The zephyrs play, the nodding cypress bends,
> A little hillock stands on either side,
> O'verspead with evergreens, the garden's pride.
> Promiscuous here appears the blushing rose,
> The guava flourishes, the myrtle grows,
> Upon the surface earthborn woodbines creep,
> O'er the green beds the pointed sturtians peep,
> Their arms aloft triumphant lilacs bear
> And jessamines perfume the ambient air.[6]

Shrewd, ambitious, and well liked by fellow islanders, the master of The Grove likely determined as a young man that he and his family could and should dominate the colony. In 1738 Henry Tucker won the hand of Anne Butterfield, daughter of General Nathaniel Butterfield, Bermuda's chief justice and head of another powerful island clan. His marriage to Anne proved not only socially and politically advantageous but also prolific. During the 1740s and early 1750s, the couple had six children, all of whom reached adulthood: Frances (1740–1825), Henry Jr. (1743–1808), Thomas Tudor (1745–1828), Elizabeth (1747–1837), Nathaniel (1750–1807), and St. George (1752–1827). Tucker's main ambition dur-

Colonel Henry Tucker Sr. of The Grove, painting by Joseph Blackburn. (Courtesy of Bermuda National Trust Collection)

Anne Butterfield Tucker with two of her children, Frances and Nathaniel, painting by Joseph Blackburn. (Courtesy of Bermuda National Trust Collection)

ing these years was to advance the political status of his growing clan. He therefore won or purchased a colonelcy in the island's militia. Throughout the 1740s and 1750s, he served as the Speaker of the Bermuda Assembly and even spent several years as the colony's agent in London.[7]

Economic aspirations also drove Colonel Tucker. The "consumer boom" of the eighteenth century opened the doors of opportunity to ambitious men who sensed the possibilities contained in the Atlantic's emerging economic order. Establishing a merchant-shipping business, Colonel Tucker had his eye on participating in the empire's expanding trade. The Seven Years' War and the extraordinary resources the metropolis poured into the conflict bolstered opportunities for traders throughout the British-Atlantic world. During that war Colonel Tucker won the friendship and patronage of Bermuda's Governor William Popples, who guided many government contracts the family's way. Following the triumph of British arms in 1763, Tucker likely expected his economic horizons to continue expanding. Little is known about his specific activities, however, for businessmen of that period were not in the habit of keeping paper records of their dealings. Soon after the war ended, he brought his eldest son, Henry Jr., into the family business and formed the partnership of Henry Tucker & Son, with its countinghouse located in the colonial capital of St. George's.[8]

Recent studies of the family in the period surrounding the Revolution have greatly sharpened our understanding of its role and function in the Atlantic world. But scholars have disagreed regarding the course and timing of familial development. Some historians argue that the mid to late eighteenth century saw the emergence of the "modern" family, which concentrated on the conjugal unit inside the household and on the expression of love and affection among its members.[9] Others contend that from the colonial era to the Civil War, the family remained rigidly patriarchal, broadly structured, and well integrated into the larger society, especially in predominantly agrarian regions of the New World.[10]

The Tucker family at The Grove defies precise categorization. Like other elite clans within the empire, its members accepted the eighteenth century's traditional values and mores. Believing that all living entities, including human societies, were organized along hierarchical, not egalitarian, lines, they embraced the monarchy and their monarchical social order. In fact, the Tuckers understood and accepted what David Hume labeled the "long train of dependence" that descended downward from the king's person and linked all within the realm from George III at the top to African slaves at the bottom. In his *Commentaries*, William Blackstone listed over forty gradations of rank in British society.[11]

Family members believed that hierarchy and rank shaped relations inside the household as well. Indeed, British Americans generally considered their families to be reflections or microcosms of their larger social order. Therefore, members of The Grove recognized Henry Tucker Sr. as their sole patriarch, with all household members (including white servants and black slaves) arranged beneath him in a descending order of place and responsibility. Patriarchalism gained particular strength in the colonial world because of the overall lack of established legal and social institutions. Household heads imbued with great authority, it was thought, could better maintain order and gain a legitimacy they would have otherwise lacked.[12]

Although the Tuckers accepted patriarchalism within their household as perfectly natural, emotional relations among members of The Grove were warm, close, and affectionate. Some historians have argued that late colonial parents and children significantly restrained their love for one another. With strong authoritarian fathers at the helm, individuals communicated sentiments "formally" and used "mannered" and "stilted" language to express themselves to their closest loved ones.[13] Relationships within the Tucker family, however, point to a softer and gentler household environment. Throughout the late colonial era, family members did avoid passionate expressions of sentiment, but they clearly felt an abiding love for one another which they rarely hesitated to communicate. Indeed, they appeared happiest and most contented in each other's company. Anne Butterfield Tucker created a loving domestic environment at The Grove in which her children's well-being came first. Her sons and daughters reciprocated this love, often expressing their gratitude for having "experienced the inexpressible Tenderness of her Affection." Obedience to Tucker Sr.'s patriarchal commands, moreover, derived more from love than fear of his authority. Repeatedly calling him the "best of fathers" and "the most indulgent of fathers," Tucker's sons and daughters seemed primarily concerned with not hurting his feelings.[14] Colonel Tucker, in turn, attempted to exercise his power with compassion, restraint, and moderation. Only on rare occasions, when he felt unjustly slighted, did he demand outright deference as household head.[15] St. George, therefore, wrote largely of uninterrupted harmony at The Grove. When he briefly returned to the island after an extended absence, he wrote in his journal of "the Rapture" he anticipated "at the prospect of clasping the best of Parents, the most affectionate of Brothers, and the tenderest of sisters to my Breast. . . . In a few Hours shall I enjoy the most exquisite Happiness." [16]

The Tuckers were aware, though, that their family extended well beyond The Grove. Never seeing the nuclear unit as a refuge from the surrounding world, they embraced a broadly defined family unit with love, obligations, and duties expected of all kinsmen. Thus uncles, aunts, cousins, grandparents, and affinal kin gave and received affection as well as provided economic and political assistance. The Tuckers' attitudes reflect general trends within colonial society, for broadly defined families were present in the New World from the beginning of colonization. The unhealthiness of the southern and island colonies particularly demanded strong kin networks. During the seventeenth century two-thirds of the children there lost at least one parent before their eighteenth birthday; one-third lost both. As a result, colonial America had numerous orphans, widows, and widowers. Frequent remarriages created extraordinarily complex kinship ties, which, far from being tenuous, were strong in order to compensate for the fragility of nuclear relationships. These ties did not weaken when conditions became healthier in the early eighteenth century but grew stronger as colonial arrivistes imitated the patterns found in the mother country, where family connections and ties often determined an individual's success or failure. [17]

The Bermuda Tuckers expressed their familial loyalty and corporate identity as a clan in a number of ways. Members handed down traditional names with loving pride and affection—from father to son, mother to daughter, uncle to nephew, aunt to niece—with repetitions occurring even within the same generation. Colonel Tucker christened his first daughter Frances after his mother, while first son Henry was named after both the Colonel and his father. Anne and Henry Tucker chose the name Thomas Tudor for their second son to honor various kinsmen who lived in both Bermuda and New York. St. George inherited the name of his great-grandfather, who had been named after his mother's family. As in other eighteenth-century British-American families, the repetition of key names helped to perpetuate the Tuckers' lineage and provided continuity for members over the generations. [18]

Beyond names, Henry and Anne Tucker raised their children with the knowledge that they belonged to a broadly defined family unit and could identify closely with all inside it. A cousin of the Tuckers, Henry Hinson, once confessed: "Now my dear St. George, you know you and I have always liv'd more like Brothers than any thing Else. I have told you several secrets which [I] do think you never told them to any one." Frequent visits and dinners all together added to this intimacy. Nathaniel once joked to St. George that "Sister Bet [Elizabeth] has eaten so much of Aunt Hinsons roast Pig that she is quite lazy." Gifts between extended kin only increased this familial closeness. After several nieces and nephews had been born, St. George purchased children's spellers and readers for them, earning both their pledges of "Duty" and lifelong affection.[19]

Marriages both strengthened and extended familial bonds throughout the island. Recent scholars have argued that the heart played an increasingly significant role in marital decisions during the late colonial era, with economic considerations diminishing in importance.[20] Although love and affection greatly influenced the Tuckers' choices of mates, the needs of the corporate family still commanded attention. In the late 1750s the Colonel's eldest daughter, Frances, married her distant cousin Henry Tucker of Sandy's Parish or (as he was more commonly known) of Somerset Bridge. The marriage was a harmonious one until Henry's death in 1796, but more importantly the match brought these two branches of the Tucker clan closer together, a key consideration because Henry of Somerset was a partner in the successful Bermuda merchant-shipping firm of Jennings, Tucker & Company. In 1770, probably with the Colonel's strong encouragement, Henry Jr. married Frances Bruere, daughter of Bermuda governor George James Bruere. The match proved advantageous for both families. Bruere won a connection to the powerful clan and support in his dealings with the assembly; the Tuckers won government patronage. The year of the wedding, Governor Bruere appointed his new son-in-law the colony's treasurer. The next year, Henry Jr. and his cousin John Tudor earned appointments to the governor's council. Colonel Tucker later purchased the office of colonial secretary for Henry Jr. Nathaniel found himself named the council's clerk. Even St. George gained access to the governor's influence. In 1773, when the youngest Tucker was speculating about going to London for his education, Bruere informed the family, "The Governor will be very glad to find it in His power to render Him any Service either here, or when St. George goes to England."[21]

Following the Seven Years' War, Colonel Tucker had grand plans for his extended clan, but he also confronted daunting challenges. While Henry Jr. and Henry Tucker of Somerset would carry on the family name and business in Bermuda, the Colonel realized that the island offered few significant opportunities for his large brood. The island's economic situation, more-over, deteriorated after 1763 as the British Empire slipped into a severe de-pression, a downturn which hit Bermuda especially hard. Military con-tracts dried up, and the island's sloops and brigs were too small to compete with larger vessels throughout the Atlantic. The ships rotted in harbors, Bermuda's shipbuilding industry stagnated, and thousands of laborers, skippers, and mariners lost their livelihoods. Governor Bruere wrote his su-periors in London that the economic malaise caused the population to be-come apathetic and lethargic. They were, he confessed, "without art, culti-vation or agriculture."[22] Although the economy marginally improved in the early 1770s, a collapse in international markets in 1772 brought addi-tional hardships. For the Tuckers to succeed in this difficult environment, opportunities would have to be pursued elsewhere in the empire.

As Tucker Sr. looked for prospects throughout the Atlantic, he realized that his family's Bermudian roots would be serious liabilities in the eyes of Britain's ruling elite. Having lived in London for several years as the island's colonial agent, Tucker realized that social prejudices within England had grown in tandem with the empire's wealth and size. The great men and families at the center saw provincial elites as Britain's nouveaux riches who lived in crude, rustic conditions while owning and exploiting African slaves. The fact that these colonials now also aspired to genteel status was particularly galling to Britain's aristocracy. James Reid, an Edinburgh-educated visitor to Virginia, reflected the haughty attitudes that emanated from the home island. During his travels in the colonies, Reid sniffed that in America the "son" of a planter was only "made a Gentleman by the Ne-groes and land given him by his father who perhaps sprung from a race of Ignoramuses and who still continues one himself."[23]

Colonel Tucker also knew that men involved in commerce and trade en-countered social bigotry. In his book *Instructions for Travellers,* the econo-mist Josiah Tucker wrote that in contrast to a landed English gentleman, a British merchant often "failed to meet with Respect equal to his large and acquired Fortune." Stereotypes of greed and avarice followed such men throughout the empire and often undermined their genteel aspirations. But Josiah Tucker offered wealthy traders a solution: "If he [the merchant] gives his Son a liberal and accomplished Education—the Birth and Call-ing of the Father are sunk in the Son; and the Son is reputed, if his Carriage is suitable, a Gentleman in all Companies." In short, definitions of gentil-ity were changing in the eighteenth century, with behavior and education growing in importance. As one historian has written, "In the decades following 1688, the men who served the state's burgeoning bureaucracy or made fortunes from the trans-Atlantic commerce grew in number, in importance, and in the resources at their command. In response, a deportmental rather than a hereditary or professional definition of gentility gained currency: one was a gentleman if one looked and acted the part."[24] Status increasingly sprang from the cultivated behavior one had learned rather than from birth alone. It was, as Lord Chesterfield succinctly put it, the ability to "shine in the best company."[25]

Henry Tucker Sr. most certainly wanted his family to move in the highest and most genteel ranks of the empire. He invested much of his capital in The Grove to demonstrate to fellow islanders and visitors from abroad not merely that he had the money to build a large house but more importantly that his family possessed the taste and refinement necessary to construct a beautiful and imposing seat. The Colonel also followed Josiah Tucker's advice to merchants concerning a "liberal and accomplished education." In 1772 he wrote that "my Children's good has always been my principal study" and that he had always tried "to do everything in my power to give them a proper Education in order to fix them in some Reputable way in life." Whether or not Henry Tucker Sr. actually read John Locke's pivotal work *Some Thoughts concerning Education,* the Colonel's actions indicate a keen awareness of the philosopher's injunctions. Locke advocated rigorous intellectual training for young gentlemen as well as vigorous social instruction in order to develop "well-bred" individuals who could act and converse intelligently in all situations. The book gained a wide currency among colonists in the mid-eighteenth century, especially among those like Colonel Tucker who sought to overcome ingrained social prejudices within the mother country.[26]

Nathaniel's poem *The Bermudian* provides some details about the Tucker children's formal education on Bermuda: the Colonel hired a demanding tutor who held classes for a time in a small outbuilding near the mansion house. "Near yonder Hill, above the stagnant Pool," Nathaniel wrote, "My stern Preceptor taught his little School." At the age of sixteen, St. George left The Grove to attend a grammar school run by the Reverend Alexander Richardson in the island's capital. Richardson was the popular rector of St. Peter's Church and likely provided Tucker with basic instruction in writing, rhetoric, and arithmetic.[27]

The Tucker children's instruction was strong if one judges by the results. They were keenly familiar with the great writers of their day and often entertained one another in the mansion's garden reading aloud their favorite authors, including Goldsmith, Gray, and Pope.[28] They also articulated the dominant and optimistic ideals of the Enlightenment. The Colonel's sons and daughters believed man to be an inherently rational creature endowed with great "moral sense." Yet man also had to master his emotional passions and physical appetites. Thus he needed restraint, self-discipline, and moderation in all things.

To achieve this balance in life, the Tuckers turned to rational religion. Whenever family members raised spiritual matters in letters to one another, deism served as a means to control and limit their passions. "Above all things remember your Religious duties," Colonel Tucker once advised St. George, "knowing that there is a Being to whom you must Account for all your Actions." His son's external "Actions," not his internal beliefs, would determine God's final disposition toward him. Although the Tuckers viewed God as "gracious," "all wise," and "benevolent," they also saw man as a free agent in this world guided by the moral compass provided to him by the Lord. "I can scarcely persuade myself," Thomas once wrote, "that we are under any Obligation to the Being that gave [us existence]." Indeed, a man's fate was determined solely by his own actions. "I am much of a Pythagorean," he concluded, "and believe every Animal will make gradual Advances toward Perfection and happiness." St. George also debated man's free agency, and he too concluded that "the Creator," in "his Godly wisdom," did not constrain man in any way.[29] Nathaniel probably best summed up the family's religious outlook with a verse he titled *The Optimist.* Consciously imitating Alexander Pope, Nathaniel explained that happiness lay in accepting the minor vagaries of life as long as one realized that in the world God had created, man would make inevitable progress up the scale of civilization:

> Thus worldly ills for ever tend
> To man's advantage in the end.
> Be patient—leave to Heav'n the rest,
> And know *whatever is, is best.*

The only exception in the family was Anne Butterfield Tucker, who believed in a harsh Deity and in a terrible judgment day for mankind.[30]

Parallel with their formal education and religious instruction, the Colonel taught his children the ways of sociability and genteel conduct, determined to make them "well-bred" individuals who could correspond and converse in all circles throughout the empire. His motives were far from aesthetic. Throughout the eighteenth century the realm's citizens recognized that they lived in a society stitched together via patronage connections between individuals and families of different rank. Throughout colonial America prominent leaders had long used their power to sponsor aspiring, talented, and polite men. Just before the Revolution, John Adams told an ambitious Boston lawyer that to get ahead he needed "the Friendship and Patronage of the great Masters in the Profession." In Philadelphia, Benjamin Franklin's meteoric rise occurred under the gaze of influential patrons; and in Virginia's Northern Neck, George Washington began his climb into the highest ranks of that colony's gentry through the patronage of Lord Fairfax.[31]

As his sons matured, Henry Tucker taught them to adopt polite and respectable personas when in public in order to gain the attention of their society's most influential citizens. He paid particular attention to St. George's social demeanor long before the youth left the island. In the late 1760s, when young Tucker attended the Reverend Mr. Richardson's grammar school on the island's east end, his father kept close tabs on him. Realizing that his son had a penchant for practical jokes, the Colonel forwarded regular advice to the youth on how to comport himself in the company of important people: "As you are now from us, I think it necessary to remained [remind?] you of your behavior, let it always be such as to gain you the Esteem of every one. . . . above all things be cautious of your Company. Youth are too apt to be drawn away by folly. Let not that be your case. . . . Let all your Actions be dictated by Honor and Virtue and then you are sure of being right." Because his son's every word and action would be noticed and because "a character once lost is hard to retrieve," Tucker Sr. demanded that St. George behave at all times with "utmost Circumspection," avoid the "low class," and "be Choice in [his selection of] Intimates." If he did not, his reputation would be sullied and future prospects gravely threatened.[32]

St. George was never altogether successful in controlling his love of jokes. His brother Nathaniel wrote in *The Bermudian:*

St. George appears with Bus'ness fraught—
Th' electrical Machine is brought . . .
The Wire touch'd, you feel the Shock—
One cries, 'twas a confound Knock!

While Saint declares 'tis all a Joke,
Says he, there ha'nt been such a Stroke
As that I felt at first alone—
It almost broke my Finger Bone.

Nevertheless, with the constant flow of paternal advice from the Colonel, the youthful St. George quickly grasped the necessity of presenting a genteel persona before the "great men" he met. Upon being invited to dinner by a well-respected gentleman, he noted in a journal he periodically kept, "I replied with a Bow down to the Ground, Mr. Dunbar[?] is what the world calls an extremely polite, well-bred Gentleman so it was necessary to take him in his own way."[33]

Sociable letter writing was another skill Colonel Tucker emphasized. Their surviving epistles demonstrate that the Tuckers dedicated many hours to composing their letters. While correspondence helped to cement bonds of family and friendship, articulate and expressive letters also demonstrated refinement, graciousness, and gentility. The eighteenth century's "familiar letter," as it was called, was an emerging literary mode among the Atlantic world's elite which sought to imitate in written form face-to-face conversations. Thus contemporaries likened letters to a theatrical performance where one displayed intelligence, civility, and good breeding to the larger world.

The motives behind such efforts, again, were hardly aesthetic. People earned respect and attention within the empire through witty, eloquent, entertaining epistles. A genre of "how-to" books emerged in Great Britain to train ambitious individuals in the art. One work, published in 1775, urged letter writers to adopt "an easy complaisance, an open Sincerity, and unaffected Good-nature." Excessive ornament in style must be avoided, or else one would come off "like a Fop admiring his own Dress."[34]

The Tuckers' letters reflect these trends. In an empire where less than half the population could sign its name, the family's epistles are not only expressive but beautifully written, indicating that much effort was directed at the art of writing itself. George Washington's "Rules of Civility" noted that fine penmanship was a mark of polite conduct.[35] The Tuckers, too, saw exceptional handwriting as important and well worth the trouble. The substance of their communiqués also reflects their efforts to shine and to achieve gentility. In letters to both kin and non-kin alike, the Tuckers attempted to convey not only the daily stuff of their lives but also their cleverness, fluency, and good sense.

In the late 1760s, as the Colonel taught his children the ways of gentility, he also launched his sons into the world. His eldest, Henry Jr., would take over the family shipping business as well as extend the Tuckers' political power on the island through his tie to the royal governor. The economic depression after the Seven Years' War, however, made it necessary for second son Thomas to seek opportunities elsewhere. Interested in the medical field, he decided to pursue a career in medicine. Not only did Thomas possess a genuine interest in the subject, but medicine was one of the eighteenth century's learned professions, occupations that required specialized training but no manual labor. Such well-educated individuals, the Colonel understood, usually were looked upon as respectable gentlemen by the rest of society. To give his son every advantage, Tucker Sr. sent Thomas to the University of Edinburgh in the late 1760s. Everyone realized that instruction in the mother country would provide the young man with both superior training and the opportunity to make social connections. The costs of such an education, however, were staggering. By the time Thomas completed his studies in 1771, they had set the family purse back fifteen hundred guineas. The Colonel's third son, the poet Nathaniel, had also decided to enter the medical profession, and thus he would need the same expensive training.[36] In 1771, however, the economic downturn still gripped the empire and so forced the family to curtail its ambitions temporarily. One trading venture after another failed during this period, compelling the Colonel to confess that he could no longer afford such schooling. Elizabeth bemoaned, "Fortune seems to take pleasure in disappointing the plans he [Tucker Sr.] makes for fixing [his sons] genteelly in life."[37]

Having taken his degree and finding no prospects in Bermuda, Thomas decided to open a practice in Charleston, South Carolina. Brother Nathaniel, bored on the island and with no professional education immediately in the offing, decided to go along as a sort of apprentice. Although many Bermudians had moved to Charleston by the mid-eighteenth century, Thomas confessed that he and Nathaniel arrived in South Carolina "without a single Recommendation to any Person." Indeed, he elaborated, "We have no Relation whose consequence might make us respected."[38]

From a broad family perspective, however, the decision to move to South Carolina makes some sense and perhaps reflects the elder Tucker's paternal input. Because Bermudian merchant-shippers largely plied the intercolonial trade of the western Atlantic, a Tucker family presence in the southeastern seaboard's largest city seems a wise move. Recognized as the commercial capital of the lower South, Charleston possessed 10,000 souls and 1,300 houses in 1771. Moreover, the city's increasingly wealthy elite consciously imitated British models of gentility through the pursuit of both landed and mercantile enterprises.[39] It was the ideal spot for a British-educated doctor from a well-respected and refined imperial family. Thomas could build a medical practice of consequence and at the same time construct social ties to the city's great men that would prove useful to the family's mercantile enterprises.

Occupying a small house on Tradd Street, the two brothers lived with a slave brought from home and a widowed Bermudian housekeeper. Although they gained enough notice to win coveted invitations to the royal governor's annual ball, Thomas found himself unable to attract many patients. By late 1771, he confessed that he had made only "a small Beginning with a few Bermuda Negros" and that his practice remained "very inconsiderable."[40] The ongoing economic depression throughout the Atlantic world made him realize that no more financial help could come from his father. The following year brought only more hardship as Thomas's efforts to establish a practice continued to sputter.

In 1773 the pair hit bottom. Thomas became involved in a public feud with a prominent attorney named Robert Williams which nearly ended in a duel. The dispute erupted in the summer when Thomas treated a male slave infected with smallpox. Realizing that he needed to get the man to a quarantine ship anchored in the harbor, Tucker transported the slave through one of Charleston's most populated sections in order to reach the docks. Williams saw what was going on and accosted Tucker in the streets, accusing him of endangering the entire city.

Several days later the *South Carolina Gazette* published a letter from Williams directly attacking Tucker's professional judgment and competency. Remembering his father's injunctions linking personal reputation to success in life, Thomas felt he had little choice but to challenge Williams to a duel. Instead of fighting, however, the attorney obtained an indictment against the doctor for violating South Carolina's law against dueling. After a brief trial the judge found Tucker guilty and gave him a stiff fine.[41] From Bermuda, Colonel Tucker admitted that he was "glad Tommy has supported his Character with so much Spirit," but he regretted the lengths the dispute traveled. It proved costly in many ways. Not only did Thomas go far in debt to pay his fines and legal expenses—totaling £320—but he also found himself humiliated in the city's newspapers and courts. Establishing a genteel medical practice among Charleston's elite now seemed out of the question. Thus the brothers gave up on the city. The following year Nathaniel sailed home while Thomas moved to Dorchester, a small village twenty miles away, hoping to buy some land and start a rural practice. Soon afterwards he met and married a country girl of modest means named Esther Evans. Frustrated by his inability to break into Charleston society, Thomas wrote that his new bride possessed few of the city's artificial refinements. Esther "has had but little Opportunity of Improvement either by Schools or Society."[42]

As Thomas and Nathaniel struggled in South Carolina, the Colonel's youngest son, St. George, was preparing for his own career beyond Bermuda. In the late 1760s, while attending Richardson's grammar school, Tucker decided to pursue the law. Such a course made great sense for a younger son from a genteel business family. Not only was the law one of the learned professions, but as trade and commerce spread throughout the Atlantic, well-trained lawyers who could resolve property disputes were needed. Hence they began to enjoy a "creeping respectability" among the wealthy and powerful. The prestige of lawyers grew as well because of improvements in their technical training and education.[43]

Still eager that his sons be educated at the empire's center, Colonel Tucker initially wanted St. George to attend London's Inns of Court. But the lasting burden of Thomas's education and the anticipated expenses of Nathaniel's training made such a course impossible. To get his son started, Tucker Sr. persuaded John Slater, Bermuda's attorney general and St. George's uncle, to apprentice the youth at his law office. Although young Tucker did not much like his relative, he worked diligently. A year later the Colonel met a Virginia gentleman named Stark, probably Bolling Stark, who was visiting the island. Mentioning his son's quandary, Tucker learned about the College of William and Mary in Williamsburg, Virginia. Stark boasted about the quality of the school's instructors and that the college itself was "under the particular Inspection of Lord Botetourt," the Old Dominion's popular royal governor. What most caught the Colonel's ear, however, was Stark's assertion regarding the school's "cheapness" when compared to London. Taken by the prospect, Tucker offered his son a Virginia education, at least until the Inns of Court became feasible. Unhappy in his uncle's office, St. George jumped at the chance and prepared to sail overseas.[44]

As with Thomas's move to Charleston, St. George's relocation to the tidewater probably reflected both individual and family ambitions. Colonel Tucker certainly wanted his youngest son to gain a strong professional education in order to situate himself independently. In addition, living in Williamsburg, the capital of Britain's largest American colony, and training alongside the sons of Virginia's great planters presented a marvelous opportunity to expand the Tuckers' mercantile connections into the Chesapeake region.[45]

Armed with letters of introduction from his father and other Bermuda dignitaries, St. George left the island in the fall of 1771. He sailed first to New York City to visit with the Tudor family, Bermuda kin who had moved to the continent a number of years before. Arriving at the city's great harbor on 27 October, Tucker spent several weeks in the town. He then traveled south down the eastern seaboard, stopping for a time to see Philadelphia before reaching Virginia at the end of 1771.[46]

The first person St. George contacted after his arrival was yet another Bermuda relative, his uncle Archibald Campbell. A merchant in Norfolk, Campbell knew the region well. Norfolk was one of the few mercantile towns in the Old Dominion, an entrepôt for goods from the metropolis and the point of departure for Chesapeake tobacco and wheat. Because Virginia and Bermuda belonged to the same empire, the colonies had many similarities. Both depended on commercial networks that radiated out of London, and each relied on the labor of African and African-American slaves, who made up approximately half the population in each. Beyond economic ties, the gentry elite of both enthusiastically embraced the cultural norms of the mother country, and hence the wealthy saw themselves as refined, cosmopolitan, and outward-looking. Dress, manners, and conversation in Williamsburg resembled the patterns St. George knew in Bermuda. Like Colonel Tucker, moreover, Virginia planters had built large and luxurious homes—"seats"—to demonstrate their families' wealth, taste, and power within the empire. Finally, the ruling clans of the Old Dominion, like those in Bermuda, had thoroughly intermarried into one another, creating a tight web of closely allied and powerful families.[47]

Tucker obtained a room in Williamsburg as a lodger in Margaret Campbell Eustace's home and soon enrolled in the college. He initially met with the Reverend Thomas Gwatkin, one of the school's faculty, who determined that the Bermudian was not yet ready for study in the law. There-fore, Gwatkin designed a course of instruction in natural and moral phi-losophy, a move which startled the Colonel, who had expected his son to embark immediately upon his legal training. "When you went from hence," he wrote that April, "I did not expect that you w[oul]d have enter'd upon an Academical Education[.] a little Logick, Rhetorick, and a Small Notion of Mathematics are all that ever can be Necessary for one that is to study the Law." The Colonel also noticed his son's mounting bills. "I can-not forbear mentioning my surprise at what you say in regard to your Ex-pense, which had I forseen I sh[oul]d never have tho[ugh]t of sending you to Virga. as the same sum w[oul]d near maintain'd you in London at the Temple where you might have immediately enter'd upon the Study of the Law." So that St. George would not have to call on his father's credit so fre-quently, his uncle Campbell quietly provided Tucker with several cash ad-vances. The Norfolk merchant understood that his nephew needed a strong intellectual foundation in order to succeed with Virginia's elite.[48]

Throughout 1772, while St. George pursued his "Academical Educa-tion" with Gwatkin, his Bermuda kin wrote letters that focused mainly on his developing social contacts. Most family epistles asked not "How are your studies progressing?" but rather "In what manner have you been rec[eiv]ed?" After several months in the Old Dominion, young Tucker be-gan writing back that he had met with "many Marks of Politeness" from "some of the principal Families of Virginia." Applauding his initial suc-cesses, Tucker's father, mother, brothers, and sisters all urged him to con-tinue "cultivating" these "Friendships." Henry Jr. particularly cheered St. George on. "Your own good sense," he counseled, "will easily suggest the Necessity of cultivating [the] Acquaintance [of the colony's great men] and of engaging their Friendships by a propriety of Conduct and invariable Re-gard to the Dictates of Integrity and Honor. The Continuance of Esteem of People of Character and Distinction in that Province will not only be use-ful to you during your Residence among them but may perhaps be service-able at some future Period. Advantages of this Sort, however remote or un-certain, shou'd nevertheless not be blatantly disregarded."[49]

The Tuckers first hoped that St. George would build a clientage friend-ship with Colonel George William Fairfax of the Northern Neck, a busi-ness acquaintance of Tucker Sr. Fairfax's departure from his proprietary in 1773, however, ended that expectation.[50] One relative talked about "a Connection at the Blair Family," but nothing profitable developed on that front either. St. George did strike up friendships with a number of fellow students at William and Mary. He joined a college group called the Flat Hat Club, led by James Innes, known as "the Major" because of his large physique. Modeling it after London's polite social clubs, the members pursued sociability, intellectual prowess, and good fellowship. In the process Tucker befriended John Page, heir to Rosewell, north of Williamsburg. Not only was Rosewell the grandest mansion in the colony, but the Page family owned over 4,000 acres surrounding the great house and more than 150 slaves. Although Page was nine years older than St. George, the two men instantly took to one another and became lifelong friends. Tucker also became the companion of two sons of Thomas Nelson of Yorktown, a member of the governor's council and Virginia's colonial secretary. In early 1773 Tucker wrote about his "great intimacy" with the two youths as well as of his growing "friendship" with the elder Nelson.[51]

This all came as glorious news to the Bermuda clan. St. George's information arrived amid ongoing reports about the dismal state of trade throughout the Atlantic world, even further straining the family's shipping business and purse. Connections to the Page and Nelson families thus raised hopes at a difficult time. Brother Henry wrote of the "inconceivable pleasure" everyone felt, while the Colonel chortled at the prospect of patronage, telling his son that it was "greatly in [Secretary Nelson's] power to serve you as he has 52 counties in his gift." Three weeks later, the elder Tucker again urged his son to cultivate his ties, especially with the Nelsons, reminding St. George that the secretary "has many pretty things in his gift."[52]

In early 1773 St. George Tucker finished his studies under Gwatkin and began to read law with Williamsburg's most eminent lawyer, George Wythe. Although Tucker never wrote specifically about his training under Wythe, both Littleton Waller Tazewell and Thomas Jefferson described a rigorous regimen. Wythe required his students to be at his door at sunrise and to remain at work until after sunset. Working from an extensive reading list, they grappled with the great theorists of English law, such as Coke, Bacon, William Sheppard, and Blackstone. Students also abstracted case reports from Britain as well as the statutes of Parliament and colonial assemblies. Finally, Wythe demanded that his pupils read a "fair sampling from classical literature, the natural science, history and philosophy." Tucker's liberal arts education, therefore, continued. Wythe further required students to assist him in his law practice during sessions of the General Court.[53] As a result, throughout most of 1773 and into early 1774, Tucker gained a broad knowledge of the law while getting to know some of the colony's most talented attorneys.

As St. George completed his training, his friendship with the Nelson family began to pay dividends. In January 1774 Secretary Nelson wrote a letter to Tucker Sr. lauding St. George's "good sense, chearfulness of disposition, and goodness of heart." Such genteel attributes, Nelson stressed, "have recommended him in a strange country to the notice of some of the most respectable persons among us." He concluded that the Colonel must be "one of the Happiest Men in the world" to have such a refined and well-thought-of son. Two months before, the secretary expressed his fondness for the Bermudian in a more tangible way when he offered St. George a deputy clerkship in the county court of either Gloucester or Dinwiddie. Ever mindful of the source of this appointment, Colonel Tucker urged his son to accept the Gloucester clerkship because its county courthouse was just across the river from the secretary's home in Yorktown. St. George, however, took the more lucrative Dinwiddie post.[54]

In the spring of 1774, Tucker presented himself to George Wythe and Attorney General John Randolph as a candidate for admittance to the bar. After performing satisfactorily in the traditional oral examination given to all budding lawyers, Tucker received his law license. He then prepared to move approximately fifty miles westward to Petersburg in Dinwiddie County. In the small but growing mercantile town, Tucker expected to begin practicing law and to take up his clerkship. As he packed, the young lawyer also looked into purchasing two fine horses and a slave boy. Tucker realized that he needed to demonstrate to potential clients his independent status, even if he did not actually possess many resources. Given the great planters' obsession with outward appearances, Tucker had to look prosperous in order to attract genteel planters.[55] From Bermuda, though, Colonel Tucker warned his son about spending too much too quickly. He also pleaded with St. George to maintain his contacts with Nelson, exclaiming, "I am truly sorry that you are obliged to remove to so remot a part of the Country."[56]

After completing his preparations, Tucker started a long-planned round of visits to his relations along the eastern seaboard. In April he traveled south to visit his two brothers in South Carolina. He then made his

way northward to New York City to see his Tudor cousins again.[57] Returning to the Old Dominion in late October, Tucker found a number of dis-
turbing letters waiting for him. During his absence Henry Tucker of Somerset had written from Bermuda, "We have by Way of the Leeward Islands
a blind Account that the Bostonians have thrown into the Sea some three
hundred and odd Chests of Teas." Reflecting on the political explosion that
followed the Boston Tea Party, Henry concluded, "I am warmly attached to
Liberty as any Man, but I cannot say that I like the Proceedings."[58]

The intelligence must have been old news to St. George but probably
served to remind him of the growing imperial crisis. A letter had also arrived from Nathaniel, further pointing to escalating troubles. "The Boston
Port Bill makes a great Noise here," he exclaimed. "Every body is turn'd
Politician. Spirited Measures are talk'd of and it is even conjectu'd that Resolutions will be enter'd for Putting an entire Stop to all Export and Import
whatsoever." Realizing the devastating impact this would have on the family's shipping business, Nathaniel concluded: "The Storm seems to be gathering over America. God knows what will be the Event."[59]

Other bad news awaited Tucker in Williamsburg. Four months before,
Virginia's royal governor, Lord Dunmore, had dissolved the House of
Burgesses because of its support for Massachusetts in the wake of Parliament's Coercive Acts. The dissolution, however, occurred before the
burgesses could renew the colony's schedule of court fees. Thus the power
of courts throughout Virginia to assess commissions expired, which caused
them to shut down.[60] At a time when a continental embargo hung over his
father's merchant-shipping business, St. George's law license and clerkship
had become worthless.

Despite these mounting threats to its interests, the Tucker family by
this time had come to adopt a staunch pro-American view. From the beginning of the crisis, the Tuckers openly condemned the London government's various measures, labeling them all "unconstitutional Acts." Having served as Speaker of the Bermuda Assembly, Colonel Tucker had no
trouble realizing how Parliament was impinging upon the long-established
prerogatives of the colonies. Moreover, because of their determination to
rise and accumulate wealth, the Tuckers especially feared measures that
threatened property rights. In July 1774 the Colonel condemned the king's
ministers for their ongoing "Obstinacy" and barked, "I think the Collonies
ought to hazzard every thing rather than to Submit to Slavery, . . . for if the
Parliament of great Britain have a right to dispose of the American's prop-

erty as they please, call it by what name you will there can be no greater marks of Slavery."[61]

Like all conflicts, America's approaching war against the mother country presented both perils and opportunities. As always, the Tuckers' primary concern centered on the family's collective interests and well-being. Perils soon materialized not only in the Parliament's Coercive Acts but also in the Continental Congress's response, the trade embargo slated for implementation in 1775. Family members throughout the Atlantic immediately saw that a trade shutdown threatened both the family's pocketbook and Bermuda itself with starvation. Because the island lacked enough arable land to sustain its population, it had long imported food from North America. Although this dependence drew many islanders closer to the cause of the continental colonies, Bermudians naturally feared military retaliation by the Royal Navy.

By spring 1775 the embargo's impact was already being felt, with food shortages developing. Colonel Tucker wrote an urgent letter to St. George telling him to inform Virginia's patriot leaders that Bermudians "wish well to the American cause" but could do little to assist them given their great vulnerability to royal warships.[62] By the summer, shortages on the island had grown more acute, compelling the Colonel himself to sail to Philadelphia along with several other Bermudian leaders to plead their case. Before the delegation landed, Virginia delegate Peyton Randolph reported that he had learned (from St. George no doubt) that a significant cache of gunpowder was stored on the island. Thus when Tucker Sr. and other islanders arrived, congressional leaders slyly informed them that if ships from Bermuda loaded with munitions and other crucial war supplies arrived on the mainland, they would most certainly return home with needed provisions. The message was clear: the war supplies had to be turned over to the Americans. In late July, therefore, soon after the delegation returned home, the Colonel and other family members helped plan and execute a nighttime raid on the colony's stock of gunpowder. The action came off without a hitch, and the 112 barrels of powder soon made their way to the colonies. The raid, however, caused an open and permanent rift between the Tuckers and Governor Bruere. The family's pro-American politics had already strained relations with the governor, and the Tuckers' obvious role in the seizure of the powder was the final straw. Bruere groused to officials in London about the Tuckers' disloyalty, and he even labeled St. George a "mere rebel." Nonetheless, the raid had its intended effect. The following

November, Congress voted to exempt Bermuda from its trade embargo as long as islanders did not reexport provisions to loyalist colonies in the West Indies.[63]

Several weeks before the gunpowder raid, Henry Tucker Jr.'s four-year-old son, Henry St. George, stayed overnight at The Grove. Very late in the evening, the youngster saw what he thought was a robber breaking into the house. Years later, after Henry had become the treasurer of the East India Company, he recalled in his memoirs: "I perceived a strange man, muffled up to the ears, suddenly rush from the garden into the house, and I expected every moment to see him present a blunderbuss, or some other deadly weapon. But, to my surprise, the females of the family immediately threw themselves into his arms!" The "strange man" was St. George, the boy's uncle, back from the Old Dominion. With the Virginia courts closed, America descending toward war, and the family purse nearly empty, the Colonel had demanded that his son return home, telling him that his "Golden dreams of Virginia are vanish'd."[64] Although happy to be among his loved ones again, St. George resented having to return, telling his brothers that his departure from the colony had utterly destroyed his "Advancement in Life." He did obtain his law license to practice on the island in July 1775, but he had few cases and remained depressed. Family members tried to console him and pleaded that he not "yield to the impulses of Despair." Thomas promised his brother that every "Obstacle" he now confronted would only be "temporary."[65]

Thomas was right. Within months, opportunities for gain began to emerge out of the conflict. After Lexington and Concord, rumors flew throughout the Atlantic about privateer owners amassing easy fortunes through smuggling. John Page wrote St. George about stories he had heard. "Several People in Maryland and the Northern States," he reported, had gained "immense Profit" by running essential war goods past British patrols. Thomas also heard that "many [in Charleston] have already made Fortunes in a very short Time" through smuggling. "The present Times," he concluded, "lay open a wide Field for Adventure."[66]

As rumors of easy riches multiplied, the Colonel and other Tuckers decided not to let such opportunities pass. In the first half of 1776, family sloops and brigs began to smuggle commodities out of the rebelling colonies and across the Atlantic. That June, Henry Jr. noted that the family had a supply of smuggled American wheat for sale on one of the Caribbean islands south of Bermuda. "If we cou'd sell all the wheat and receive the Cash," he speculated, "the Commission would be a pretty thing." The Tuckers also dealt in South Carolina rice. Henry Jr. told St. George, "You have smuggled so much Rice amongst you at the West End that it is become quite a Drug." From the beginning the Tucker clan expected its vessels to operate off Virginia and South Carolina, in the West Indies, and in friendly ports on the European continent. Smuggling salt, sugar, guns, munitions, and cloth into North America, the vessels attempted to bring out food commodities, tobacco, and indigo. Believing that they had at last found the way to wealth, Thomas trumpeted that "it was high Time they shou'd come in for a Share of the Good Things of this World, after having experienced so many bitter Disappointments and Difficulties."[67]

As before the war, the Tuckers stitched their trading (and now smuggling) enterprises together via family ties. Only reliable kinsmen could be entirely trusted to manage complex (and illegal) mercantile operations as well as handle large sums of money and goods. Once their ventures began, The Grove Tuckers teamed up with their "Bridge" relations, especially Henry of Somerset, who belonged to the firm Jennings, Tucker & Company. Although sometimes portrayed as rival firms before 1776, Henry Tucker & Son more than had likely joined forces with Jennings, Tucker & Company whenever business circumstances warranted. Before the Revolution, British-American shipping firms typically allied together when necessary in order to share the enormous expenses involved in outfitting ocean-going vessels and to divide the risks involved in large-scale trading ventures. Such business alliances also allowed partners to utilize one another's human resources throughout Atlantic ports.[68]

During the Revolution the Tuckers sought to take advantage of all these benefits, with family bonds serving as the glue that held the whole enterprise together. Skippers with the surname Tucker often commanded vessels for both firms. "Old Capt. Thos. Tucker" and "young Thos. Tucker" regularly plied the Atlantic in family ships. The Tuckers and Jenningses also situated trusted kin in those spots most often visited by Bermudian brigs and sloops. The Colonel sent a kinsman named John Tucker to Barbados just before the war. Henry of Somerset dispatched his brother Daniel Tucker to the same island to help negotiate the purchase of sugar from planters. Daniel Jennings, meanwhile, lived in the Dutch colony of St. Eustatius, where he arranged for the arrival and departure of family-owned vessels. As the wartime enterprise began, the Colonel, Henry of Somerset, and the Jennings brothers also brought the rising generation into the operation, even those with no mercantile experience. Both Thomas and St. George took part in smuggling efforts from the start. With contacts in South Carolina and Virginia, both men could arrange for the sale of trafficked goods as well as secure provisions for export to France and the West Indies.[69]

St. George Tucker's experiences during the Revolution's early years particularly highlight how the smuggling enterprise worked and demonstrate the overwhelming importance of family bonds to its smooth operation. His activities, moreover, show how the Bermuda clan expected St. George to place his social ties in Virginia at the family's collective disposal. In October 1776 young Tucker wrote John Page, now Virginia's lieutenant governor, to explain that the Colonel and his other Bermuda relations were involved in running essential goods into the now-independent states. The Colonel had just purchased "a large Sloop" named the *Dispatch*, on which St. George was about to sail for Virginia. On board would be "3000 Bushells of Salt besides some other trifling Articles." Hoping that his friend would use his political connections to get the state government to purchase the cargo, Tucker minced few words, noting, "If ever I am in favor with fortune it will be thro' the Interposition of Friends."[70]

Several weeks later the *Dispatch* sailed from Bermuda with St. George aboard and Captain Thomas Tucker, probably "old Capt. Thos. Tucker," at the helm. An experienced master, Captain Tucker possessed a keen familiarity with the American coastline and a good understanding of the ins and outs of Atlantic trade. He, therefore, could oversee St. George's negotiations with the Virginia government. After leaving the island, the *Dispatch* made its way to Turks Island in the Bahamas where the crew loaded the brig with 2,817 bushels of salt and 1,500 pounds of "fine ginned Cotton." Proceeding directly to the Old Dominion, the ship landed at Yorktown on 3 January 1777. Tucker immediately made his way to Williamsburg, and several days later he sold the desperately needed provisions to the state government for a profit of nearly £1,800.[71]

In addition to selling goods to the Americans, the Bermuda Tuckers wished to bring Virginia's "great men" into their enterprise. A partnership with state leaders not only would bolster the family's ability to profit from the war but also would strengthen its commercial ties to the Chesapeake region once peace returned. While preparing the *Dispatch* for the return trip home, St. George met privately with Page to explain "some proposals" that he earlier had only hinted at. The "proposals" involved the formation of a business syndicate composed of the Bermuda Tuckers, the Jennings clan, Page, and several other prominent Virginians. The Americans would put up some capital while Tucker and other Bermuda-owned vessels would smuggle tobacco, wheat, indigo, and rice out of America for sale in Europe and the West Indies. Ships would then return to the United States loaded with rum, sugar, salt, and war munitions.[72]

Page replied to the offer on 17 February, "I have serious Thoughts of accepting your offer, and putting in £200." Eleven days later the increasingly excited Virginian wrote Tucker that he and the others "were so enlivened . . . that we forgot the Cares of America and our own Situation and were as happy as Lords, or rather as the richest Jew Merchants; for we soon demonstrated that our Company would be as rich as a Jew. Our Stock we saw clearly would be doubled in the West Indies, our Importation Hence that *double,* be quad[rupled] here. Our Rice and Indigo sold high at St. Eusta[tius]." "You see," Page concluded, "how easy it was to purchase a Cargo of Tobo. Flour Coal and Iron which we know suits the Char[les]ton Market, and go the Rounds again doubling and quadrupling as long as the War lasts." At this letter's end Page acknowledged that these speculative trades were only in his imagination, but he hoped "may it prove true."[73]

The Bermuda-Virginia partnership benefited the Tucker family at once. The day after Page agreed to invest in the enterprise, the governor's council, of which he was president, awarded the Tuckers a contract to purchase £10,000 of South Carolina indigo for export to the West Indies. Proceeds from the sale would then go to purchase more salt and other commodities needed by the Revolutionary government. Upon the deal's completion, the family would receive a 2½ percent commission. Within weeks of receiving the contract, St. George traveled overland to Charleston where he purchased the indigo. Although he found commodity prices fluctuating because of the war, he organized a flotilla of four ships which he immediately sailed into the Caribbean. Within weeks, he had exchanged the dye for salt, sugar, rum, arms, and munitions. The Tuckers made a "considerable sum" off the contract, but upon his return St. George found himself scolded by Governor Patrick Henry, who believed the Bermudian had "paid too much for the indigo." When the Colonel learned about the governor's anger, he warned his son, "I hope you will not engage in any thing that may make you an object of resentment to Government" and hence undermine the family's developing ties to state leaders.[74]

Throughout 1777 the Tucker enterprise continued to smuggle essential provisions into America while taking out much-in-demand raw materials and agricultural staples. After its initial voyage the *Dispatch* sailed to Caracas loaded with Virginia lumber that Captain Tucker exchanged for more salt. After delivering the cargo, the sloop carried Chesapeake tobacco to Bordeaux, France, and returned to the former colonies loaded with additional salt as well as guns and various other "light articles." The family syndicate purchased additional ships and hired privateers whenever it could in order to satisfy the extraordinary demands caused by the rebellion. The goods Tucker vessels smuggled into the United States sold quickly and at a substantial profit. In November, Daniel Hylton, a Virginia merchant who worked for the family operation, begged St. George to hurry up with a shipment of salt that had just landed at Edenton in Albemarle Sound. "I am ready to be tore to pieces for the Salt," he pleaded, "as it will command £5 p[er]. bushle Cash. . . . For Godsake if yr. well enough, [I] shall be glad if you can hurry it up." With business so robust, the family needed more help in America. The Colonel persuaded a Bermudian cousin named St. George Tucker (referred to as St. George Tucker Jr. in family correspondence) to go to Virginia. Because British cruisers had moved to the capes, Tucker Jr. was to assist his kinsmen with the wagons of goods that regularly trekked between Virginia and Charleston. As profits came in, Colonel Tucker arranged that they be deposited with two London merchants whom he personally knew and trusted, John Strettel and John Brickwood. Despite their smuggling activities, the Tuckers apparently were not afraid that their money deposited in London might be seized by the royal government.[75]

Because of their many successes, the Tuckers attempted the following year to expand their operations. They sought new Virginia investors to provide additional capital and hoped to take advantage of St. George's close ties to the Nelson family. In January 1778 the wealthy planter Jaquelin Ambler wrote St. George to follow up on a meeting the two had just completed. "I communicated the Scheme as you advised," Ambler explained, "to Mr. [David?] Jameson and Genl. [Thomas] Nelson, both of whom expressed the greatest Willingness to be Parties. The Genl., indeed, does not think himself altogether at Liberty to engage his own Name, but was exceedingly desirous of vesting part of his younger Brother's Money in Trade.

Mr. Hugh Nelson appeared equally so of employing a thousand Pounds in the same way." Ambler furthermore told Tucker that he did not doubt the "readiness" of "our worthy Friend, Mr. Page," to invest additional funds with the Tuckers, although Ambler had not yet asked him.[76]

The venture appeared to promise additional profits, but it never materialized. Although 1777 had been a year of financial successes, the family operation started to unravel in 1778. Some members' lack of mercantile experience proved costly. Thomas's assistance in South Carolina hurt as much as it helped the syndicate. From the beginning of the war, Thomas had provided the family with important intelligence about southern markets, and he periodically hired ships and skippers to transport goods. However, he found himself incapable of dealing with rapidly fluctuating commodity prices in wartime Charleston. In April 1778 this shortcoming cost the operation dearly. The previous January, St. George had purchased 200 hogsheads of Virginia tobacco at £65 apiece for export. As cousin St. George Jr. transported them overland by wagon, rumors spread through Charleston that a peace accord had been reached between the royal government and the American Congress, and tobacco prices plummeted. Knowing his kinsman was on his way, Thomas panicked and sold the hogsheads at only £45 each. When the news proved false, prices moved up again. Mortified, Thomas admitted, "We lost much by the Agreement."[77]

Rather than ending, the Revolutionary War intensified in 1778, particularly on the high seas. Smuggling operations became significantly more dangerous and costly. The Colonel had noticed the previous year that more British men-of-war plied Caribbean waters, making it more difficult to obtain salt and other needed provisions for sale. In mid-1777 a family sloop named the *Fanny,* commanded by "Capt. Tucker," was surprised and seized by the twenty-gun HMS *Daphney.*[78] The next year, the Royal Navy stepped up its patrols off the United States coast, and the Tuckers' losses on the seas mounted alarmingly. On 1 July 1778 the British captured the family's brig *Sally Van* as it left American waters bound for Bordeaux. On board, the Royal Navy discovered 290 hogsheads of tobacco. The Colonel later groaned about further losses. He told St. George, "Capt. Thos. Tucker in a small Sloop we are concerned in was beat off the Coast ab[ou]t a month past with the loss of his Mast and Bowsprit." The ship, he concluded, was "a perfect wreck."[79]

In 1779 the news went from bad to worse. The *Dispatch* ran aground inside the Chesapeake Bay and was pounced upon by a British cruiser. Another family brig, the *Sullivan,* was also taken after a brief skirmish with an enemy patrol.[80] Communication difficulties and mix-ups proved costly as well. St. George Tucker, for example, on his own initiative sold the family's sloop *Adelphi* when it was docked in Virginia for £500 sterling, only to discover that his father had purchased insurance for the vessel for £300.[81]

Obtaining new ships to replace those lost was extremely difficult. After exploring the shipyards of Gloucester one morning, Jaquelin Ambler reported to Tucker that new sloops were not available at any price. "I inquired very particularly . . . whither *proper* Vessells cou'd be procured, but was sorry to find that all agreed in opinion that there was no Chance of getting them unless by contract with the Builders, all of whom I found were fully employ'd." Ambler further wondered if the rewards were worth the risks as enemy "Men of War and Arm'd Vessells are so numerous in our Bay." The extraordinary amounts of capital lost in the Tuckers' captured vessels in 1778–79 probably ate deeply into the profits they won during the war's early years. Insurance costs on smugglers also eroded gains. By the war's middle period, premiums often reached 50 percent of a cargo's value. And if a ship was lost, a claimant then had to gather a wealth of documentation before a policy would be paid off. After 1779, insurance could rarely be had at all, and several uninsured Tucker vessels became complete losses.[82]

The family's correspondence by 1780 becomes a train of dismal reports. In February, Henry Jr. lamented to his brother about how the family's losses had mounted over the previous two years. "I was sorry to hear of the Fate of your Brig," he sighed, but in keeping with the family's genteel moderation, he concluded, "Resignation is a Lesson we must all endeavour to learn." St. George Tucker Jr. decided to return home that spring. As the war moved south, few trading vessels were either leaving or arriving in the Chesapeake.[83] Difficulties also mounted when Colonel Tucker had to travel to London at the behest of Bermuda's assembly. Because food shortages throughout the war had remained acute, assembly members wanted Tucker Sr. to ask ministry officials to permit islanders to trade with the Americans. As a result of these numerous problems, the Tuckers gradually wound down their operation and decided to wait out the war. Henry of Somerset best summed up the family's sentiments when he wrote his cousin in 1781, "I shall forbear Politics further than to wish for Peace, when the Intercourse between Friends and Countries may be conducted without Hazard of

Interruption for thieves Robbers and such Pests of Society of which among the Cruisers of the present Times there are too many to be met with."[84]

Although it ultimately failed to rescue their finances, the Tuckers' smuggling operation reveals the complex and multifaceted nature of late eighteenth-century family life. Extended clans served both public and private functions, and individuals understood their responsibilities to the entire familial unit. Members not only gave and received love between spouses, parents, and children, but they bestowed affection and comfort upon extended and affinal kin as well. The Tuckers, moreover, realized that material success in their society required an unwavering sense of loyalty to one's clan and a willingness to work hard to advance its collective interests. St. George Tucker's efforts in Virginia throughout the 1770s further reveal that an individual's social connections were always to be placed at the disposal of the complete family. However, with the Tuckers little better off at the end of the Revolution than before, the Colonel's children recognized that they would have to adopt new strategies in order to survive the future. They also understood that family members needed to look well beyond Bermuda in order to make their mark on the world.

Two

Revolutionary Times: War, Marriage, Opportunity

S t. George Tucker's life took an unexpected turn in the autumn of 1777 when General John Burgoyne surrendered his 6,000 British troops to Horatio Gates's American army at Saratoga. As patriots throughout the nation celebrated, Virginia's Governor Patrick Henry proclaimed a day of thanksgiving with a prayer service held in Williamsburg's Bruton Church. Then in the state capital organizing yet another smuggling venture, St. George entered the chapel late, and as he later wrote, "I happened unwittingly, to take my seat next to a pew in which all the Ladies were kneeling most devoutly." Although Tucker claimed that he had pledged "never to marry a Widow," he "discovered a face I had seen some years before, with an infant in her Arms: she was now a Widow! And from that moment, had I been a Roman Catholic I should have applied to the Pope for Absolution from my Vow." [1] Within a year, Tucker married the widow named Frances Bland Randolph and entered the inner ranks of two great Virginia families. Tucker's wedding forever changed his life and guaranteed that he would permanently make the Old Dominion his home. Once a young Bermudian on the make, Tucker now became through marriage a respected and formidable member of the state's landed gentry. And even before the Revolution ended, he determined that he would establish a new family dynasty in America based upon the customs, values, and practices of Virginia's ruling elite.

St. George Tucker made a successful entry into this world of tidewater plantations. After they took their vows, he and Frances, along with her three children from her first marriage, settled at Matoax, a 1,300-acre Chesterfield County estate nestled along the Appomattox River's northern bank near Petersburg. With the war still raging, Tucker soon joined the Virginia militia to defend his new home from British invaders and to advance a Revolutionary cause that he sincerely believed would bring a more enlightened way of life to American society. Despite the Revolution, Matoax functioned in these years much like tidewater households of the late colonial era. Members of the great house continued to define the family in the broadest terms. Crucial emotional ties and utilitarian responsibilities extended well beyond the household to kin members throughout the state. The couple saw their interests as tightly fused with those of their extended kin, and familial assistance was essential to the smooth operation of their plantations. Finally, the life of St. George's new wife, Frances, demonstrates how elite women conceived of their role within the family and how they contributed to its social and economic advancement.

St. George Tucker's courtship of Frances Bland Randolph and their marriage in September 1778 allowed him at a stroke to fulfill his "Golden dreams of Virginia." While his connections beforehand had been good, this match firmly established his place in the state. The use of marriage to gain social position was not unusual in British-American society. Virginians had long understood that winning the hand of an elite woman often led to "the top of the province." Bermudians too recognized that tangible benefits came with such bonds. Although Elizabeth Tucker once had written that "mutual Attachment" should provide the "principal Ingredient for Happiness" in marriage, she and others had witnessed the political benefits gained by her brother Henry Jr. following his wedding to the daughter of Bermuda's royal governor.[2]

During their courtship not only did St. George Tucker discover Frances Bland Randolph's charming, dynamic personality, but he also learned the extent and reach of her family connections. Her father, Theodorick Bland Sr. of Prince George County, possessed a distinguished genealogy and abundant wealth. Her mother was Frances Bolling Bland, herself a member of a prominent gentry clan from Prince George. Their magnificent and imposing seat, Cawsons, sat on a promontory where the Appomattox River turns northward to join the James. Although of limited education, Theodorick Bland had earned respect, influence, and power over the years, serving as Prince George's county lieutenant and as a member of the House of Burgesses. Like Colonel Tucker in Bermuda, Bland also had great ambitions for his family and expected its members to continue advancing up Virginia's social ladder. In the 1760s he sent his son and namesake to London for medical training, an education that he understood would confer both knowledge and status. On the eve of the Revolution, Bland's wealth was so great that he gave his daughter and her first husband, John Randolph of Matoax, twenty adult slaves as a dowry, a number that apparently caused the old gentleman little hardship in making his annual tobacco crop.[3]

Frances's marriage to John Randolph from 1770 until 1775 appears to have been a harmonious one but should be viewed in its broader context. In the decades leading up to the war with Great Britain, Virginia's great clans became more closely linked to one another. Marriages between important families helped secure property and enhance power. John Randolph was the youngest of the four sons of Richard Randolph and Jane Bolling Randolph of Curles Neck. In the mid-eighteenth century Richard Randolph had gained extraordinary wealth within Virginia's tobacco economy and served for a time as the colony's treasurer. At his death in 1748, his 40,000 acres were divided among his boys, with John inheriting three large productive estates: Matoax on the Appomattox River, Bizarre to the west in Cumberland County, and Roanoke, an enormous farm in Charlotte County. Ten years older than his bride, John Randolph already had an important blood tie to the Bland family, for he and his new mother-in-law were cousins.[4]

After the couple took their vows at Cawsons in 1770, the two clans became even closer. Members frequently visited one another's plantations, performed work and favors, and exchanged slaves in order to assist with field labor and chores around their mansions. When war began, all backed the American cause. John Randolph, Bland Sr., and his son, Theodorick Bland Jr., together offered forty slaves for sale to raise money to replace the colony's gunpowder seized by royal governor Lord Dunmore.[5] However, a decaying rot underlay much of this wealth and grandeur: debt. Soon after his marriage in 1770, John Randolph unwisely endorsed notes made out by one of his brothers to English creditors. When his sibling defaulted, the debt fell to John, who lacked the cash to retire the liability. Unwilling to liquidate his family's lands, he let unpaid interest expenses mount until the debt appeared greater than the value of his plantations. Once the war started, however, the problem moved to the back burner and was safely ignored. When John Randolph unexpectedly died in 1775, all in Virginia viewed his surviving wife as a beautiful, well connected, and above all, wealthy widow.[6]

St. George Tucker certainly recognized Frances as such at their chance meeting in Bruton Parish Church, and he immediately pursued her. Marrying a woman for her money was not an unknown impulse for the young Bermudian. Before the Revolution he had briefly courted a "Miss Galloway" from Philadelphia. Her main asset, he told his brothers and sisters, was her family's "very considerable fortune," which he hoped might save him "the Trouble of prosecuting the dry and tedious Study of Law."[7] Romantic love, though, played an increasingly important role in late eighteenth-century matches, often paralleling financial considerations. St. George's words and actions mirrored these developments, for he not only considered Frances's wealth and connections, but a few months after the courtship began, he felt enormous passion for her. By early 1778 he confessed that all "Reason" had deserted him. "Think what the man must feel who can not think of Happiness but for you," he pleaded. "Oh! my Fanny, do not steel your heart against me."[8]

Yet at first Frances did "steel" her "heart" against Tucker. In January 1778 she merely pledged her "Esteem" for her ardent suitor, but no more. Virginia's marital laws may have given her pause. The Old Dominion adhered to England's common-law practice of coverture, which severely limited a woman's legal freedoms and social identity. Through coverture, a bride became legally "covered" by her husband. As a result, she could not bring suits in court, make binding contracts, or even testify in judicial proceedings. Most importantly, when a woman took a husband, she lost the right to control her property. When St. George began his pursuit, Frances had ruled her estates alone for nearly three years, directing the plantations' slaves and white employees. Regardless of her sentiments for the young Bermudian, the possibility of surrendering this control likely made her hesitate.[9]

But Tucker had much to recommend him. A dashing and well-known smuggler for the patriot cause, he possessed impeccable manners, which demonstrated a refined and genteel family background. He also had powerful connections to the state's leading men. Companionship and passion were no less important to Frances, and she found Tucker's charm, sociability, and open earnestness irresistible. By the spring of 1778, her "Esteem" had blossomed into a fervent love, at which point she finally accepted his repeated proposals of marriage. Several months later Frances longingly wrote her betrothed, "You left us so early I cou'd not for sometime think you ware gone, but was soon convinced of the sad truth, and found I have nothing left of value, but the hair I rob'd you of, which has been my Bracelet and constan[t] companion." [10] After their September wedding the couple's affection for each other grew even stronger. A year after the ceremony, Frances playfully teased her then-absent husband: "My lips have not been touched since you blessed them. do not be as good, or I will retaliate two fold." On the couple's third anniversary, St. George exclaimed: "Happy, happy, happy Day. The anniversary of the happiest Event of my Life! Blest be the Day and blest ever the Event!" [11]

Following their wedding, the couple settled in Matoax's white-framed great house, along with Frances's three sons, a number of white servants and overseers, and dozens of black slaves who labored inside the mansion as well as upon the plantation's 1,300 acres. War, however, still raged beyond the estate, and in the spring of 1779, Tucker decided to enlist. Although he volunteered as a private in the Virginia militia, his ties to the gentry again came to his aid. That May, General Thomas Nelson Jr., the secretary's nephew, noticed Tucker's low rank and provided the Bermudian with a major's commission. [12] As a soldier, Tucker undoubtedly wanted to protect his adopted homeland from a marauding enemy. As a new member of the gentry, moreover, the twenty-six-year-old planter likely believed that he had to contribute to the cause militarily in order to maintain his reputation. In 1779 two of his brothers-in-law served as colonels in Washington's army: Frances's brother, Theodorick Bland Jr., and John Banister, who had married Frances's sister Elizabeth; unlike Bland and Banister, Tucker claimed that his marriage to Frances precluded his enlistment in the Continental army. [13] However, another of her kinsmen, Beverley Randolph, commanded a regiment of Virginia militia. Joining the latter force would allow Tucker to maintain his dignity within the family.

Tucker likely placed his life on the line also because of his staunch commitment to the Revolution's liberal principles. Genuinely convinced, as Virginia's Declaration of Rights proclaimed, "That all Men are by nature equally free and Independent," he wanted to help create an enlightened and stable republican government, one selected by a majority of freeholders with officeholders (Tucker expected) drawn from the ranks of the Old Dominion's educated elite. A successful war would, furthermore, free America at last from the corrupting hands the London ministry and Parliament.

Finally, Tucker entered the military because a war for liberty proved an irresistible adventure. At the outset John Page told him that America's struggle had the "Attention of the whole world" and "well deserves the Laborer [Laboring?] Pen of a Livy or Polybius."[14] Tucker saw the Revolution in the same grand way. During the war he wrote an epic poem titled *Liberty* in which he confidently predicted that a great empire would arise in the New World. With the muse of Liberty safely ensconced in America, a better and more virtuous nation soon would emerge:

If Liberty thy Board shall deign to grace
And smiling peace adorn thine humble Cot,
Columbia, thus, shall live to deathless Fame,
Unrivall'd or by Rome, or Britain's vaunted name![15]

Tucker's own chance for personal fame came in May 1779, soon after he received his commission. During that month twenty-eight British ships with 1,800 enemy troops aboard entered the Virginia Capes and anchored near Norfolk. The force, commanded by Commodore Sir George Collier and Major General Edward Mathew, immediately launched a series of raids in the Norfolk-Portsmouth area. The enemy troops burned and destroyed patriot ships and a number of warehouses filled with salt and other supplies. St. George mustered in with nearly a thousand troops to repulse the invaders, even though Frances was seven months pregnant with the couple's first child. The British, fortunately, withdrew before any severe action took place.[16]

The following year, 1780, Tucker again took to the field to defend the state from British general Alexander Leslie's 2,200 troops, who entered the Chesapeake that autumn to divert American attention from Lord Cornwallis's campaign against the Carolinas. Like Collier and Mathew, Leslie departed before any major action occurred. That December, though, British forces returned once more, this time under the command of the traitor Benedict Arnold, now a British general. As soon as Arnold's men landed, they rapidly pushed up the James River toward Richmond and Petersburg. The invasion caught the tidewater by surprise, including everyone at Matoax. Having just celebrated the birth of their first son, the Tuckers found themselves directly in the path of British arms. In early January 1781 St. George scribbled in his almanac: "This year began with the news of an invasion by the British under the Command of Arnold. On the 5th of Janry. it being presumed that their efforts were directing toward Petersburg, I removed Fanny with her Child but seven Days old from Matoax to Mr. B. Ward's Junr. at Wintopoke in Chesterfield proposing from there to remove to Cumberland." [17]

The Tuckers traveled westward to Bizarre, their 800-acre Cumberland County estate sixty miles west of Matoax. The winter journey over the badly rutted roads was difficult and painful, especially for the still-recovering Frances. Traveling with the couple were their newborn son Henry St. George, his seventeen-month-old sister, Anne Frances, the three Randolph boys, two white servants, a number of black slaves, and as much of Matoax's furniture as their wagons could carry. Because turmoil still reigned in Petersburg, Tucker rushed back eastward to help his father-in-law at Cawsons escape the advancing enemy. Although he rescued Bland Sr., Tucker noted to his brother-in-law that the "old gentleman" "has suffered much by the absconding of his negroes." Tucker himself lost property to British pilfering: two hogsheads of rum stored in a Richmond warehouse. He joked that "it was too trifling a quantity for a man to break his heart about." [18]

With his wife and children at Bizarre and his other kinsmen now safe, Tucker mustered in with Beverley Randolph's militia regiment, which was attached to General Robert Lawson's brigade of Virginians. Late in February 1781 the unit marched south into North Carolina to bolster General Nathanael Greene's army of Continentals as it sought to turn back Lord Cornwallis's legions. Several weeks later, Tucker fought with Greene's troops at the battle of Guilford Courthouse. Even though the Virginians ran away from advancing British regulars, Tucker himself performed bravely and even received a bayonet wound in the leg while attempting to stop a fleeing soldier. As he recovered at Matoax, he learned that he had received a lieutenant colonel's commission and the command of a regiment of Virginia volunteers. [19]

During the summer Cornwallis punched his way into Virginia, forcing Tucker's regiment into the field. The British assault also compelled another hasty evacuation of his family from Matoax to Bizarre, which St. George still worried about being overrun by the British. As the enemy marched up the James River valley, Tucker learned that the British had not overrun any of his abandoned properties. His kinsmen, however, were not so lucky. Cornwallis's troops sacked Theodorick Bland Jr.'s plantation at Farmingdell, pillaging his corn, tobacco, and livestock and making off with a number of his slaves. Tucker's brother-in-law John Banister sustained even greater losses. Not only did he abandon his plantation, Battersea, before the advancing invaders, but the British consumed nearly £1,000 of bread and flour produced at Banister's mills and left with "82 of my best negroes, including all my tradesmen," some of whom he got back later that year.[20]

Despite such losses, the final American victory at Yorktown took shape early that fall. Tucker clearly saw the war's end at hand, a prospect which filled him with joy. In September, as American forces concentrated around Williamsburg, he celebrated the arrival of their commander-in-chief with some uncharacteristically passionate prose. "Acknowledgments to this protector," he wrote Frances, "their Deliverer, and to the Savior of their Country, implore an uninterrupted Profusion of Blessing on the head of the glorious and immortal WASHINGTON!" Several days later he rather sheepishly tried to explain his lack of moderation. "Can you assign a reason my dear Fanny why my style in several of my late letters so often breaks out into bombast? I wish I could avoid what I so cordially condemn . . . in others." "I will endeavour," he at last promised, "to drop it though my Fanny is the only person to whom I address myself."[21] The reasons for Tucker's uncontrolled joy are not hard to fathom. Victory not only would guarantee American patriots their independence but also would provide Tucker the opportunity to cultivate his position in Virginia within a stable and peaceful environment. With the war over, he finally could tend to increasing his family's wealth, property, and social position.

In mid-September, Tucker's militia unit found itself in the trenches surrounding the British garrison. At the height of the siege, his superior connections again proved useful. On 16 September, General Thomas Nelson, now the Old Dominion's governor, asked Tucker to join his staff—"my family"—as his interpreter to the French army. The appointment pleased Tucker for it allowed him to move in the highest circles at allied headquarters. The position may have also paid tangible benefits. During the month's third week, Tucker learned from French officers that Admiral de Grasse's provisioners, loaded with chests of gold and silver, had set off up the James River valley to seek supplies. After suffering through hard economic times, inflation, and a shortage of specie throughout the war, Tucker could not resist the opportunity.[22] He secretly wrote Frances, who was then back at Matoax, telling her to wait for French agents before selling their estate's wheat crop. While not to disobey a direct requisition order if American foragers arrived first, she was not to hand over any produce voluntarily. Whether Frances sold to the French in return for specie is unknown, and within a month Cornwallis had surrendered.[23] Except for a slight wound to his nose from an exploding shell, Tucker came through the campaign unscathed. In late October, as he packed his equipment to go home, he completed a journal he kept during the siege, writing several lines that expressed his hopes for the future:

> "Let there be Light!" then spake th' eternal Word,
>   And darkness fled before thy heavenly Ray.
> To Peace the jarring Firmament restored
>   While Chaos humbly yields his wonted Sway.[24]

Though the Revolution had caused much dislocation to their lives, St. George and Frances had reasons to be optimistic at the war's conclusion. In a state of 700,000 people, Tucker's family stood near the apex of Virginia society. The Bermudian was "just off the list" of the state's one hundred wealthiest citizens. Important Virginians, moreover, respected him as a genteel landowner, slaveholder, and militia officer. Soon after Cornwallis's surrender, the leading men of the General Assembly named Tucker to the governor's council.[25] Thus, as 1781 came to a close, he and his wife looked to the future with confidence. As an influential gentry couple, they expected wheat and tobacco markets to improve with peace. The state's social scene also would recover as the great houses across the state, including Matoax, once more had their doors thrown open, with sociability and conviviality returning to the tidewater. Finally, St. George and Frances looked forward to having more children, who one day would take possession of their extensive properties.

Although late eighteenth-century Virginia is sometimes labeled a rigidly patriarchal society with strong and powerful men in charge of the households, the Tuckers' home at Matoax offers a different picture. Laws of course continued to favor males, but close cooperation and collaboration marked St. George and Frances's life together. In most undertakings the couple saw their marriage as a partnership with great (though never complete) equality existing between the two. Scholars have vigorously debated, however, the Revolution's overall impact on women and their opportunities. Some historians argue that Revolutionary ideology, with its implicit revolt against patriarchy and hierarchical relations, significantly reshaped women's relationships with their husbands. They suggest that the War for Independence gave birth to "companionate" wives and "republican mothers," cultural constructs grounded in a definition of women as near-equal

St. George Tucker at the time he lived at Matoax, c. 1785, painting by Asher Durand. (Courtesy of Bermuda National Trust Collection)

partners to men. Other scholars have argued that the Revolution strengthened "domestic patriarchicalism," with husbands emerging from the conflict more powerful than ever and with all notions of gender equality sys-
tematically repressed.[26]

The Tuckers' marriage offers a mixed picture of the Revolutionary era.
Within the Tucker family circle, women generally accepted that they lived
in a male-dominated society, a situation they seemed little inclined to
change. Frances sometimes lamented her own personal limitations, which
she saw as grounded in her sex. "I never regretted any thing more than my
not possessing the talent for writing," she once told her husband. While St.
George's letters always seemed witty, clever, and interesting, she believed
her own were anything but. "It wou'd afford me infinite satisfaction," she
finished one, if "I cou'd confidently scribble on, knowing that it wou'd be
entertaining to you." During the war, moreover, Frances felt compelled to
apologize to her spouse for her constant "Womanish fears" about his safety.
Clearly, men possessed fortitude and bravery, while women were more
fainthearted.[27]

Frances and other women in the family, however, did not timidly retire
into the background. Having received solid educations, they time and
again asserted their opinions while demonstrating a broad knowledge of
history, literature, and philosophy. Planters in the neighborhoods surrounding Matoax widely acknowledged Frances as a woman of "quick intelligence."[28] And she frequently demanded that she be treated as such.
During the siege of Yorktown, she chastised St. George for addressing her
as someone ignorant of the great events then occurring: "Don't think because I have not mentioned it that we are unacquainted with the arrival of
the French Fleet and *they say* 3000 land forces. we have already captured
Cornwallis in imagination and done every thing else that Sanguine Whigs
cou'd wish."[29]

The couple largely managed their household together as partners with
each relying upon and seeking input from the other. Child rearing was seen
by the two as their most important responsibility, and they approached the
task jointly. From the beginning of their marriage, the Tuckers wanted
many children. Large families were common in late eighteenth-century
America. Numerous children ensured the continuity of a clan's name and
provided security to parents against indigence and loneliness during their
elderly years. St. George once asked a married yet childless friend: "Pray do
you intend to pass all your days without ever hearing yourself called

papa? . . . Pray remember the danger of growing old in Wickedness [i.e., alone]."[30] Children were also recognized as innocent beings who brought great emotional happiness to their parents' lives.

Although men and women desired children, everyone recognized the inherent dangers of pregnancy as well as the pain involved. Virginia women naturally viewed reproduction with anxiety and trepidation. Frances's sister-in-law, Martha Bland, once commiserated that in her mind pregnancy was a *"nine-month-scrape."* In 1779, when St. George first saw his wife in labor, he was shocked by her distress. Days after the birth of their daughter, Tucker wrote Theodorick Bland, "From the moment of conception to that of delivery the throes were incessant and sometimes too violent to be endured. nor have the after-pains totally subsided yet." But he concluded, "The Sight of my beloved babe amply compensates for all the ills I Suffered in producing her."[31] More babies arrived at Matoax following Anne Frances's birth. Frances Tucker gave birth to Henry St. George at the end of the next year. The spring after Yorktown, she had another son whom the couple named Theodorick Thomas Tudor. In 1784 another boy was born and named Nathaniel Beverley.

Both Tuckers recognized the paramount importance of land to their family's ambitions. Land had long been seen as "the basis of wealth and power" in the Old Dominion. Even before her marriage to Tucker, Frances taught her boys "the moral significance of this economic fact." Land "must be held onto" at all costs. While the sons of her first marriage would eventually inherit the Randolph estates of Matoax, Bizarre, and Roanoke, what about the children she had with St. George? The couple realized that they needed additional plantations, and even before their first child arrived, St. George began accumulating more. He first purchased from their kinsman Beverley Randolph a 1,200-acre Cumberland County plantation named Green Creek. In 1779 Tucker searched for additional estates but met with frustration. "My expectations of purchasing Land," he complained that year, "are from many Circumstances likely to be disappointed."[32]

After the Revolution ended, however, Tucker had more success. In the early 1780s he purchased a plantation which he called Bermuda Forest as well as four city lots in Blandford, a village several miles east of Petersburg. At least one of these lots was utilized as a blacksmith's shop, operated by one of his slaves. St. George also obtained a 900-acre tract in Dinwiddie County. He even discussed with several acquaintances the possibility of speculating in land in Georgia, but nothing ever materialized. Finally, late in the decade he bought a 500-acre farm in Lunenburg County, southwest of Matoax. Rather than personally manage this more distant property, he rented the plantation to tenant farmers in order to supplement his family's income.[33]

Within their home at Matoax, St. George and Frances worked hard to create a warm and affectionate atmosphere for their family. Frances ensured that her daughter and sons grew up believing in a kind and benevolent Lord. Rejecting the notion of a detached "Supreme Being," she told her children that a caring, loving, and generous God ruled the universe. She vigorously inculcated these views to the entire household through regular family prayer and Bible readings. John Randolph throughout his life vividly remembered his mother's religious instructions. "Every night after I was undressed, and in the morning before I rose," he recalled in 1813, "I kneeled down in the bed, putting up my little hands, and repeated after my mother the Lord's Prayer and 'the belief.'"[34]

Frances Tucker pressed her religious sentiments not only upon the children but also upon her husband. Although Tucker believed in a rational Creator before and after his marriage, many of his friends noticed a change in his religious attitudes during his years with her. Robert Andrews, a college chum and an ordained Episcopal minister, wrote, "I was pleased to observe that amongst the Benefits you have derived from Matrimony, some Knowledge of what the Scriptures contain is one, and I hope you will in Time become an Example of Piety and godly Wisdom to the Husbands of this degenerate Age."[35]

St. George always showed himself to be a tender and devoted father, especially when their children were young. Even before his marriage to Frances, he wanted her sons to feel secure in his love. "How do my dear Boys?" he asked in July 1778. "Are they disposed to love the person from whom they shall ever experience the utmost paternal Care and Tenderness from?" Outsiders even noticed Tucker's affection for Frances's children. One frequent visitor to Matoax declared, "Mr. Tucker must be the best father-in-law [i.e., stepfather] in the world, or his stepchildren would not be so fond of him."[36]

Seeing their children as inherently good, innocent creatures, the couple derived enormous satisfaction as parents and often wrote one another about first words, winsome tricks, and precocious actions. During Cornwallis's campaign Frances wrote St. George about their daughter, "Fan is a sweet cross Puss and shakes her fist at the English for Carrying Papa from her."

Several years later when the couple left for a trip to New York City, St. George noted with pride his daughter's growing maturity. Although five-year-old Henry St. George shed "some tears" on his parents' departure, eight-year-old Fan bore the separation with "tranquility."[37] Other letters are brimming with affectionate terms for their young ones, such as "monkey, toads, pugs and sluts," the last word a term for "a child who was not yet toilet trained."[38]

Even when overwhelmed with work and chores, the couple filled their letters with affection for their children. Frances once wrote at the end of a difficult spring day: "The Children are very well, but intolerable noisy and troublesome. it is a hard days work to attend to them and the drudgery of the house. their interruptions at this moment are so frequent I scarcely know what I write." Yet she then made a loving observation on each: "Beverley wants to know who b[r]ought this letter and must sit by my elbow to see the light. Tudor has just come in as dirty as a Pig from Toms house with his arms full of wood to make me a fire. Fan and Hal are rather more decent, say their Books tolerably well, and often. Fan smiles at the thought of learning Musick, but I fear she will not be very fond of applying to it." St. George Tucker found this letter so charming that he forwarded it to Theodorick and John Randolph, then away at school, noting "these particulars, of little importance but to yourselves and me, I thought it might entertain you to hear." Although the Tuckers always avoided the passionate rhetoric often associated with nineteenth-century romanticism, the open love they expressed for their children was hardly unusual. The Bermuda Tuckers repeatedly wrote about their young ones in a similar manner. In 1780 Henry Jr. explained to his brother: "Our Plants [i.e., children] begin to want Room to expand themselves in. Hal and George are as promising as we cou'd wish them. Tom is as fat as a Dutchman. Nan is a downright Amazon. . . . What a Catalogue is here! Aren't you frightened at it?"[39]

The love that the parents felt for their children naturally spilled over into concerns for their futures. Although usually perceived as a paternal responsibility, education and schooling at Matoax involved both St. George and Frances. The couple together oversaw their children's early training, frequently discussed the contents of their instruction, and made key decisions together. When the couple wed, they especially worried about the three Randolph boys' schooling. Wartime turmoil had repeatedly frustrated their efforts to find an acceptable tutor, even though they and the boys' uncle Theodorick Bland Jr. had searched far and wide for one.

St. George and Frances anguished over these lapses in their sons' instruction. In the summer of 1781, Frances wrote her husband that she had interviewed a Dr. Armstrong about educating the children, "but I think he seems to be averse." As a result, "my poor boys . . . (like all other children who are without employment) are grown quite Idle and troublesome." St. George agreed. "Tell my poor Boys," he wrote back, "that I am unhappy whenever I think of the valuable time they are losing. Beg Dick in my name to set his Brothers a good example by minding his Book, and tell them I am sure they will follow, poor Fellows! I am more anxious for them than they will ever believe at a future Day." Several months later he urged Frances to remind them, "Only by minding their books would their future success be assured."[40]

The couple's joint efforts regarding education can best be seen in how they together dealt with Richard, the eldest of the Randolph children. Following the Revolution, St. George and Frances decided to send all three boys to a grammar school operated by Walker Maury, one of Tucker's college chums. When Maury moved the school from Orange County to Williamsburg, the couple noticed a distinct change in Richard's behavior. Like many sixteen-year-olds, Randolph's obedience to parental commands declined during his teenage years as he focused more attention on his appearance, dress, and social schedule than on his studies. In 1786 he misspent ten dollars his stepfather had specifically sent him for a tuition payment. Although St. George strongly "rebuked" the boy, he particularly wanted Frances "to write him very seriously on the subject."[41] The youth promised his mother several months later, "I have not taken up nor shall I be in any thing but in attending to my studies." The boys also reported to their mother about the precise contents of their studies and their progress in each subject.[42]

The following year the Tuckers pulled Richard and his two brothers out of Maury's school in the old capital, with St. George condemning "the Corruption of the place." The couple then enrolled their children at the College of New Jersey in Princeton. During the summer of 1786, St. George and Frances had visited the school during their trip to New York City. They met the college's headmaster, John Witherspoon, who assured them that the boys' behavior would be closely monitored and regulated.[43] Although convinced that Witherspoon would keep Richard diligently at his studies, the parents were soon disappointed. Immediately upon arrival Richard purchased an expensive set of clothes (with the bill forwarded to Matoax), and he once again misspent money earmarked for tuition, this time to attend a public ball. When Frances learned the news, she sent a stern letter to her son, demanding that he abandon such profligate habits. He must instead, she insisted, follow "the example of both [his] fathers," one who "possessed every virtue" and "the other [who] is all a father can or ought to be." In October 1787 a contrite Richard wrote a full (almost embarrassing) confession to his mother demonstrating her powerful influence over him. He had concealed his misbehavior, he pleaded, "not because I was really afraid of you. . . . But I assure you it was the fear of making you unhappy, but miserable I am in making you more so. It was what I most wished to avoid and that I ought to have thought while I was acting."[44]

St. George and Frances viewed raising their children and securing their futures as their primary responsibility. Yet they also looked at the genteel presentation of Matoax as an essential duty, vital to maintaining the family's social influence throughout the state. Understanding the critical importance of appearance and reputation, St. George upon his marriage to Frances tried to shed his mercantile roots by assuming the demeanor of a landed gentleman. He realized that the stereotype of traders being greedy and filled with avarice was especially strong in Virginia. He thus grew quite perturbed when friends reminded him of his commercial background. During the war, after paying a high price for some goods brought into the state from a Tucker smuggling ship, St. George's friend the Reverend James Madison teased him about "being metamorphosed into that Thing called a Merchant." Deeply offended, Tucker sharply rebuked his friend about the joke, forcing him to apologize. Tucker also became highly sensitive regarding the status of his credit, which he considered a reflection of his reputation. When a store clerk once refused his credit, a furious Tucker demanded the establishment's owner immediately step in and rectify matters.[45]

Tucker also sought to present himself to his fellow planters as a refined, well-educated, and cosmopolitan gentleman. He always possessed an interest in science, history, and literature and over the years invented such things as a steam-powered water pump. He wrote dozens of poems on various topics and drafted extensive treatises on astronomy, a topic that one historian has labeled "the great favorite of the *virtuosi*."[46] Tucker understood, however, that these intellectual "accomplishments required public ratification" if they were to enhance his status.[47] He therefore actively disseminated his ideas and writings among his friends and acquaintances. His literary efforts did magnify his prestige. For instance, after sending his poem *Liberty* to the South Carolinian politician William Pierce, Tucker received the reply he had likely hoped for. "I doubt not your success" with the poem, Pierce wrote back, "for it is universally acknowledged that you are a Man of taste." [48]

St. George also used his wit and charm to strengthen his reputation for sociability among the tidewater elite. After a neighbor failed to show up for a dinner party at Matoax, Tucker composed a verse for the absent guest—doubtlessly written on the spot and shared with the other visitors—describing the missed feast:

> Though you expected naught to eat,
> We could have given you some meat,
> Veal that had sucked two well-fed cows,
> Lamb that was fattened in a house,
> Bacon well-fed on Indian corn,
> And Chicken crammed both night & morn,
> Sturgeon likewise adorned the board,
> Of Pears we had a monstrous hoard. . . .
> We ate, we drank, we went to bed,
> And slept as though we all were dead. [49]

Tucker also participated in the less intellectual aspects of gentry culture after his marriage. He frequently took part in horse racing, Virginia's leading sport throughout most of the eighteenth century. Always fond of fine horses, Tucker maintained an impressive stable of racers at Matoax. He also gambled with his fellow planters on race days. His interest in horses may have been sparked by his intimacy with the Nelson family, many of whom raised horses and gambled on them at races during the prewar years. [50]

Tucker's social status and influence in the new Republic were repeatedly confirmed by the state's gentry leaders in the years immediately following the Revolution. Although his tenure on the governor's council was brief, the College of William and Mary appointed him to the Board of Visitors late in 1782. Two years later, after a reorganization of the state's militia statutes, Governor Patrick Henry and his council named Tucker the county lieutenant of Chesterfield. Although the governor's militia plan collapsed due to protests from members of the bypassed county courts, Tucker's appointment nevertheless reflects the weight with which the state's ruling class regarded him. [51]

Frances too believed it crucial for the family's reputation that she present herself as a gracious and charming mistress. Like other eighteenth-century great houses, Matoax was an open home which offered generous hospitality to all gentry visitors. Entertaining respectable guests in such a manner remained an important duty among the tidewater gentry during and immediately after the Revolution. Planters and other distinguished callers entered the couple's home above the Appomattox River at all times. During the British invasion in the summer of 1781, while St. George fought with the militia, Frances explained that she had not written to him sooner because "I am obliged to steal every moment from company. the house is always full."[52]

Unlike later nineteenth-century plantation wives, Frances believed it essential that the couple's parties, teas, and dinners be integrated affairs with men and women socializing together. Although she had close female friends, she almost always made sure that the sexes mingled whenever possible at Matoax's formal gatherings. At times she was forceful about this. Once when she learned that the wife of "Mr. N." would soon arrive at her home, she pleaded with an absent St. George to somehow get the visit put off until he himself could return. "For of all things," she wrote, "defend me from a female tète a tète unless there be a particular intimacy." Explaining that she had "nearly fallen a sacrifice last year to Metaphysicks" during a previous visit with this woman, Frances ordered her husband, "for heavens sake contrive to be at home."[53]

Neighbors surrounding Matoax always remembered Frances as a graceful and substantive hostess. One frequent visitor recalled her as "delightful in Conversation, elegant in Manners, and beautiful in Person."[54] Benjamin Watkins Leigh later reminisced, "It was the joy of my boyhood to sit at [my tutor, Mr.] Robinson's knee and listen to his conversations with my father and John Randolph's mother, who lived at Matoax. The world thought that her son spake as never man spake; but *she* could charm a bird out of a tree by the music of her tongue."[55] Frances Tucker undoubtedly possessed a natural charm about her, but she clearly felt a responsibility to appear lovely before her guests, to engage them in intelligent conversation, and to make all gentry visitors welcome within her family's home.

In addition to their own personal refinement, St. George and Frances took great care to ensure that Matoax physically mirrored the family's social elegance and independence. Like others of their class, they realized that furniture and other household articles were much more than func-

Frances Bland Tucker while mistress of Matoax, c. 1785, copy of Asher Durand portrait, probably painted by William James Hubard. (Courtesy of Raymond D. Kimbrough Jr.)

tional items. They were reflections of the couple's taste and gentility. Thus the Tuckers worked together to fill their home with beautiful objects. In 1779 St. George explained to his wife that he had just "made the extravagant purchase of a couple of Teapots and some other Articles . . . [at] which you will be very apt to smile." Several years later he announced to her: "You will get a genteel set of chairs, I hope, for your parlour. . . . another of the Vessels is to furnish your dining room with some green chairs, and there is a probability that your new chamber will be decorated with an elegant mahogany Bedstead." [56]

The Tuckers' estates were, above all, economic units of production. Indeed, they had to be in order to sustain the refined elegance inside Matoax's great house. As in most aspects of their marriage, St. George and Frances closely cooperated and worked together in this regard. In 1782 Tucker wrote or carefully copied an opinion piece entitled, "Letter 2nd. To the Farmer," which likely expressed the bright hopes the couple had about Virginia's plantation economy now that the war had ended. Its author contended "that Tobacco is a never failing Source of riches to the planter, and that that Commodity will always command Specie. To illustrate this, I mention . . . that a Gentleman in [Virginia] about a fortnight ago received near fifteen hundred pounds in Specie for James-river Tobo. sold by him in Baltimore." With their own estates each producing 20,000 to 25,000 pounds of tobacco annually, St. George and Frances confidently expected their properties to bring them "ease and independence" in the years ahead. [57]

But close collaboration would be essential to their success. Frances Bland Tucker certainly intended to assist her husband with the family's economic endeavors. And St. George greatly counted on his wife's skills to help manage their five estates, totaling nearly 9,000 acres, with over 100 slaves and numerous white employees and contractors. Plantation mistresses throughout Virginia had long held key responsibilities beyond the household. In 1770, when eighteen-year-old Frances Bland married John Randolph of Matoax, her mother explained that a gentry family could live "handsomely" in the Old Dominion only if the mistress of the household carried out her many duties with great "care and frugality." If a wife fell short, disaster awaited. Frances's mother noted that without a strong female hand, "the best Estates in Virginia soon dwindle and come to Little." In essence, the success of plantations depended largely on women consistently and faithfully carrying out their obligations. Frances's mother concluded by pointing out how daunting her daughter's new responsibilities would

be: "I hope my Dear Fan you will distinguish your self by making a Virtuous tender affectionate wife and parent, a humain Mistress and a kind
Neighbour. For blessed is she of whom many worldly deeds are recorded."[58]
Despite such challenging duties, Frances had likely been raised and educated with the knowledge that much eventually would be expected of her.

After her first husband died, Frances gained considerable experience in
managing the family estates on her own. She received frequent assistance
from her nearby tidewater kin, but she nevertheless made most of the key
decisions regarding Matoax, Bizarre, and Roanoke. Frances practiced typical housewifery duties between 1775 and 1778: food preparation, child-
care, cleaning, and gardening, as well as dairying and raising poultry. She
also oversaw the plantations' cloth production. In 1776 she hired a white
woman named Massy Gwyn "to come live with me at 30 pound p[e]r year."
In an account book she kept, Frances noted, "She engages to teach my
[black] weavers and spinners and to weave all the fine Cloath I may want."
In addition to these duties, Frances also had responsibilities beyond the
great house. She collected rents from tenants living on her lands, supervised
various plantation managers and overseers at work, purchased supplies
for the household, and hired white artisans and laborers to perform certain tasks.[59]

When Frances married St. George, her responsibilities did not dimin-
ish. Although the couple at times operated within their own specific
spheres, they more often than not shared plantation duties and closely cooperated with one another. Merchants and planters almost always dealt
with St. George concerning tobacco crops and/or slaves, but both husband
and wife frequently issued orders, requested information, and asked advice
from one another. Once when away from home, St. George wrote Frances,
"I have agreed with Clarke for the tools, provided Jimmy on Inspection
shall find the Bellows to be good. Will you give him orders to look at
them." Another time, when alone at Matoax, he carefully listed for his wife
a number of instructions he had just given to the slaves regarding the plantation's livestock and food supply. He concluded, "Thus far I have endeav-
oured to execute your Commands, in the morning I shall proceed to the remainder." Tucker later received a letter from Frances urging him to market
ten hogsheads of their tobacco immediately through her brother, Theodorick, probably because of a sudden spike in prices. "It was," she stressed, "of
too much importance to be neglected."[60]

Because of St. George's military service during the war and his legal practice in the 1780s, Frances Tucker had to engage in numerous tasks beyond the immediate household. She helped maintain the plantation's finances by keeping records and copying pertinent business correspondence. She also demanded that local debts be promptly paid to her. She kept a close eye on the estates' white employees. When one overseer at Bizarre embezzled some of the family's money, a furious Frances criticized her brother, who perhaps had hired him. "It was ever my opinion," she lectured Theodorick, "that it was wrong to entrust any one without an annual Settlement." She informed her brother that she had taken full charge of the situation. "As I am on this plantation I shall take care there shall be no more Embezzlement." As for the overseer, "so far from requesting him to continue in the business I shall with pleasure see him resign it."[61]

Several years later the family hired a new estate manager for Bizarre named Phil Halcombe, who quickly realized that power in this marriage lay equally with St. George and Frances. Throughout his tenure he reported to both the Tuckers about business matters. With Frances, he periodically discussed the varying condition of the estates' crops and livestock, the frequent need for cash, and information concerning runaway slaves. In 1787, when the family sought a new plantation "Steward," one applicant even applied to Frances and not St. George for the position. Other tasks she performed included purchasing foodstuffs from local farmers, obtaining iron for the plantations' blacksmiths, and negotiating contracts for grinding the estates' corn.[62]

The wives of late eighteenth-century Virginia planters have been portrayed in some recent histories as highly leisured individuals who spent their days reading, writing, playing music, and doing needlework. One scholar has even claimed that such women were primarily "wall-decorations for society."[63] Frances Tucker's activities, however, provide a more complex and well-rounded illustration of the plantation mistress's role. While expected to be a well-read, genteel, and entertaining hostess, she also had many duties critical to the smooth functioning of the household's enterprises. Contemporaries understood the great challenges such women confronted. Richard Randolph once admitted to his mother his growing "uneasiness" in witnessing "your many Disturbances in Managing so large a family." Such difficult and "perplexing" duties, he warned, may be "dangerous to your health."[64]

One of the most "perplexing" responsibilities Frances and St. George faced was managing their African-American slaves. Although the family as a whole supported the Revolution's liberal principles, the couple had grown up surrounded by slaves in their homes, fields, and towns, laborers who were regarded as property and subject to taxation. Both Bermuda and eastern Virginia had populations that were roughly half black and economies that depended upon the muscle of African Americans. The Tuckers demonstrated little concern for the freedom of their bondpeople during these years and probably agreed with their close friend the Reverend James Madison, who asked in 1779, "How can [a family] subsist in this Country without Slaves?"[65] The planter elite as a whole exhibited little inclination to see the institution disappear, even while fighting for their own political liberty.

Although indifferent to the cause of black freedom, the Tuckers had few illusions about slavery's cruelty. Even though most Chesapeake slaves were born in the region and lived in family units, whites realized that African Americans despised their bondage and were quite capable of resistance. Revolutionary planters "did not expect their slaves to be content or submissive; the myth of the happy and docile slave was not an eighteenth-century invention."[66] The Tuckers time and again experienced their slaves' unhappiness firsthand and dealt with it as they saw fit. Many of the family's slaves engaged in truancy, abandoning the quarters for weeks at a time. Frances's father, Theodorick Bland Sr., wrote from Cawsons in 1779: "Simon was runaway for three weeks. . . . Mr. Sturdivant [Bland's overseer], very justly, I think, gave him a whipping before I saw him." But he reported that another slave named "Tom Baker is still out," and the infuriated Bland bellowed, "I have had him outlawed, and offered a reward of one hundred dollars for apprehending him, and two hundred for his head." St. George and Frances felt little sympathy when their slaves misbehaved or wished for freedom. During the raids of 1781, many Tucker slaves tried to escape to the British. After two unfortunates were recaptured, St. George ordered them immediately sold, no doubt as an example to his remaining bondmen. Other slaves who displeased their masters also fared badly. St. George owned one African American named Hammond and used him as a personal servant before his marriage to Frances. But this slave possessed a taste for liquor and a sharp tongue, traits his new mistress refused to tolerate. Soon after the couple's wedding, Hammond disappeared entirely from the family's correspondence, indicating that he was sold off.[67]

Although the Tuckers were not harsh masters by contemporary standards, indifference about African Americans permeates their letters. The couple largely placed blacks on the far periphery of the family's collective experience, rarely mentioning their slaves apart from their duties or acts of disobedience. Even when slaves performed well, they received only vague and cursory notices. In March 1781, while campaigning in North Carolina with General Greene's Continental army, Tucker made only a passing reference to his personal servant, Syphax, who had accompanied his master into the field. Frances was highly pleased with her slaves during the family's escape from British raiders, but she only wrote, "My faithful Servants are every thing I cou'd wish them, and are willing to follow my fortune." Nor did the Tuckers seem especially concerned with or even aware of the black family networks that had developed in the Chesapeake by the late eighteenth century. In 1784, while looking for a runaway slave named John Braxton, Ryland Randolph, a kinsman of the Tuckers, had to explain to an apparently unaware St. George that this slave had many children then living at Matoax. Because of this, Randolph suspected the slave was hiding somewhere on the plantation.[68]

Even when they attempted to prevent what they considered to be excessive and unnecessary cruelty, the Tuckers' concern was always the protection of the family's property. In November 1787, when seven months pregnant, Frances traveled sixty miles over bad roads from Chesterfield to Cumberland County because of the "Anarchy" then reigning at Bizarre. "The extreem, and repeated cruelty of the Overseer," she explained to her husband, had led to a "Mutiny" among the slaves. Although Frances pitied these "miserable creatures" and "their cruel situation," she especially noted that "the most Valuable Negroes" had fled the farm, which had caused great "injury [to] the plantation."[69]

Though St. George and Frances Tucker closely cooperated in governing their children, land, and slaves, they never saw their household as an isolated entity. As in Bermuda, members of the Virginia gentry relied upon a dense network of kinship ties to achieve happiness, success, and advancement in their lives. Although historians assert that eighteenth-century planters wished for "independence" from the outside world, they also greatly depended upon a wide array of trusted kinsmen for utilitarian assistance and emotional support. Complex blood and affinal ties, therefore, stretched throughout eastern Virginia during the eighteenth century and were a key component to the planter class's power. Before the Revolution the Bland and Randolph families frequently called on one another both socially and to help manage their plantations. In October 1772 Theodorick Bland Sr. informed his son-in-law John Randolph that two hogsheads of

Matoax tobacco had just arrived at "Boyds Warehouse." "Let me know," Bland wrote, "what you would have done with them and your directions shall be complyed with." A month later Bland again wrote to Randolph, telling him that the finished "Ironwork" slated for Matoax would be delayed because the blacksmiths at Cawsons lacked the "proper Iron."[70]

The Blands and Randolphs also exchanged family slaves when certain tasks needed to be completed. John Randolph once asked if his father-in-law's "little Tom" could be sent to his estate to paint the great house. Several months earlier Randolph had sent one of his slaves named Phill Anthony to Cawsons to be trained by Bland's bondsmen as a carpenter or wheelwright. Bland periodically updated his son-in-law about this slave's progress: "Your Waggon is done and the whole work performed by Phill I think is well done, however, I don't believe he is yet master of his Trade tho' a few months more will Compleat . . . his education."[71]

This indispensable web of familial assistance remained in place following St. George Tucker's entrance into these clans. In particular, kin members continued to market and sell one another's tobacco. In 1780 Theodorick Jr. arranged for £650 worth of his brother-in-law's crop to be carted to Archibald Robertson's warehouse in Petersburg. John Banister also assisted his kin at Matoax, at times purchasing the Tuckers' tobacco and consigning it with his own for sale overseas.[72] St. George performed various duties for his kin as well. In 1784 Theodorick Bland Sr. needed four hogsheads of tobacco sold at once so that he could pay his state taxes. Expecting Tucker to perform the task immediately and without question, the old man grumbled that the cash had to be in hand "by the first of next week." The previous year Tucker had sought to find "a Tenant of good Character" to rent Theodorick Jr.'s Farmingdell plantation in Prince Edward County. Then in Philadelphia as a member of the Continental Congress, Theodorick expected his brother-in-law also to collect debts due to the family from planters around the area. "Capt Benet," Bland explained in one letter, "is to pay me some money which I sh[oul]d be obl'ged to you to receive and remit to me."[73]

Tucker did not forgot his responsibilities to his Bermuda clan. Whenever possible, he used his kinsmen's vessels (likely commanded by trusted skippers he already knew) to ship the produce of his farms overseas. In October 1780 the brig *Charity,* owned by Jennings, Tucker & Company, docked at Blandford near Matoax. The captain, Thomas Gordon, immediately applied to Tucker for his tobacco to fill the ship's hold. Several months beforehand, St. George had personally supervised the loading of another family vessel, the *Porgy,* with hogsheads of his "James River" tobacco.[74]

Tucker assisted his relations in other ways as well. In 1779 a cousin from Bermuda named Elizabeth Colbert lived in Hampton, Virginia. Married to a brutal man, she confessed to St. George that her husband "abuses me in the vilest manner . . . [and] denies that he is married to me." Moreover, he had begun "beating me." Colbert called upon her kinsman as "the only friend I have in this Country." Tucker at once offered his cousin "as much money as may be necessary" to enable her to obtain a legal separation and transportation back home to Bermuda. If she wished to stay in Virginia, Tucker promised to support her with £150 to £200 annually out of his own pocket. Several years later St. George traveled to New York City at the behest of another Bermuda cousin named John Tudor, who believed that he had a claim to some land within the rising metropolis. Needing a lawyer to go through New York's land records, Tudor called upon his Virginia cousin to perform the task. In 1786 St. George spent several months in the city, but his search proved fruitless. Despite the time and travel he put in, Tucker never received or expected any financial recompense. It was simply a familial obligation he was expected to fulfill.[75]

The functional nature of these kinship ties during the Revolutionary era was, above all, grounded in close emotional bonds between members. As before the War for Independence, love and affection reached throughout the entire familial network. St. George Tucker, for example, constructed very close ties to his tidewater kin. His brother-in-law Theodorick Bland once bemoaned to Tucker about having to leave "my more than Friends at Matoax" because of his congressional duties in Philadelphia. But "I shall bear along with me," he concluded, "a warm and affectionate remembrance of them patterning myself with a *reciprocity* of affection." Bland also lavished attention upon his niece and nephews, repeatedly writing to them as well as frequently sending them presents. Beverley Randolph too remained close to the Matoax clan after his cousin John Randolph died. While devoted to both St. George and Frances, Beverley took special delight in the children. He once requested Anne Frances spend "a year or two" with him and his wife on their nearby plantation of Chatsworth. He paid particular attention to his namesake, Nathaniel Beverley, born in 1784. Randolph closed one letter: "My Love particularly to my sweet little namesake. The strong attachment which he discovered to me has perfectly won my Heart and I beg that when he shall deserve Punishment for some of the almost involuntary transgressions of childhood a Part at least of the Penalty may be remitted on my account."[76]

Close ties of affection ran between Bermuda and Virginia as well. Soon after her marriage Frances found herself warmly embraced by all of The Grove Tuckers. Elizabeth assured her brother, for instance, that the fact "that you have a wife, will be sufficient for me to love her as a Sister, and to wish a Sister's Place in her Affection." Henry Tucker Jr. told Frances in his first letter to her: "Nobody loves their Friends with more Tenderness than I do. Give my Leave, My dear Sister, to seat you in the little Circle of those I love best."[77] Several years later, when the couple's "dear little Prattlers" began to arrive, St. George's mother urged her son to "teach them to know they have friends in Bermuda that are very Anxious about them." She need not have worried. As soon as he took his vows, St. George made sure that his Virginia family would come to know and love his kin in his homeland. He constantly urged Frances as well as his stepchildren to write letters to their Bermuda relations. He demanded, moreover, that his own nieces and nephews in Bermuda write to him regularly in the Old Dominion. Tucker fully realized that if these familial ties were to survive, letters, good wishes, and gifts needed to flow across the Atlantic.[78]

These bonds of affection between Virginia and Bermuda were experienced firsthand in 1785 when the Matoax household traveled to the island for a five-month visit. The trip occurred in part because of the precarious health of St. George's youngest stepson, John Randolph Jr. The eleven-year-old boy had a frail constitution, and in 1784 his parents thought Bermuda's temperate climate would strengthen him. When young Randolph arrived at The Grove, the Colonel and the women in the house warmly cared for him. After a time St. George and Frances decided to take the rest of the family from Matoax over for a visit.[79] By mid-1785 the arrangements were finally completed, with the Tuckers' Virginia kin agreeing to oversee their slaves and plantations in the couple's absence. John Banister would monitor affairs at Roanoke while Beverley Randolph would keep tabs on the other estates.[80] Ship accommodations out of Norfolk also were set by this time. In addition to the children and several house slaves, St. George arranged to bring his finest bay horse with him to show off to friends and family.

The family visit was a rousing success, culminating in November with the celebration of Colonel Tucker's seventy-second birthday. As he grew older, St. George would look back and remember these months as the happiest of his life. His children especially seem to have been the center of much attention and activity. St. George's sister Elizabeth asked soon after the clan's departure: "How do they all do? Does my dear lively Fanny keep her health and Spirits? Does my good little Harry love his book as well as ever? To my sweet tempered Tudor as full of emulation, and as fond of praise as he used to be? and is that wild, sprightly rogue Nat Beverly likely to credit to my prediction by growing a handsome fellow? Heaven bless them all! Tell them their Aunt will always love them with the greatest tenderness." Colonel Tucker also wrote after the departure of the Matoax household, but in a more serious vein. Realizing the improbability of ever seeing them again, he told his son: "I shall say little on the subject of our parting, it is of too tender a nature to dwell upon. however severe it was I wou'd not have foregone the happiness I had of seeing Mrs. Tucker and the Children for any Consideration."[81]

True to his premonition, the Colonel never saw the Virginia clan again. After a brief illness he died in April 1787. Henry Tucker Sr.'s death, however, was only the first of two blows to strike the family following their return. Nine months after the Colonel's demise, Frances Bland Tucker died following the birth of a second daughter. These two unexpected deaths, coming so closely together, spawned a powerful reaction among surviving members that marked a dramatic turning point in the family's emotional life and outlook. The Tuckers had theretofore always attempted to face death the same way they confronted life's other challenges: with balance, moderation, and restraint. In 1779 Colonel Tucker had noted with admiration how his wife's brother, Frank Butterfield, had died "like a Hero." Suspecting the end to be near, Butterfield had carefully placed his papers in order and executed a will. Then after consuming a bit of bread and drink, he "laid himself on the bed and dyed immediately." Several years later, after Archibald Campbell's "much respected" wife passed away, everyone at The Grove observed how her husband "bears his misfortune with Christian Fortitude." The only discernible reaction, they noted, was the "silent tears rolling down his venerable Cheeks."[82]

After the Colonel and Frances died, however, the family's emotional state entered a period of change and flux. Henry Tucker Sr. began his seventy-fourth year in reasonably good health, but in the spring of 1787 he contracted an illness that quickly proved fatal. Afterwards, the family

attempted to act with traditional restraint and resignation. Henry Jr. re-
layed the news to Matoax that "the good old Gentleman" had "given up the
Ghost." Although everyone felt "great" pain at his demise, Henry insisted
that there was no need to dwell on "our Affliction." The family had hoped
the Colonel would live to an older age, but "Heaven has thought fit to order otherwise, and it is our Duty to submit," Henry concluded. "It affords
us too inconceivable Comfort to reflect, that he met . . . his Dissolution
with a Fortitude and Steadiness which wou'd have done Credit to . . . the
Romans." Others soon chimed in. All celebrated the Colonel's noble life,
complimented his dispassionate death, and repressed the grief that everyone felt. Elizabeth wrote that her father died fully conscious "of a well spent
life." Recalling the death scene, she told St. George, "I see him patient and
resigned calm and collected to his latest moments."[83]

As the months passed, however, family members found that their traditional moderation had left them empty and wanting. Six months after the
Colonel died, Henry Tucker of Somerset's son wrote to his Virginia uncle
that everyone's grief at the Colonel's passing had not abated but rather had
grown "almost insupportable." The Tuckers in Bermuda seemed no longer
to care about Tucker Sr.'s well-spent life. They wanted only to focus on the
hereafter when "the Almighty" would, as his daughter Frances hopefully
wrote, "send us all [to] a joyful meeting with him in a happier place." The
language of restraint also disappeared from their letters. Seventeen months
after the Colonel's death, Elizabeth confessed how "my soul was harrowed
up" after he died, "and I sank under the distress." Though God "had called
him to a better life," she had "wept abundantly." Her "grief" had diminished over time, she admitted, but not because she had reflected on his good
life. The pain eased only when she "dwelt on that future state of blessed-
ness, where I have the most lively hopes of one day meeting my dear departed friends who go before."[84]

The second blow to the family came in January 1788 when thirty-six-
year-old Frances Bland Tucker died at Matoax following the birth of a
daughter the family named Elizabeth. Frances's health had been declining
for several years. Possessing a frail constitution, she was badly shaken and
weakened during the family's very rough passage home from Bermuda in
late 1785. The next year her health worsened after she endured an exhaust-
ing pregnancy only to lose the baby at birth. The following spring Frances
discovered she was again pregnant, for the ninth time in seventeen years.

As the due date approached, she grew progressively weaker in part because of her constant work on the family's plantations. That summer, moreover, she accidentally fell off the porch that wrapped around the great house at Matoax, badly injuring herself.[85] In mid-December she gave birth to a healthy girl, but only after a difficult labor, and she did not recover as in the past. Instead Frances grew steadily weaker and died on 18 January 1788.

Several weeks after her death, Frances's brother, Theodorick, attempted to console everyone at Matoax with traditional moderation. "Alas my Friend," he explained to St. George, "our plaints are unavailing, and the calm reasoning of Philosophy and time alone must reconcile us to heaven." This advice, so common beforehand, now went entirely unheeded. Few family members even tried to hide their grief at her death. An inconsolable St. George took to his bed, not emerging for weeks. John Coalter, a young man from Augusta County recently hired as the children's tutor, tried to find out if he would remain with the family, "but Mr. Tuckers grief will not permit him to say anything." From South Carolina, brother Thomas exclaimed at the news, "The Anguish of my Soul is unspeakable." "Gracious God!" Henry Jr. opened his letter of consolation. "I see your Agonies. I hear the Groans you strive in vain to suppress." No one mentioned Frances's noble and well-spent life. Immediately all thoughts turned to the grief everyone felt and to the afterlife "beyond this transitory Scene of Wickedness," as Thomas wrote. "Indeed our only Consolation," Henry Jr. cried, "seems to rest on the Hope, that we are all hastening to the same blissful Abode, where we shall recognize each other and dwell together in perpetual and endless Delight."[86]

The deaths of the Colonel and Frances Tucker in quick succession unleashed a torrent of passion and agitation within the clan. The response of family members, so out of character when compared to earlier times, points to the centrality of these two figures to the family's collective life. But the survivors' efforts to cope also hint at broader strains and pressures afflicting their lives that were only now beginning to emerge. Throughout the 1780s, as St. George and Frances attempted to manage Matoax and their other plantations, Virginia and the United States were changing at a rapid rate. Many of these transformations were deeply ominous ones for the family and for the Old Dominion's planter class in general. The Tuckers' unmistakable loss of moderation in 1787–88, therefore, reflects not simply

personal bereavement but a broader sense of loss at the changes manifest-
ing around them. They had become people whose lives were being unexpectedly "harrowed up" on a variety of fronts. In the process they began to
lose that enlightened balance for which they and the Revolutionary gentry
overall had been so famous. The Tuckers at this point started to become
very different people living in a world whose axis was rapidly turning.

Three

Surviving the New Republic: New Strategies, New Educations

In the summer of 1788, the events of the Revolution intruded once more into St. George Tucker's household. On 25 June, after much debate, Virginia's Ratification Convention narrowly approved the plan for a new national government drafted in Philadelphia the previous year. Four days later Tucker wrote his stepsons: "You will have heard that the Constitution has been adopted in this State; that Event, my dear Children, affects your interest more nearly than that of most others. The recovery of British debts can no longer be postponed, and there now seems to be a moral certainty that your patrimony will all go to satisfy the unjust debt from your Papa to the Hanbury's." Much of the land and property with which the Randolph boys had expected to make their way in the world soon would be seized to retire their father's long-standing liabilities. Tucker concluded with blunt advice: "The consequence, my dear boys, must be obvious to you—your sole dependence must be on your own personal Abilities and Exertions."[1]

In 1788 St. George Tucker was a shaken man. He remained emotionally distraught over his wife's death in January. During the final years of his marriage, moreover, he had begun to witness numerous changes across the land that threatened his family as well as the state he had come to love. In particular, Tucker saw Virginia's gentry class dangerously teeter in its position of power. The Revolution's aftermath brought so many unexpected social, political, and economic changes to the Old Dominion that Tucker became convinced that the great planters' authority and place had been fatally compromised. In order to maintain his family's position near the apex of society, he told his stepchildren that they would have to adopt new values and principles. As Virginia and the nation adjusted to the transformations unleashed by independence, he predicted that individual self-reliance and self-sufficiency would be the keys to success in the future.

This chapter examines the Tucker family's response to the post-Revolutionary years. Expecting few significant changes after the conflict, St. George and Frances initially had reached back to the practices of the late colonial era to guide their lives and households. They firmly believed that land, slaves, and family bonds would guarantee their prosperity. Soon, however, St. George Tucker saw ominous changes sweep through the state that economically destroyed many within his circle and politically weakened the gentry's overall domination. Amid the flux he reevaluated and eventually abandoned his commitment to the traditions of the past, including the elite's fundamental belief in land and slaves. Tucker concurrently groped for new strategies that would protect his family's place and wealth. Time and again, Tucker explained to his sons that the ways of the past no longer ensured success and affluence. Nor would membership to a great family automatically bring prestige and fortune. Instead, in the years ahead only "personal Abilities and Exertions" could deliver happiness, position, and property.

In the years before Frances Tucker died, an ambitious St. George Tucker had sought to enter the first ranks of Virginia society through a combination of connections, gentility, and landownership. Yet before her death, he began to witness startling changes in the state's economy that eventually led him to rethink his commitment to the Old Dominion's traditional order. At the time of the Revolution, a number of great planters, particularly those living south of the James River, stood heavily in debt. Most had spent exorbitant amounts of money on mansions, carriages, clothes, slaves, china, and furniture, in part to prove their financial strength and independence. By the 1770s their liabilities were staggering.[2]

Wartime destruction deepened the crisis and further undermined the solvency of many planters. During Benedict Arnold's raid across the James River valley in 1780–81, British troops looted numerous plantations, burned tobacco warehouses, and freed thousands of slaves. Later in 1781 Lord Cornwallis's raiders returned to the tidewater and destroyed more property, including Theodorick Bland Jr.'s Farmingdell plantation. In September 1781 St. George wrote to his brother-in-law, "Your furniture, I was told, was totally destroyed or pillaged, your corn &c., wasted, your stock of cattle and sheep greatly damaged if not totally destroyed." Tucker's brother-in-law John Banister also suffered greatly at the hands of the enemy. Both men realized that their losses would not be easy to recoup.[3]

After the war, moreover, Virginia's economy did not recover as many had expected. Tobacco prices did spike upward following the Treaty of Paris, but this merely encouraged planters to resume their prewar spending habits. Finished goods from Great Britain again poured onto Virginia wharves. But the Old Dominion's staple economy remained as vulnerable as ever to outside forces well beyond the gentry's control. Thus, when demand for tobacco fell off and prices collapsed in 1785, many planters found themselves more deeply in debt than ever. Throughout the decade the gentry also had to learn to operate outside the protective walls of the British Empire as well as to cope with other European nations that refused to open their markets fully to American produce. The state's economy ground almost to a halt. Banister helplessly wrote Tucker, "I do not know in such Circumstances how business can go on, for Confidence is totally lost." Another friend from Petersburg described common scenes of economic malaise. "Our Planters and Merchants are much dispirited," he wrote. "The first cannot pay what they owe and the Last cannot sell the goods they have on Hand. The dulness of Trade and the Scarcity of Money are Expressions which in the common Intercourse among our Citizens you may expect to hear about a thousand times a Day." Planters also became aware of just how serious soil exhaustion had become throughout the tidewater, adding to their economic woes.[4]

As Virginia's economy deteriorated, Tucker witnessed the great planters endure frightful losses. John Banister's world collapsed after the war. In 1787, after struggling for years, Tucker's brother-in-law confronted heavy debts, restricted credit, and diminished tobacco yields. He cried to family members that he could not even pay his state taxes. As a result, "my Chariot horses and several of my best Negroes are taken in execution which will prevent my making a Crop." As his debts mounted, Banister grew acutely aware of his crumbling reputation. When St. George once pressed him for payment of a small debt, he lost his temper: "As to Punctuality I trust you have no complaint about as I have always answered every demand you ever made. The reverse of what I have experienced to a great amount from many." The following year Tucker's demoralized kinsman died.

Within months the executors of Banister's will auctioned off thirty-six slaves to satisfy the many waiting creditors. Yet the estate still remained £4,000 in debt, which forced the final liquidation of his family's lands.[5]

Particularly painful for Tucker was the collapse of his former patrons, the Nelsons. Hard economic times and long-standing debts overwhelmed the once-powerful clan. St. George attempted to assist the struggling family, but nothing halted its precipitous decline. In 1786 Governor Thomas Nelson's brother Nathaniel Nelson left Virginia and sailed to Bermuda to test his fortunes there. St. George probably provided the Virginian with generous letters of introduction, and Nelson resided at The Grove after landing. But he had caught a fever during the voyage and died six weeks later. In 1789 the ex-governor himself died, forcing the liquidation of more property. St. George soon afterwards loaned the family money, hoping that the cash would tide the clan's survivors over until the state's economy improved. Getting repaid, however, proved to be a long and painful task, embarrassing to all sides. For years Tucker repeatedly applied to the governor's oldest son, William, simply for interest due on the loan. St. George usually received only testy replies, perhaps hiding wounded family pride. "I have no money at present," Nelson snapped in 1794, "and I have had none since your last application to me, or I should have made the payment before this time." A year later little had changed. "I rec'd your Letter . . . yesterday and am extremely sorry that I have it not in my power to comply with the contents of it. . . . The wheat crop of the last year was so bad that my Mother was obliged to make use of the money received for . . . necessities for her family." The Nelsons did not pay Tucker until 1800, nearly a decade after the original debt was contracted.[6]

John Banister and the Nelsons were not the only members in Tucker's circle to encounter financial difficulties. His brother Thomas in South Carolina faced numerous troubles after the war, especially after several unwise land investments floundered. Unable to pay a vast array of obligations, he confessed that he was reduced to "the Condition of a Beggar." Other friends and family expressed similar complaints. His brother-in-law Theodorick Bland Jr. as well as Archibald Cary, Beverley Randolph, John Page, and William Fitzhugh all spoke of their growing woes. Each of these planters had to liquidate portions of their landed and human property in order to retire their debts. During these years Tucker likely agreed with Virginia merchant William Allison's assessment that "we have not only had a revolution in Political government but also in many peoples private circumstances." According to Allison, many individuals of "good credit" before the war now confronted poverty and hardship, while those of modest means "are now the most opulent."[7]

In this uncertain environment St. George Tucker confronted his own family's possible ruin. Although Frances Bland Randolph had brought land and slaves to her marriage, she also conveyed the great debts incurred by her first husband, John Randolph of Matoax. Such liabilities were ignored during the war, but St. George had to deal with them now. Well-known among family members for his great "dread" of "poverty," Tucker realized that he needed additional income beyond faltering agricultural enterprises to preserve his family's economic viability.[8] Thus he reluctantly returned to the bar as a county court lawyer in 1782. Although truly interested in the law, Tucker told acquaintances that he detested his new situation. One friend, Robert Innes, sympathized: "You complain of your being oblig'd to turn County Court Lawyer. It is true the fall from a gentleman of ease and pleasure to one Laborious occupation is disagreeable."[9]

Despite Tucker's concerns about his change in status, his legal practice during the 1780s became highly successful, a product of talent, timing, and connections. Already well-known and respected in the counties surrounding Matoax, Tucker found that his friendship with Jerman Baker paid particular dividends. Baker had long been Chesterfield County's most prominent and successful attorney, but after the war he wanted to practice only before the General Court in Richmond. Therefore, he asked St. George to assume his pending county court suits. This immediately provided the new lawyer with hundreds of cases in Chesterfield, Dinwiddie, and Amelia Counties and made his practice an instant success.[10]

Tucker's heavy caseload throughout the 1780s ironically reflected Virginia's growing instability. Like many county court lawyers, he handled mainly debt cases and, as a result, witnessed repeated scenes of hardship. Because the courts had been closed for the greater part of the Revolution, Virginia creditors were desperate to get their money, and they "commenced actions with a vengeance, pressing for debts in several courts at once." Tucker handled an avalanche of cases for both creditors who demanded quick action and debtors who pleaded for relief. One client in Dinwiddie County lamented that the county sheriff had cleared his house out because of a £127 debt. He wrote that the sheriff had "seiz'd on my house Servants,

Bay horses, household furniture, he has not left me a Chair Table or a Bed to ly on." He begged Tucker to get the public sale of his property postponed until he could raise the money.[11]

Although he had much business, Tucker's financial worries multiplied as the years passed. Uncertain markets for his family's crops, the frequent inability of clients to pay for his legal services, and John Randolph of Matoax's outstanding debts all weighed upon his mind. In 1784 the Colonel had noted to his son, "You complain much of your Finances." So great had his money problems become that St. George had to call periodically upon fellow planters for outstanding debts, a task that "much embarrassed" and "pained" him. To his wife he confessed that he felt overwhelmed by "all my perplexities" and wished for "ease and independence."[12] Several months after Frances's death, Tucker once more complained, this time to his brother, that he felt "much straighten'd in pecuniary Circumstances."[13]

As hard economic times shredded Virginia's social fabric, great political changes unfolded. In many respects social, economic, and political matters all became thoroughly intermixed during the 1780s. Tucker and others saw that excessive debt, high taxes, and the dismal economy consumed the minds of both leaders and freeholders alike. And the difficult climate spawned great suspicions and bitterness between them. A large part of the problem was that few people understood the true causes behind the decade's depression. Though the reasons were complex, the downturn was triggered particularly by a profound shortage of money in the state. Like most in the eighteenth century, Virginia politicians believed that paper currency should only be used in times of dire emergencies. Thus when the Revolution ended, the state government began redeeming its wartime currency without regard to the economic impact of such a move. Within a year of Yorktown, state paper in circulation dropped from £60 million (in face value) to under £1 million. At the same time the resumption of British imports drained the state of specie. Adding to these woes, the state government continued to require that all taxes be paid in coin. The result was severe deflation and a near halt to economic activity.[14]

From the gentry's point of view, one of the most serious consequences of the financial crisis was the political instability it engendered. Throughout the decade great planters deeply feared that politicians drawn from the ranks of the yeomanry, such as Patrick Henry, would use the downturn to increase their personal power and to force the General Assembly to overturn legal contracts in the name of debtor relief. Even more troubling were

the direct forms of protest against established authority that were beginning to occur. In the eastern counties of King William and New Kent,
courthouses mysteriously burned down right before their quarterly courts
met. In Greenbrier County to the west, three hundred farmers joined together and stoutly refused to pay all debts and taxes.[15]

The depression also undercut nearly everyone's confidence in the federal
government established under the Articles of Confederation. With the
Continental Congress wholly unable to respond to the nation's economic
woes, Virginia leaders called for a general meeting of the states in 1786 to
strengthen the Articles' commercial clauses. The General Assembly named
Tucker as a delegate because, as James Madison wrote, he was a "sensible
federal and skilled in commerce." The five state delegations that attended
the Annapolis Convention called for another meeting to convene the following spring in Philadelphia. Although the state legislature did not name
Tucker to the Constitutional Convention of 1787, he eventually supported
the new federal system. He concluded that a stronger national government
was essential to bring order to the nation's economy and to its foreign
trade.[16]

Despite the establishment of a more powerful central government,
political changes detrimental to the gentry continued to unfold within
the state. Planter authority unraveled within the county courts throughout the 1780s. Long a bastion of gentry power, the state's local judiciary
nearly collapsed following the Revolution when planter magistrates found
themselves overwhelmed with numerous complex cases argued by lawyers
trained in the law's intricacies. The number of untried cases mounted
alarmingly while many other disputes were successfully appealed to the
state's higher courts.[17] St. George Tucker possessed only antipathy for this
ancient institution of Virginia law. His animosity, however, stemmed not
from the unrepublican nature of the local courts' power but rather from the
planter justices' utter inability to resolve cases efficiently. Without competent jurists in command, respect for the courts vanished, and more importantly, deference toward gentry magistrates eroded. Recalling his own experiences, Tucker wrote:

My Acquaintance with [the county courts] has shewn them to be
places of general resort for idle and dissipated, as well as for those
whose business may call them thither: the latter are far less numerous than the former. Drunkenness, quarelling, and fighting keep

pace, at least, with the Administration of Justice, at these places. Lawsuits and Dissipation are alike promoted and encreased thereby. Many who have no other Business repair to Court in the hope of getting a drink at the expence of some other person, or with the design of spending the only shilling they can command in Liquor.[18]

Instead of being a stabilizing force for their uncertain times, the county courts increased social instability by encouraging open disdain for men in authority. An appointment to the state's bench in 1788 only confirmed Tucker's grim view. That January he learned that the legislature had appointed him a judge to the General Court. Although he at first hesitated because of Frances's death, Tucker eventually accepted the position. The judgeship required him to travel throughout Virginia to attend district court sessions, a process that took him to all corners of the Old Dominion and vividly revealed the social, economic, and political transformations at work.[19]

Thus, as the first decade of independence drew to a close, Tucker believed that he confronted two crises: one private, involving the reputation and solvency of his own family; the other public, concerning the declining position, status, and authority of the state's planter elite. Although he refused to blame the Revolution for the turmoil he saw, he significantly altered his vision of the Old Dominion at this time. Determined both to create a more stable political and social environment and to preserve his family's wealth and influence, Tucker embraced new strategies and principles that he believed would bring prosperity to Virginia, stability to its government, and security to his kin.

In the wake of these changes, Tucker grew convinced first and foremost that land—that bulwark of the old gentry's status and power—had become a dismal, dead-end investment. Not only did he see his own land values decline in the late 1780s and into the 1790s, but he witnessed the near-total collapse of others, including John Page's once-glorious plantation of Rosewell, which shrank from 4,000 acres to 1,750. In his notes to *Blackstone's Commentaries,* published in 1803 but drafted in the 1790s, Tucker explained what he saw happening. The best lands in the "country below the mountains in Virginia" had all been cleared and cultivated, largely "without improvement, till they are not more productive than fresh lands of far inferior quality." He estimated that barely one tidewater planter in twenty now made enough "for the support of himself and his family."[20] As a result,

Tucker decided to sell off the plantations he had acquired during his marriage to Frances. He liquidated Green Creek by selling it back to Beverley Randolph. He also sold off Bermuda Forest and his 900 acres in Dinwiddie County. He never again considered a major land purchase.[21] Tucker later explained that instead of promising security and independence, his estates had only brought him "continual losses."[22]

At the same time he abandoned landownership, Tucker purchased three lots and a house facing the Palace Green and Market Square in Williamsburg from his stepsons' distant cousin Edmund Randolph, who was completing a term as Virginia's governor. St. George moved there with his children and house slaves in the autumn of 1788. He left Matoax and relocated to the former capital, he later wrote, "for the benefit of educating my Children at the College without parting with them from under mine own Eye."[23] He also moved because his stepsons were approaching maturity and would soon take control of their lands. But Tucker left Matoax, above all, because he perceived the economic folly of remaining on decaying estates. Tucker's remarriage in 1791 even reflected his new attitudes about landed property. Tucker began courting twenty-four-year-old Lelia Skipwith Carter, the daughter of Sir Peyton Skipwith and widow of George Carter, in the fall of 1790 soon after she began tutoring Tucker's older daughter, Anne Frances. The couple became engaged the following spring, and in October the two were wed.[24] Lelia shared many of her predecessor's traits: she found herself widowed at a early age with young children, she possessed important connections to two powerful Virginia families, and she brought landed property to the marriage, the sizable Lancaster County plantation named Corotoman, once the domain of Robert "King" Carter. Unlike Frances Tucker, though, Lelia did not insist that they live on this country estate. She instead willingly and happily moved into her new husband's town home, where she cared for the judge, her new stepchildren, and her own two children, Charles and Mary "Polly" Carter. The couple clearly found a city lifestyle compatible with their mutual tastes and needs.

Tucker repositioned his family's property in other ways to respond to changing times. By the early 1790s he saw many tidewater planters and other Virginians migrating westward into the piedmont and even regions beyond, seeking new lands and opportunities. Although tobacco markets modestly improved during the decade, demand for wheat and other grain crops surged when European wars erupted in 1793. Most farmers in the western counties eschewed Virginia's traditional staple crop and chose instead to cultivate less labor-intensive food grains.[25] Although St. George Tucker maintained that land could no longer serve as the foundation of elite power in the state, he still envisioned America as a great agricultural empire. As a good republican, he believed that the United States should and could remain an agricultural society "for ages," peopled by a "hardy, independent yeomanry" class that nobly worked the land and remained free from corruption. This was possible, he held, because of the "great abundance" of "low price[d] land" available to the west. Tucker understood, however, that migrating farmers also needed access to reliable credit to develop their lands. He recognized that tobacco factors, who had served as "a kind of Petty Banker" before the Revolution, could no longer adequately serve Virginians at a time when the state's economy was expanding and growing more complex. Only properly regulated and heavily capitalized banks could facilitate Virginia's sustained economic development, particularly as lands away from the state's navigable rivers were cleared and opened for cultivation. Recognizing the potential for profit, he began to invest heavily in state banks, purchasing stock with capital likely raised from his own land sales. He ultimately purchased over $10,000 worth of stock in the newly chartered Bank of Alexandria, and he bought additional shares for his children.[26]

When Tucker sold his landed property, he also began to reevaluate his commitment to human property. Before 1790 he had dealt with slaves simply as workers and had remained mute about the system's morality. Blacks in bondage had been part of his everyday life, always present. After he sold off most of his lands and moved to Williamsburg, however, Tucker began to argue that the time was right for Virginians to live up to their Revolutionary ideals.

Shortly after he relocated to the former colonial capital, Tucker accepted an offer to become the College of William and Mary's law professor. The judge replaced George Wythe, who resigned after becoming the sole chancellor of Virginia and in a few years moved to Richmond. The new position allowed Tucker to continue in his post on the General Court and provided him with a stage from which to pose difficult questions he believed whites now had to face in the Revolution's wake. Troubled by the hypocrisy of slavery in a republic of liberty, he asked his law students in 1790 if there was "due consistency between our avowed principles and our practice" with regard to "those unfortunate people." After further reflection, Tucker more pointedly asserted, "Whilst America hath been the land of promise to Europeans, and their descendants, it hath been the vale of death to millions of the wretched sons of Africa." [27] Yet it was slavery's incompatibility with the Revolution's universal tenets that disturbed him the most. That all men are created equal, he affirmed, "is, indeed, no more than a recognition of the first principles of the law of nature." Therefore, in the name of compassion and ideological consistency, he urged whites to "regard [African Americans] as our fellow men." [28]

Convinced of the fundamental humanity of slaves, Tucker saw much that both encouraged and disheartened him since the Revolution. During the war northern states began to eliminate the institution, while at home Virginia's General Assembly liberalized manumission laws.[29] Concurrently, some prominent Virginians put forth serious emancipation plans, and many evangelicals maintained their staunch commitment to slavery's eradication.[30] Yet attitudes also hardened in many corners of the state. In 1784–85 more than twelve hundred ordinary citizens signed petitions asserting that in their minds African Americans were nothing more than chattel.[31] Several years later the Constitution's three-fifths clause regarding slaves significantly augmented Virginia's political power at the national level and thus convinced some not to challenge the institution, regardless of the injustice to blacks.

Amid these mixed signals, Tucker decided to prepare a serious emancipation proposal of his own. Like all Americans, he was horrified at the bloody slave revolution that broke out in St. Domingue in 1793. The successful rebellion in western Hispaniola convinced him of the need for quick action at home. He remained confident, moreover, that "a very large majority of slave-holders among us would cheerfully concur in any feasible plan for the [institution's] abolition." Because the current decade was the first period "of constitutional health and vigour" since the Revolution, Virginians ought to "embrace" the opportunity.[32] Tucker initially looked to the North for precedents. He corresponded at length with Jeremy Belknap, founder of the Massachusetts Historical Society, to learn how his state had freed and integrated African Americans into the general population. He also exchanged letters with Connecticut congressman Zephaniah Swift about the issue.[33]

Tucker completed his proposal in 1796 and had it published by the Philadelphia printer Mathew Carey under the title *A Dissertation on Slavery*. In it he sought a middle ground on which to reconcile liberalism's twin beliefs in basic human equality and the sanctity of all property. In short, he wished to eliminate slavery while not impinging upon the property rights of his fellow slave owners. He soothingly explained, "The abolition of slavery may be effected without the *emancipation* of a single slave; without depriving any man of the *property* which he *possesses,* and without defrauding a creditor who has trusted him on the faith of that property." To achieve these multiple ends, Tucker proposed that Virginia adopt many elements of Pennsylvania's plan for gradual emancipation adopted in 1780. All existing slaves would continue in bondage for the remainder of their lives, and all African-American males born to the current generation would also be enslaved for life. Females born after the plan's adoption would be free, although in servitude until their twenty-eighth birthday. These second-generation females then would transmit their free status to all their children, both male and female.[34]

Like many in his society, Tucker assumed slavery had so debased African Americans that once freed, they would not work unless compelled by force. Because "the earth cannot want cultivators," he proposed that all freedmen subsequently be coerced into laboring for the white ruling class if they did not do so voluntarily. Moreover, believing that whites would never permit blacks to participate in society on terms of equality, Tucker proposed excluding them from most civil and political rights, hoping that over time they would voluntarily migrate to western lands beyond the United States. Although admitting that his plan "savour[ed] strongly of prejudice," Tucker confessed that he chose to "accomodate" racism in order to "avoid as many obstacles as possible to the completion of so desirable a work, as the abolition of slavery." From the date of its inception, the plan would take 105 years before Virginia's last slave would die.[35]

After Carey printed the *Dissertation on Slavery,* Tucker confidently submitted it to the state legislature for consideration. To the Speaker of the House of Delegates, he solemnly wrote, "The Representatives of a free people who . . . have declared that all Men are by nature equally free and independent, can not disapprove an attempt to carry so incontestible a moral Truth into practical Effect." The reception in the General Assembly proved disastrous. Despite Tucker's many concessions to white racism, most delegates refused even to consider his proposal. "Such is the force of prejudice," one sympathetic member wrote, "that in the house of delegates, characters were found who voted against the letter and its enclosure lying on the table." Stunned by the virulent reaction, Tucker indignantly told Belknap, "Nobody was prepared to meet the blind fury of the enemies of freedom." Tucker despaired over whether the nation's Revolutionary principles would ever be fulfilled. He continued to distribute the *Dissertation on Slavery* to his friends and family and to lecture his law students about his plan. He also reprinted the essay in his 1803 edition of *Blackstone's Commentaries*. But he never again approached the legislature about the matter.[36]

Despite his failure to move the Old Dominion's leaders toward emancipation, St. George Tucker clearly had altered his beliefs about the institution's legitimacy in a land of freedom. However, the numerous bankruptcies around him and the precarious financial situation of his own family led Tucker to believe himself as yet unable to free his own nineteen bondpeople. Too much of his net worth and his children's future inheritances were wrapped up in these individuals. Family loyalty, therefore, compelled him to keep some slaves, while he sold off others for cash. On 2 December 1796, only two days after he had submitted his emancipation plan to the Virginia legislature, Tucker wrote Petersburg slave trader William Haxall that he wanted to sell four slaves—a mother and her three daughters—all of whom Tucker had previously hired out in that city. Confident in this merchant's "adroitness and punctuality," Tucker demanded £200 for the family, explaining, "The high price of negroes at present encourages me to hope that you will dispose of those for more than [that] sum." But the foursome drew no offers, nor could Haxall even hire them out. The trader suspected that no whites wanted the slaves because they "have so long had their own time and lived without controul." As a result, he urged Tucker to sell them separately at public auction, a course the judge resisted, not wishing to break up the family. Finally, in March 1797, after "much plague and trouble," Haxall announced that he had sold the foursome to a neighbor. Tucker afterwards used the cash to purchase more shares in the Bank of Alexandria for his daughter Anne Frances. Although he received less than he had originally hoped, the transaction greatly pleased him, and he utilized Haxall's services repeatedly over the next four years.[37]

Although Tucker placed his family's financial well-being before his stated principles, he had dramatically changed his vision of Virginia as an agrarian society. Land and slaves, he realized, no longer guaranteed a family economic power and social prestige over the long term. Tucker therefore rigorously prepared and trained his children for a very different world in the early Republic. Because he saw dangerous rocks strewn everywhere, he concluded that only a strong, practical, and utilitarian education could preserve their elite status into the future. Like his father, St. George

stressed morally upright and honorable behavior to his sons in order to gain
the respect of peers. Unlike the Colonel, however, St. George Tucker em-
phatically underscored the importance of a rigorous formal education. In
the early 1770s Tucker Sr. had never demanded that his son diligently master his studies. Only four months after St. George's arrival at William and
Mary, discussion in the family's correspondence regarding his academic
work ceased. Colonel Tucker and other family members instead focused on
St. George's "friendships" with members of the colonial aristocracy. Such
attitudes reflected not a lack of interest in schooling but rather a common
set of pre-Revolutionary priorities. In Virginia's plantation society, as in
Bermuda's mercantile-shipping economy, the need for liberally educated
gentlemen was limited. Theodorick Bland Jr. once explained that he was
"well convinced that learning is not confined merely to books and schools."
Although "learning is not a despicable acquirement when rightly understood," "the Paltry Jargon of schools constitute the smallest part of a Gents.
Education." Even as committed a republican as George Washington admitted that he did not believe that "becoming a mere scholar was a desirable education for a gentleman."[38] These men clearly grafted prewar con-
ceptions about genteel behavior onto the new Republic. In the past, those
taught to display the highest degree of social refinement and virtue won the
approbation of equals and superiors as well as the continuing deference of
those ranked below them.

Yet in the eighteenth century's final two decades, as important tidewater families declined and migration to the West accelerated, Tucker
grasped how markedly Virginia had changed. What a person knew and
how well he knew it had become much more important. One of the first in-
structional changes Tucker made regarding his children involved the complete elimination of language concerning "connections" and "cultivated
friendships." Although he never explicitly stated why he came to shun such
language, it conceivably stemmed from the sudden collapse of so many
powerful clans, particularly his old patrons the Nelsons. As prewar debts
eroded their wealth and influence, Tucker must have realized the folly of relying on such bonds.

In addition to rejecting the language of patronage, Tucker strongly emphasized the need for his children to master their formal studies through
hard work and self-discipline. The new realities that emerged out of the
Revolution in part explain the change. St. George recognized that American citizens (adult white males, of course) possessed "perfect equality of

rights" in this new Republic. As a result, nature would eventually reorder property ownership and social rank. "Equality of rights necessarily produces inequality of possessions," he later wrote, "because, by the laws of nature and of equality, every man has a right to use his faculties, in an honest way, and the fruits of his labour, thus acquired, are his own. But, some men have more strength than others; some more health; some more industry; and some more skill and ingenuity, than others; and according to these, and other circumstances the products of their labour must be various, and their property must become unequal." [39] Therefore, if the family's elite status was to survive into the future, the Tucker children must possess knowledge, industry, and self-reliance, not refined manners and patronage connections. In later years Tucker pointedly wrote to a young cousin about the need for self-sufficiency amid the instability of their times: "If ever there was a period in the History of Man which demonstrated the necessity of a Man's being able to place his reliance on *Himself,* the last thirty years may be considered as furnishing the most awful and instructive Lessons upon that Head. Thousands born to Affluence have in a moment been reduced to wretchedness." [40]

These fears led St. George and initially Frances Tucker to oversee their children's instruction closely. When the three Randolph boys attended Walker Maury's grammar school in the 1780s, their parents demanded regular updates on their progress. They later sent Richard, Theodorick, and John to the College of New Jersey in Princeton to be trained under the watchful eye of John Witherspoon. Best known for his treatise *Letters on Education* published in 1775, Witherspoon stressed moral development, intellectual attainment, and social refinement in all of his students. While Witherspoon worked on developing the boys' intellects, the Tuckers repeatedly told them that the route to happiness lay solely through hard work and effort. "Your own happiness through Life my boys," St. George wrote, "depends upon the conduct you now pursue. The boy who diligently attends his studies . . . will, when he is to move on the larger theatre of the world be careful attentive and diligent in his business." Tucker also sought to inspire them through the examples of America's Revolutionary heroes. Stressing that "every man is respectable in proportion to the Talents he possesses to serve it," Tucker urged his stepsons to emulate such luminaries as "General Washington," "Doctor Franklin," and "Mr. Rittenhouse." Frances also enticed her children to work hard with promises of gifts if they met their parents' academic expectations. The year after she died, St. George transferred the boys to Columbia College in New York City so that their uncles Thomas Tudor Tucker and Theodorick Bland Jr., then congressmen in the new federal government, could personally oversee their ongoing training and development.[41]

The Tuckers' intense management of the Randolph boys' education made a considerable impression on them all. In letters home, they always mentioned their industrious work habits and strong self-discipline. On Christmas Day 1788 fifteen-year-old John Randolph anxiously wrote to his stepfather: "Brother writes to you that I am lazy. I assure you, dear papa, he has been egregiously mistaken." John insisted that far from being indolent, he awoke daily at five o'clock, read assiduously, and attended every lecture. All remaining "leisure time," he asserted, was devoted to his "college duty."[42]

During the following decade, when it came time to educate his own daughter Anne Frances and sons, Henry St. George, Thomas Tudor, and Nathaniel Beverley, Tucker continued to stress intellectual development and self-discipline. Weeks before Frances's death, the couple decided to hire a private tutor "at all costs" instead of sending their young children away to boarding school where they could not monitor their progress. They retained a nineteen-year-old Augusta County man named John Coalter, whom Tucker later took to Williamsburg with the family in the autumn of 1788.[43] In the old colonial capital, Coalter instructed the children in their lessons three hours a day while Tucker traveled throughout the state as a district judge. The family and Coalter grew quite close during this period. St. George especially took to the young man, admiring both his intelligence and his diligent work habits. Tucker convinced Coalter to pursue the law as a career and arranged for him to read with George Wythe. The following decade, Coalter would marry Tucker's daughter Anne Frances.

In 1790, after completing his legal training, Coalter left the Williamsburg household to begin his own law practice. Henry, Tudor, and Beverley, then ages ten, eight, and six respectively, began to attend the Reverend John Bracken's grammar school on the William and Mary campus. The following year they were joined by their stepbrother, Charles Carter. As Henry grew older, he assumed most of the family tutoring responsibilities and oversaw his siblings' intellectual progress. Tudor, whom St. George thought the brightest of his boys, died in the spring of 1795 after an extended illness, but Tucker kept an exceedingly close watch over his surviving children. When time for college arrived, he made sure that the boys enrolled at William and Mary, a mere half mile from the family's house.[44]

The Tucker house in Williamsburg, Virginia,
from a late nineteenth-century photograph. (Courtesy of Colonial
Williamsburg Foundation)

Not only did Tucker rigorously oversee his children's formal education,
but he remained a sharp disciplinarian. When displeased with their work
or actions, he invoked their deceased mother's memory, refused to let them
sit by him at meals, and (when traveling his court circuit) would not answer their letters from home. The judge even drafted rules—which he
called "Garrison Articles"—regulating behavior in the Williamsburg
house. The children labeled (perhaps with some tongue-in-cheek) their
home "Fort St. George." Like their half brothers in the previous decade, the
Tucker children throughout the 1790s also had to assure their father that
they spent their time profitably engaged in substantive endeavors. Henry
once promised his father that he diligently kept at his books during a summer vacation on the Bizarre plantation with his half brothers. "I am perfectly confident of the truth of your observation," he finished one letter,
"that perseverance is necessary for the attainment of true knowledge."[45]

When his sons considered careers, Tucker pointedly steered them away from land and agriculture. The decline of so many gentry families, his own difficulties with landed plantations, and rapid westward expansion all convinced him that tidewater estates would never again bring substantial returns. Nor would such property ever convey again the same social authority that it had in the past. Tucker told his stepsons and his own children that only the learned professions, particularly the law and medicine, offered individuals significant opportunities. Men in these occupations, he repeatedly emphasized, rose or fell solely according to their own talent, education, and industry. These individuals also could avoid crippling debts and declining markets for tobacco, both of which had so greatly undermined landowners throughout the state. In 1786 Tucker ordered fifteen-year-old Theodorick Randolph to "begin to reflect on your future mode of Life." St. George explained that he soon wanted to know from his stepson "whether you will pursue a learned profession or a labourious Occupation [i.e., planting]. Should the former be your choice, (and it appears to me you can not avoid giving it the preference) you must pursue your studies in the Interim with great diligence." Because Theodorick's interest lay in medicine, Tucker planned to send him to the University of Edinburgh to obtain "a profession that will set you above the frowns of fortune." Although Theodorick died in 1792 before he could be sent overseas, Tucker maintained his views about the worth of the learned professions. In 1809 he lectured a young cousin in his charge, "However averse you may now be to the plan of Education I have uniformly proposed for you, I flatter myself you are too sensible of the Advantages to be derived from a liberal, and let me add, a *professional* one, to decline the Idea altogether."[46]

Although Theodorick intended to pursue medicine, the judge thought the law the most important and prestigious of the learned professions in the new Republic. As movement to the West accelerated, agricultural diversification and internal trade in Virginia and elsewhere significantly increased. Overseas markets for American food products, moreover, continued to develop because of the wars of Napoleon. These new economic realities created much more complex commercial relationships both inside the Old Dominion and throughout the Atlantic world, leading to an essential need for well-trained lawyers capable of resolving property disputes quickly and efficiently.[47]

Tucker saw the legal profession's social prestige rising for other reasons. He must have noticed the respect immediately granted him and other judges on the reorganized General Court, all of whom possessed fine educations and superior legal minds rather than great landed estates. While planter justices serving on the county courts were still traditionally referred to as "Gent." by the rest of society, the General Court's jurists quickly earned the much more respected appellation "Esquire." This esteem for highly educated attorneys occurred in large part because the Revolution's political rhetoric had been so manifestly legalistic. The natural right of rebellion and liberal notions of individual equality often stemmed from expressions found by members of the judiciary in the common law, colonial charters, and eventually the Declaration of Independence. Well-read lawyers and judges became the nation's republican spokesmen: they defined proper citizenship and educated the people about their fundamental rights and liberties. During his tenure Tucker worked hard to maintain the General Court's (and the legal profession's) dignity through a grave and solemn demeanor on the bench. He always demanded the utmost respect from disputing attorneys and parties for his judicial rank and position. Tucker and his fellow jurists also kept the county courts in their place by often scolding untrained gentry magistrates when they refused to cooperate with the higher court as well as when they badly mangled legal decisions.[48]

Tucker saw in the profession's growing importance and stature the solution to his many public concerns about social change and his private fears about the future of his family. After he assumed the law professorship at William and Mary, Tucker drafted a series of appendixes to his main text, Blackstone's *Commentaries on the Laws.* In his essays on Virginia and American laws, Tucker embraced the notion put forth by the philosophers of the Scottish Enlightenment that all societies move through distinct stages toward ever-increasing complexity. Post-Revolutionary America, he asserted, was no longer "a most simple machine," but rather like "a seedling oak, that has just burst the acorn and appears above the surface," it grew larger and more complicated every day. The United States one day might even be regarded "as king of the forest."

As America expanded, however, the danger to freedom and liberty grew proportionally. With expansion, the judge noted, "the machine of government becomes necessarily more complex." Thus it would become easy over time for "those who administer" government to manipulate the levers of power secretly toward corrupt ends. Yet exceptionally well trained jurists—men who regarded the law and government as a "dispassionate" science—could prevent such abuses. In *Blackstone's Commentaries,* Tucker wrote that legal training in the "science [of government] counteracts this mechanical monopoly of knowledge [by officeholders and administrators], and unfolds to its votaries those principles which ought to direct the operations of the machine." Indeed, he explained, "those nations which have been most distinguished for science, have been also most distinguished for the freedom they have enjoyed."[49] Tucker envisioned the legal profession filling the social and political vacuum left by the gentry's decline. Scientifically educated in the intricacies of the law and government, members of an independent, disinterested judiciary would protect the Republic and ensure its perpetual stability. Rendering impartial judgments both in and out of the courtroom, such men would preserve America's "republican government in its full tone and vigour, and . . . prevent that degeneracy into which the best forms of government are apt to fall."[50]

Superior legal training had another, more immediate purpose, Tucker believed. Although the prestige of the judiciary was on the rise, he and other observers concurrently saw the profession becoming overloaded with newcomers, often ill-prepared, ill-trained novices who showed little deference toward their better-educated counterparts. Tucker repeatedly warned his sons and law students that they would encounter severe competition from such attorneys when they began to practice in the county and district courts. One pupil, Chapman Johnson, even joked to an attorney friend, "Do you think there is any probability that many of your lawyers will die, or that the Court Houses will be made larger, in the course of two or three years? Because unless one or the other event takes place, you will have no room for me . . . and I should hate to speak to the Court and Jury through the windows."[51]

Tucker's concern for diligence and industry become clear in this broader context. He sought to make of his sons and students exceptional jurists whose scholarly learning and professional expertise would set them above other aspirants in the profession and would guarantee the Republic's stability through their disinterested service. Toward this end, Tucker favored increasing the requirements for taking a law degree at William and Mary. John Coalter concisely summed up how Tucker had come to view the profession after the Revolution. After resolving to become a lawyer, Coalter wrote his father, "The Law is of infinite importance to a man in his civil capacity, especially in a free country." Parroting his new mentor, Coalter asserted that "it does not therefore appear unreasonable that I should spend some time at what may stand a chance to turn out a *public advantage,* . . . to my own private *emolument* and securing a *subsistence, three things* of great importance in life."[52]

With these several goals in mind, Tucker vigorously pushed his own children as well as other sons of the gentry into the profession. In the mid-1780s his eldest stepson, Richard, read law with George Wythe in Williamsburg. John Randolph later read with Edmund Randolph, who was serving as attorney general of the United States in Philadelphia, and briefly studied at William and Mary. Both young men, however, had more interest in land and agriculture than in the law, and much to their stepfather's chagrin, neither completed their training. Therefore, when the Tucker boys began their legal educations in the mid-1790s, they remained firmly under their father's control. Tucker kept his sons and his other law students at work from sunrise to sunset, six days a week, attending lectures, reading, and abstracting important cases. Henry quickly became well known at the college as a student of remarkable diligence. Although Tucker's youngest son, Beverley, had more difficulty mastering the law, both eventually received licenses to practice.[53]

Throughout the 1790s, as Tucker educated his children, changes in public life continued at a rapid pace. The Constitution's establishment of a new national government fundamentally altered politics. Tucker initially had hoped that the new order would bring stability and consistency to federal operations, but he saw party factionalism and corruption quickly emerge in Philadelphia. Well versed in the writings of Britain's Augustan "commonwealthmen" who had lamented the corruption of London, Tucker and other Virginians kept close tabs on events in the nation's capital. They soon grew convinced that history was repeating itself in America.[54] In particular, Washington's secretary of the treasury, Alexander Hamilton, seemed bent on re-creating Robert Walpole's insidious system of political bribery, national debt, and financial manipulation. Appalled at Hamilton's actions and ambition, Tucker even thrust himself into Philadelphia's partisan battles. In 1793, at the urging of John Page, now a congressman, he drafted a collection of scathing verses entitled *The Probationary Odes of Jonathan Pindar,* all of which appeared first in Philip Freneau's *National Gazette.* Derisively calling Hamilton "Atlas," Tucker accused the secretary of sitting atop a "paper throne," around which he had gathered all power in the nation. Like Walpole earlier in the century, Hamilton even supposedly controlled the national legislature by surreptitiously bribing members. Thus, Tucker cried, "Your faithful Janizaries all / Shall muster thick in

Congress Hall / To guard their leader's side." "Liberty," meanwhile, had become nothing more than a "castoff mistress."[55]

Events in Virginia gave further cause for alarm. Like many elite supporters of the Revolution, St. George at first expected the Old Dominion's freeholders, if properly educated with reason and virtue, to select only "the most respectable men" to fill state offices. Under the state constitution of 1776, however, the number of elected positions significantly increased. After the war the legislature continued to establish new counties, adding more seats in the General Assembly. Finally, the federal regime in Philadelphia required multicounty congressional elections as well as legislative appointments to the new national Senate. Therefore, the number of political offices after the Revolution sometimes outran the number of "respectable men" available to fill them.[56]

Tucker noticed too that ambitious men from the state's lower and middling ranks, infused with the Revolutionary ideology of popular sovereignty, increasingly dropped their traditional deference and challenged gentlemen politicians at election time. Regarding them as ill-bred upstarts, Tucker believed that these men lacked the birth, training, and disinterestedness needed to govern their society in a stable fashion. In the 1790s he bitterly lamented the growing presence of "men who court popularity, in preference to the prosperity of their Country." Their excessive politicking "at Elections, at Musters, and other public Occasions" "tend[s] to beget & encourage a spirit of idleness, dissipation, and extravagance in the poorer class of people, and less to generate & promote the practice of Servility."[57] Walter Jones, an acquaintance of Tucker's from the Northern Neck, also noted these changes at work. In January 1793, while running for a congressional seat, he wrote St. George that not only was he going "Cap in hand to the Electors of five Counties," but he faced "a very active opponent in Johnny Heath." Apparently of modest means, Heath played up his humble roots to freeholders, as "his addresses are principally, in his own Language, *to the yeomanry*." Thus, Jones noted, "I am not to secur, and never lose sight of Shakespeakes excellent expression, that 'an Habitation, giddy and unsure / Hath he that buildith on the *vulgar Heart*.'" John Page also found himself challenged for political office despite his long service to the state. But Page adamantly refused to change his old ways. He recognized the growing need for candidates to speak from the hustings because aspirants for office and freeholders rarely knew one another in these large multicounty districts. Yet he balked at soliciting votes in such a manner, arguing that he was "not qualified by habit or education to harangue" the electorate. With growing frequency, as Tucker wrote, these men "of inferior pretensions to the confidence of the people" were winning elections against members of the gentry whose "minds had been properly enlightened by study and application."[58]

Land offered neither protection nor "independence" from such politically charged times, Tucker discovered. Although he had sold his own estates following Frances's death, Corotoman, the Lancaster County plantation of the Carter family, legally had to pass to the two children Lelia Skipwith Tucker had with George Carter. Thus St. George was forced to manage the tidewater property, and the experience only confirmed his distaste for land. Like John Randolph of Matoax's estates, Carter's plantation was heavily encumbered at his death, and throughout the 1790s the couple received no proceeds from the estate's tobacco and rents. Periodic droughts, soil exhaustion, and especially unreliable overseers added to Tucker's headaches. At one point he cried that although "I never did or could, pretend to be any Judge of the proper mode of managing a Virginia estate, . . . miserable experience has fully convinc'd me that few things are so difficult . . . as to meet with an *honest, industrious* Overseer or Manager."[59]

Only the legal profession seemed to offer the security, stability, and status that Tucker craved for his family. Ironically, however, his career as a lawyer and judge often separated him from his home, wife, and children, and thus began the transformation of his patriarchal position as household head. When Tucker became a member of Virginia's General Court in 1788, he wrote of the necessity that every justice in the state be paid a respectable salary, not merely to avoid "the temptation of avarice" but more importantly to allow a judge to "devote his whole time and attention to the duties of his office." Tucker realized that the law had become a full-time profession in the early Republic, requiring jurists to dedicate their complete attention to dispensing the law inside the courthouse and engaging in "those studies" outside of it "which are necessary to qualify him for a proper discharge of" his responsibilities.[60] No longer could a planter magistrate dispense justice several days per month at a county court while devoting the bulk of his time to his plantations, slaves, and tobacco. This professionalization of the judiciary, however, fundamentally altered the rhythm of family life inside Tucker's Williamsburg home.

As a district court judge throughout the 1790s, he traveled every spring and fall among five circuit courts set up by the state legislature. The judges of the General Court additionally met in Richmond for collective conferences each June and November. After several years of this demanding schedule, Tucker lamented to one correspondent, "My avocations are such during the Spring, Summer and Autumn as to make me almost a stranger to my own house." He found himself especially distressed by his long separations from his children. Writing to Theodorick Randolph, he cried: "I am extremely anxious to see my poor babies again. it is ten days since I was at home, and I have not seen Beverley these six weeks." The following year he told Theodorick, then heading back from college, "I shall have the mortification of being from home . . . when you arrive, as I shall be on the circuit." The children saw their father so infrequently during these years that the youngest ones sometimes failed to recognize him. In 1790 the family's housekeeper, Maria Rind, wrote John Coalter about two-year-old Elizabeth Tucker: "What think you at my D[ea]r bet? . . . She call[s] you every day her papa."[61]

As Tucker lamented the many absences from home required by his profession, the makeup and composition of his family changed considerably, among both his Virginia and Bermuda kin. The deaths of Colonel Tucker and Frances Bland Randolph marked the end of the 1780s. The next decade, in 1792, Theodorick Randolph died at age nineteen after a long wasting illness. Twelve-year-old Tudor Tucker died three years later. The next year he was followed by two more members of the Williamsburg household: his sister Elizabeth, eight years old, fell mortally ill early in the year only to be followed several months later by Lelia and St. George's three-year-old St. George Jr., nicknamed "Tutee." In December 1796 Lelia and St. George had one more child, but the baby was born lifeless. Thus grief became an everyday reality with which all had to cope. From Bermuda, Tucker's eldest brother, Henry Jr., sympathized with his Virginia relatives. These tragedies, he concluded, made life itself seem little more than "a Tissue of Troubles and Sorrows."[62]

Death also pulled at the Tucker clan beyond the Williamsburg household. In 1790 Frances's brother, Theodorick Bland Jr., died after a brief illness. His widow Martha remarried several years later and left the tidewater forever. Before moving, she and her new husband sold the Blands' great estate of Cawsons, and so the plantation passed out of the family's hands. In 1797 Beverley Randolph, who had served alongside St. George in the ranks of the Virginia militia and later became Virginia's governor, also fell ill and died. Tucker tenderly eulogized his friend as the ideal Virginia gentleman:

"He was just, honourable, liberal, polite, affable, candid, and unaffected in his dealings and intercourse with mankind; sincere, ardent and steadfast in his friendships; tender, affectionate, humane and gentle, in his domestic relations; and manly, patient and resigned in his sufferings."[63]

St. George's Bermuda kin also changed considerably in the years after the Colonel's death. In 1796 Elizabeth lamented that the family had recently lost "the urbanity, and social friendship of our worthy Brother-in-law" Henry Tucker of Somerset. Their distant cousin had left behind a widow and seven children.[64] In 1797 death again visited The Grove when Anne Butterfield Tucker—"the best of mothers"—succumbed after a long period of declining health.

The Bermuda clan's economic position also deteriorated in the 1790s as the island became something of a commercial backwater within the empire. Tucker of Somerset's business partners, the Jennings brothers, saw their financial fortunes rapidly dwindle in the late eighteenth century. Brother Henry's shipping business plodded along, but with few substantial rewards. He once confessed to St. George that he had experienced few trading successes after the Revolution. The family's connections to England, however, remained strong enough to permit him to launch of his numerous sons "into a busy World." Henry reported that his eldest, Hal, had gained a position with the British East India Company. The post, though, required the lad to sail off to Calcutta, never to return to the island. Two other sons, George and Thomas, through connections had purchased lieutenant's commissions in the Royal Navy. Although their father wished they held higher ranks, he noted that more substantial "Appointments . . . are handsome" and were now well beyond the clan's modest means. Therefore, the pair "have little to expect, but from their own Talents and Industry." "Poor Fellows!" he exclaimed. Although he appreciated the help his sons received, he realized that the need for it pointed to the family's declining position. "Without the Assistance of Friends," he lamented, "I shou'd have been sadly puzzled what to have done with them, for little is it I have in my own power." Elizabeth too noted how things had changed since America's independence. She wrote St. George that if he should ever visit the island again, he would find everyone "much altered." "You would miss," she explained, "that cheerfulness . . . of happy young persons, unhurt by misfortune, [which] used to diffuse among us."[65]

Thomas and Nathaniel also struggled throughout these years. Like their Virginia brother, both established lives and careers outside Bermuda after the Revolution. Thomas continued to practice medicine in Dorchester Parish near Charleston, where he earned a reputation for honesty and integrity. The parish's freeholders twice elected the doctor to the new federal Congress. Respectability in the new Republic, though, did not bring much income. Throughout the 1790s Thomas depended on his congressional salary merely to subsist, and he struggled to cope with his debts. Time and again he had to stave off aggressive creditors, much to his mortification. Brother Nathaniel decided to settle in the old mother country in the seaside town of Hull near York. There he established a modest medical practice, worked in a local charity hospital, and married a serious-minded woman from a modest family named Jane Wood. Together the couple had six children and became devout followers of the Swedish theologian Emanuel Swedenborg.[66]

Although none of the Tuckers found themselves seriously wanting as the eighteenth century closed, the family as a whole was "much altered" from earlier days. Not only had their living standards declined, but they increasingly realized that their familial network—so important in the previous age—now provided few tangible benefits. Only connections to England offered a channel to modest positions and influence. And only St. George in Virginia still possessed the financial means to assist struggling kin. In the 1790s, when the ailing situation of his Bermuda family became apparent, Tucker started to purchase and forward to them badly needed provisions. Through merchants in Norfolk he often sent barrels of pork, flour, and beef to The Grove. He also dispatched food to his other Bermudian kin.[67] Even though he recognized their declining benefit, St. George entered the nineteenth century determined to maintain his kinship ties beyond Virginia. He was committed, however, to making sure that his children understood that they could not rely upon these bonds in any substantive way. Rather members of the rising generation would have to make their way in the world alone.

The eighteenth century's final two decades brought vast changes to the Tuckers' lives that profoundly altered how they looked at and dealt with the wider world. Having expected continuity after the Revolution, St. George Tucker found himself dramatically shifting his beliefs, property holdings, and educational strategies as the times changed. Determined not to see his family fall like so many other gentry clans, he tried to prepare his sons for professional careers in the law, away from any sort of dependence upon land and slaves. He also sternly warned them that the ways of the past, especially reliance on familial bonds and connections, no longer promised success and security. As St. George Tucker's children approached maturity, they wrote little about their father's injunctions. Nonetheless, having grown up in affluence and observed firsthand the authority once wielded by the great planter class, they must have looked upon his demands as harsh and bitter medicine. The younger generation doubtlessly pondered the elder Tucker's pronouncements. Were his dire assessments correct? Was the era of the old gentry gone forever? They must also have wondered how they were going to survive in this new world of independence. Would hard work, professional training, and self-sufficiency guarantee their well-being? Or should they move in a different direction and, contrary to their father, adhere to the traditions of the past?

Four

The Crisis of the Rising Generation

In 1801 St. George Tucker's eldest son, twenty-one-year-old Henry St. George, earned his law license and, at his father's insistence, moved west the following year to start a practice in the northern Shenandoah Valley town of Winchester. After nearly three years of hard and unremitting labor, young Tucker had little to show for his efforts, except saddle sores and depression. In the summer of 1805, his frustrations got the better of him. He traveled that July throughout the Valley from one county court to another. Shuttling among sessions in the counties between Winchester and Staunton, he found himself exhausted and yet without enough business to subsist independently. Fierce competition from other lawyers and clients who often failed to pay for services had made life difficult. Far away from family and friends, Henry sank into a deep gloom. From a tiny inn thirty-five miles north of Staunton, he wrote home to Williamsburg, "I reached this place my dearest father after a very solitary ride." He admitted that he had "scarcely spoken a dozen words" that day and that "my thoughts have been wandering to those I left behind." "I am quite alone," he concluded, "[and] the sombre tints of evening inspire an almost crying melancholy." Even nighttime brought little solace as "bugs, squabbling brats, rocking cradles" kept the young attorney awake almost until dawn.[1]

Loneliness, depression, and disappointment are common themes in the Tuckers' correspondence during the early nineteenth century, especially among members of the rising generation. Launched into a world whose axis had rapidly turned, younger family members struggled to succeed as lawyers, planters, and spouses. They all worked hard, moreover, to embrace and live by the values taught them by their parents and others. The younger generation knew that the old gentry had once dominated Virginia, and they deeply respected the spectacular accomplishments of the Revolution. As the new century dawned, however, the Tuckers and others in their circle were also painfully aware of changed circumstances in the state and of their own diminished situation within it.

This chapter explores the varied efforts of the post-Revolutionary generation to enter the larger world as independent figures and to prosper in a difficult environment. Despite their father's advice, younger family members adopted a variety of attitudes about the changes they witnessed and struggled in diverse ways to cope. Tucker's stepsons convinced themselves that only the old traditions, grounded in landownership and tobacco cultivation, would preserve their family's position over the long term. Beverley Tucker, increasingly under the sway of his half brother John Randolph, moved in the same direction. Their sister, Fanny, tried to imitate their mother's style once she became mistress of her own household. Henry, on the other hand, dutifully followed the elder Tucker's commands. Notwithstanding their differences, all within the younger generation shared many common experiences; in particular, they lurched toward less affluent lifestyles compared to earlier elites and toward more nucleated, isolated households. Frequently pained, lonely, and bewildered by what they saw, St. George Tucker's children tried to understand exactly why their world had changed so dramatically and how they could best survive within it.

In the early 1790s St. George Tucker's two surviving stepsons entered the larger world beyond their Williamsburg home. Despite Tucker's demands that they pursue professional careers, both Richard and John Randolph wanted to gain control of their father's lands, slaves, and other properties as soon as possible. When Richard entered his nineteenth year, he resolutely told his stepfather, "The time is at hand, when I hope you will be relieved from all further anxiety . . . [in] the management of our patrimony."[2] Though extensive debts to British merchants remained unpaid and St. George continued his injunctions about the need for personal "industry" and "self-reliance," both young men confidently believed that the path to prosperity lay in following the traditions of the past. The image of the independent planter who grew tobacco and dominated his household and community powerfully resonated with them, even though both already had witnessed the collapse of many tidewater families.

Richard's first step toward "independence" came on New Year's Day 1790 when he married his distant cousin, seventeen-year-old Judith Randolph, daughter of Ann Cary Randolph and Thomas Mann Randolph of Tuckahoe. Although Richard had yet to complete his legal training, he was determined to wed. Tucker initially disapproved, believing his stepson should wait until he finished his education. Richard had briefly read law with George Wythe several years beforehand, but his inattention to assigned readings and overall lack of diligence led Wythe to break off the relationship. Randolph later studied with his stepfather but made little progress after Frances's death. Tucker's resistance to the match ended, however, when he learned that Judith's father did not object to the wedding even though he was "well acquainted with the Circumstances of [John Randolph of Matoax's] Estate."[3] Despite his stepfather's warnings about Virginia's changed landscape, Richard privately shunned all thoughts of a legal career. He instead believed that he would succeed as a great planter, regardless of the hard economic times throughout eastern Virginia. Determined also to live on the grand scale of the previous generation, Richard proudly brought Judith to his boyhood home of Matoax soon after the wedding.

Determined to live like their parents and convinced that a glittering lifestyle was crucial to their reputation, the teenage couple began to purchase expensive imported items on credit, such as new carpets, furniture, and clothes. They also lavishly entertained friends and fellow planters in their neighborhood. Within days of their arrival, the Randolphs began to use Matoax's grain supplies and livestock herds to feed their many guests. They sent for food from other Randolph plantations in order to keep their visitors satisfied. John Woodson, Bizarre's manager, anxiously wrote Tucker that January, "Mr. Richd. Randolph has made Several applications for muttons." The following month Richard informed another estate manager, "We gave out the last of our Flour last night," and asked that another barrel be sent at once to Matoax.[4]

Throughout the spring and summer of 1790, the parties continued, and demands for foodstuffs only increased. The couple began to request from their managers "a few shillings" for "the market" in order to obtain additional provisions.[5] Unable to live as they wished off their landed inheritance, they saw their debts quickly mounting. In June, Richard had to

sell Matoax's stable of horses in order to satisfy a growing number of creditors. He refused, however, to slow his consumption. The following year
tidewater merchants announced they would no longer honor his bills of ex-
change. One Richmond trader explained to Tucker: "I am placed in an awkward Situation with [regard to] Messrs. Randolphs. I do not like to refuse
these Orders, at same time I may give you reason to complain." [6]

Though deeply troubled by the lavish spending, St. George Tucker
found there was little he could do. He discovered that his authority over his
stepsons had greatly diminished since Frances's death. In the past he had
relied largely on her to discipline the boys and keep them in line. But
with her death the restraints seemed to come off. After some effort he did
eventually persuade Richard to move to Bizarre. Because the Cumberland
County bar was less crowded than Chesterfield's, Tucker convinced himself
that Richard at last would begin his legal career in the new location. Such
hopes proved illusionary as Richard had no desire to complete his training.
He and Judith continued to make new purchases and to entertain guests
and visitors. Thus the drain on the estates' resources continued, soon to the
entire clan's detriment. In November 1792 John Woodson explained to
Tucker that he could not send any "Beef" to Williamsburg as the judge had
requested. "We cannot furnish any," Woodson meekly wrote, "as Mr. Rd.
Randolph last winter had all the Roanok Beef Cattle." [7]

By this point the Randolph family at Bizarre had begun to unravel as a
gruesome and devastating rumor swept Virginia that fall. Although it cul-
minated in one of the most famous criminal proceedings of the eighteenth
century, the "Bizarre scandal" (as it soon came to be known) really reflected
the larger deterioration of the Randolph clan. The affair was a complex one,
beginning in some respects with Theodorick Randolph's long-expected
death in February 1792. The youth's health had been deteriorating for two
years, likely because of an advancing case of tuberculosis. A trip in 1791 to
Bermuda with Thomas Tudor Tucker had only marginally helped the boy.
St. George's physician brother warned that no one should be "tantaliz'd
with vain Hopes" about a recovery. After Randolph's return to the Old Dominion, his decline continued, and ongoing bouts of drunkenness accelerated it. [8]

In the last months of his life, Theodorick frequently visited Bizarre
where he apparently took up with Ann Cary Randolph, known to all as
Nancy. Nancy was Judith's younger sister and had come to live on the plan-

tation the previous year. The couple soon wished to wed despite Theodorick's health, but Nancy's father opposed the match because he now understood the full extent of the Randolphs' debts to British creditors.[9]

Following Theodorick's death, neighbors around Bizarre noticed that
Nancy soon became unusually close to her brother-in-law Richard. Carter
Page, who lived nearby at The Fork plantation, claimed to have seen the
pair "kissing" and in other ways "fond of each other." Page's wife suspected
"a criminal intercourse" between the two when "she observed Miss Nancy's
shape [begin] to alter." As Nancy herself later admitted, she had become
pregnant in early 1792. She always insisted, however, that Theodorick had
fathered the child in his last days. But rumors soon spread that she and
Richard were having an affair.[10]

The events of the fall of 1792 remain uncertain and shrouded by controversy. Nancy claimed that her pregnancy ended with a miscarriage at
Bizarre on 30 September. Others suspected, however, that it ended the next
evening when she, Judith, and Richard visited Randolph Harrison's home
Glenyvar. Nancy became violently ill during the first night of her stay,
waking the entire household with her screams. Harrison and his wife later
heard someone sneaking downstairs and then returning shortly afterwards.
Rumors started to circulate the next morning among the Harrisons' slaves
that Nancy had had a baby which Richard killed and then deposited amid
a pile of shingles near the house. The salacious story soon spread to all corners of the state.

In order to rescue his reputation, Richard appeared before the Cumberland County Court in April 1793 "to answer in the due course of law, any
charge or crime . . . against me." Imprisoned for a week to give time for the
court to assemble, Richard appeared before fourteen justices on 29 April
and was examined. Despite the damaging nature of some testimony,
Patrick Henry ably defended Randolph, and the court dismissed all charges
without a trial.[11]

Although he had been exonerated in the eyes of the law, stories about
Randolph's guilt persisted. At this point St. George Tucker stepped into
the controversy. Whatever his true sentiments, Tucker loyally stood by his
stepson and other Randolph relations. In early May he drafted an open letter in which he confessed that "the public mind is not always convinced by
the decisions of *a court of law.*" Eventually printed in Richmond's *Virginia
Gazette and General Advertiser,* Tucker's letter reminded Virginians that the
charges against his stepson had been thoroughly examined by distin-

guished magistrates and found without merit. He announced, moreover, that he had taken Richard, Judith, and Nancy into his home in Williamsburg where they had stayed for eight weeks. The conduct of all, he concluded, especially Judith's obvious love for her husband and sister, must convince "the most hardened skeptic" that the accusations against them were unfounded.[12]

Though Tucker remained steadfast in his support, the scandal exposed deep divisions and animosities among the Randolphs. In particular, Judith and Nancy's branch—the Tuckahoe Randolphs—not only failed to support Richard publicly but attacked his character. Thomas Mann Randolph, for instance, refused to institute an action of slander against several of his son-in-law's accusers. Thomas's sons were more direct in their condemnations. Thomas Mann Randolph Jr., who married Thomas Jefferson's oldest daughter, Martha, apparently told Richard: "I defy you to transfer the stigma to your deceased brother. . . . I will wash out, with your blood the stain of my family." John and William Randolph, Richard's other two brothers-in-law among the Tuckahoes, also attacked him, leading Richard to call (unsuccessfully) for satisfaction upon the field of honor.[13]

The following year, 1794, other problems for Richard emerged. In particular, legal pressures mounted from British creditors to pay off John Randolph of Matoax's long-standing debts. Faced with his own growing liabilities, Richard finally agreed with his stepfather that Matoax had to be sold. When the deal closed, the plantation on which he and his brothers had grown up and where their parents were buried brought in £3,000 sterling. But many debts still remained. After these bitter events John Randolph noticed that his brother's earlier good humor and jovial manners had disappeared. Although Judith loyally stuck by her husband and provided him with two sons, whom the couple named Tudor and John St. George, Bizarre had become a somber and depressed household. These economic and emotional crises broke his health. In June 1796 he died at the age of twenty-six, leaving Judith a widow and his two boys without a father.[14]

Beyond a grieving family, Richard Randolph left behind significant debts and a will that could not be fulfilled for many years. Likely influenced by his stepfather, Richard had turned against slavery in the last years of his life. Thus he instructed that his slaves be emancipated upon his death. The Randolphs' extravagant lifestyle while he was master of Matoax and Bizarre, however, made that impossible. In 1801 Judith explained to Tucker, "Perhaps you were not informed that the personal debts of my hus-

John Randolph of Roanoke, copy by Fred W. Wright of Gilbert Stuart portrait.
(Courtesy of Raymond D. Kimbrough Jr.)

band were very considerable; for the discharge of which there was no other resource, than in the labor of these Slaves." Richard's African Americans had to work twelve years beyond their master's death before they gained their freedom.[15]

After Richard's demise the burden of managing the remaining Randolph properties fell to twenty-three-year-old John. Some historians speculate that the youngest Randolph's unstable personality and later bouts with insanity stemmed from the traumas of these years. Although there is no direct proof that the events of the 1790s engendered a sea change in his personality, devastating occurrences did follow one after another. In 1792 not only did his brother Theodorick die, but John himself soon afterwards caught scarlet fever, which nearly carried him off. The illness permanently arrested his physical development, leaving him short and slight in stature and possessing a high-pitched voice and boyish face. Later that year the Bizarre scandal broke and brought shame to the entire family. In 1793, soon after Richard's acquittal, John began to attend William and Mary under his stepfather's eye. But he soon got into an argument with a fellow student named Robert Barraud Taylor over either politics or the pronunciation of a word. The dispute ended in a duel and Taylor's wounding. Although Taylor recovered and the two men reconciled, condemnations poured down on Randolph, compelling him to leave Williamsburg altogether.[16]

When Richard died three years later, John realized he had to manage the family's still-encumbered estates as well as care for his sister-in-law and her two children, one of whom was deaf and mute. In 1797 matters grew worse when the federal courts intervened to support the remaining claims of the Randolphs' major English creditor, the Hanburys. That April John told a friend: "I have been deprived by a sentence of the Federal Court of more than half my Fortune. 'Tis an iniquitous affair and too long to be related here." Other creditors remained, demanding payments, and John had to liquidate even more of "my fathers property." This steady accumulation of dismal events perhaps unhinged Randolph emotionally. His behavior turned increasingly erratic in the late 1790s. In the dead of night, he repeatedly galloped over the fields of Bizarre with a pair of pistols cocked and ready, as if to protect his ancestral lands from unseen enemies. Unable to sleep at other times, he paced his bedroom, muttering: "Macbeth hath murdered sleep. Macbeth hath murdered sleep."[17]

Although Richard's death may have ruined his brother's emotional stability, it nevertheless forced him to grapple with his own excessive spending, the family's crippling debts, and the exhausted lands he inherited. Randolph noted later in life that like his brothers, he as a youth spent money without care or concern. "When any bauble caught my fancy," he wrote a relative, "I would perhaps buy it on credit and always for twice as much at least as it was worth." Yet he learned from observing Richard as well as from seeing his entire family's indebted status that "the relation between debtor and creditor is that of a slave to his master." He understood, furthermore, "that a decayed family could never recover its loss of rank in the world, until the members of it left off talking and dwelling upon its former opulence." Unlike his brother, John Randolph came to grips with his situation and understood that in the early Republic material consumption had to be reined in. Only "self-denial" could guarantee one's ongoing "independence." [18]

Throughout the late 1790s, therefore, while struggling to hold himself together emotionally, Randolph worked to rescue his imperiled patrimony. Although his stepfather had counseled him to abandon land and go into the law, he had no intention of doing so. Instructed since his youth, by his mother particularly, that land stood as the fundamental linchpin of the elite's prerogatives and power, Randolph believed that any further loss of estates would signify the end of his family's influence and the demise of the planter class in general. Though Matoax was gone forever, Randolph threw himself into a desperate effort to save the remaining estates of Bizarre and Roanoke. After 1796 he introduced innovative agricultural techniques to boost productivity. He ordered the sixty-four Roanoke slaves he inherited as well as Judith's forty bondpeople at Bizarre to clear new fields, and he set them to work revitalizing acreage worn out by tobacco. Randolph purchased additional lands adjacent to Roanoke in order to enlarge his holdings. He also sought out advice from neighbors on cultivation and planting. [19]

By the century's turn his efforts had paid off. In the spring of 1802, Bizarre and Roanoke were profitable. Randolph continued to improve and enlarge his landholdings throughout his life. Fully embracing the agricultural principles of "my friend" John Taylor of Caroline, John applauded Taylor's "most whimsical sensible book," *The Arator*. "Nothing can be more just than his observations as applied to a Virginia estate. 'Ploughing—Manuring—Stock-Enclosing—Indian Corn.' There is sound sense under all his quaintness and amongst his jumble of metaphors." [20] Thus, while husbandry in the tidewater and lower piedmont generally continued to be wasteful, sloppy, and marked by increasingly lower yields, the Randolph estates were among the few to prosper.[21]

Despite their different strategies in coping with the changes of their times, Tucker and Randolph remained close in the years following Richard's death. Both men cherished their past together, and each believed in the fundamental importance of family. John visited his stepfather in Williamsburg whenever possible, and they frequently wrote to one another. After receiving one note from his stepfather, John wrote, "You know not, my dearest Sir, the unspeakable pleasure which I derive from you[r] affection and friendship, of which I experience every day fresh Proofs."[22] Randolph also maintained close ties with his half siblings. Henry, Fanny, and Beverley often took long summer vacations at Bizarre during the 1790s where their already deep bonds of affection grew even stronger.

Although the younger Tuckers watched their half brother save his landed estates during the decade's latter years, other elites were neither so skilled nor so fortunate. As St. George's sons completed their legal training, they witnessed the ongoing decline of many of their elders within their father's circle. John Page sank only deeper into debt as the new century began despite selling off most of his slaves and lands surrounding Rosewell. In 1802 the Old Dominion's legislature selected Page to be Virginia's governor, mainly as a reward to the sixty-five-year-old Revolutionary for his many years of service. Although largely a ceremonial post, the office required much entertaining, a task that added to his financial difficulties. Throughout his tenure Page complained bitterly that his meager salary and greatly diminished estate prevented him from receiving guests in a genteel fashion. When his tenure ended in 1805, Page managed to obtain the federal office of commissioner of loans for the state of Virginia. But its salary was significantly less than his pay as governor, thus placing his family under even more pressure. Page's embarrassments ended with his death in 1808. His second wife, Margaret Lowther Page, however, had to struggle afterwards through a maze of remaining liabilities. Despite her best efforts, she and her children soon had to leave Rosewell forever and crowd into a tiny rented town house in Williamsburg. For the rest of her life, she and her family struggled desperately to make ends meet on the rents from the once-great plantation. In 1809 she cried to Tucker, "I am emaciated to a Shadow—Oh! my friend! the Scorpions Hatred and Calumny, have stung me even unto Death!"[23]

Tucker and his children realized that the Pages were not the only powerful family to collapse. In 1805 one of the judge's former law students, William Munford, found himself forced off his ancestral lands by insurmountable debt. "The claims against my Father's [Robert Munford III's] estate," he explained, "are so great that they will certainly swallow up all the property he left, and will render it necessary for me to part with the plantation on which I reside." Munford's sister, Anna, who had married into the once-great Byrd family, had also fallen on hard times. She planned to relocate in Williamsburg "to live and take in boarders for her support."[24]

The Tuckers of both generations also saw the Nelson family's ongoing struggle to survive. As that clan's financial props continued to collapse in the new century, the Nelson women stepped in to find ways to avoid poverty. In 1808 Judith Nelson, the daughter of the Revolutionary governor, believed that running a boardinghouse might at least supply the family with some basic necessities. She begged Tucker for a £200 loan. "O Sir such is the reduc'd state of my finances that I am necessitated to make some exertion for the maintenance of the younger part of my Family," she wrote, "and . . . I am led to Believe that a well kept Boarding House in Richmond wou'd meet with Encouragement."[25]

Despite his stepson's success in saving his estates, St. George Tucker continued to oppose owning lands in eastern Virginia. The judge saw the state's agricultural future as located to the west—in the piedmont and beyond—where farms were more diversified and less reliant on slave labor. Rather than cultivating a single staple crop, western farmers grew a wide variety of foods and raised livestock. To profit from such changes himself, Tucker invested in the James River Canal Company in 1803. Purchasing shares from Richmond merchant Robert Gamble, the judge and other backers hoped to extend the river's navigability into the piedmont counties, better linking western farmers to markets and port cities in the East.[26]

The opening of western Virginia to commercial trade also provided Tucker with ongoing investment opportunities in state banks. He continued to extol "the little Bank of Alexandria" for providing essential capital to migrating farmers. As the bank's largest shareholder by the end of the 1790s, Tucker personally depended on both its 4 percent annual dividend and the appreciation of its stock price. In 1804 the newly chartered Bank of Virginia opened its doors for business to take advantage of growing commercial traffic between Richmond and the western counties. Tucker immediately purchased ninety-two shares for himself and organized a subscription in Williamsburg for nearly a hundred other investors. In 1809 Tucker acquired several hundred shares of the new Farmer's Bank of Virginia as soon as it was chartered by the state legislature, and in 1816, after Congress rechartered the Second Bank of the United States, he purchased one hundred shares at $113 each. A friend in Norfolk, Dr. Philip Barraud, jokingly warned, "It may happen that all you stock jobbing Folks may one day or other find out that Land is more substantial than paper money." Barraud's jabs did not undermine the judge's confidence in such investments. Not only did the banks fuel Virginia's expansion to the west and the state's economic growth, but bank stocks provided his family with a financial security he no longer found in tidewater estates.[27]

Henry St. George Tucker was the judge's first son to come of age as these new attitudes and developments emerged in post-Revolutionary Virginia. Intelligent, obedient, and eager to please, he earned his law license in 1801. Like his half brothers and other kin, Henry had repeatedly heard his father explain that eastern Virginia was no place for a young lawyer starting out. The growing presence of "new men"—ambitious, untutored, and lowly born attorneys—practicing in the tidewater's county courts, combined with the region's overall stagnation, meant few opportunities to prosper. Henry had to go west, the elder Tucker said. He thought his son should settle in Winchester, a growing city west of the Blue Ridge Mountains in the northern Shenandoah county of Frederick. Tucker had visited the town often on his General Court circuit. He saw firsthand that it had become a center of trade and commerce for the upper Valley, providing opportunities for a well-trained, industrious lawyer. Tucker also knew the local attorneys in the city and surrounding counties. Confident in his father's wisdom, Henry agreed to go.[28]

As he prepared to leave Williamsburg, however, Henry and other family members realized that his move represented a sea change in the nature of family and success in the early Republic. In spite of his connections to some of Virginia's oldest and most prominent families, only individual self-reliance and hard work now could save him from financial hardship. Though Henry packed for Winchester without complaint, his half brother lamented the situation and openly questioned its necessity. Knowing that hundreds of miles would soon separate him from his kinsman, John Randolph understood that the move threatened the entire family. "When I reflect," he told St. George, "that it is your intention to settle Henry in a distant quarter where I can . . . seldom hear from him, it brings the most mournful recollections and presages to my mind. Wherefore, my dear Sir, should we then be scattered over the face of the earth and altho' bound by the strongest ties which can connect man to man live estranged from each other?" Tucker acknowledged that he too found the prospect of Henry leaving "painful," but he believed his parental duty left him no choice. St. George's brother Thomas comforted him by stressing that in this new age "considerations of benefit to him must yield to every other."[29] The success of the individual must override any concern for the family's collective well-being.

The elder Tucker took all possible steps to ensure Henry's success. Although he had often stayed in Winchester over the years on his court circuit, Tucker had no close friends in Frederick County. Therefore, in the summer of 1802, between his spring and fall district sessions, the judge traveled to the city to oversee Henry's launching personally. The pair stayed together throughout July and August as the elder Tucker introduced his son to members of the local bar, including Hugh Holmes, Winchester's most prominent attorney. Tucker rented a small town house and purchased a library of essential lawbooks for his son. The judge also gave Henry a young slave named Johnny, who would clean, cook, and keep house for the new lawyer.[30]

As the summer closed, Tucker headed back over the Blue Ridge Mountains toward Richmond to resume his General Court duties, leaving Henry to begin his legal career. The northern Valley contrasted greatly with the tidewater. Economically, great variances existed. Although large tobacco plantations still dominated eastern Virginia, the northern Shenandoah possessed smaller, more diversified farmsteads, which concentrated on grain and livestock production. The most striking differences, though, were racial and ethnic. In 1800 the tidewater's population was roughly half slave and half free, and English surnames dominated the region. In comparison, only one-fifth of the Shenandoah Valley's population was enslaved, and the region's white community was much more ethnically diverse. Old-timers had seen in the previous decades large numbers of German and Scotch-Irish emigrants arrive in the Valley, either from Europe or from the mid-Atlantic states.[31]

The character and lack of gentility of these people shocked young Tucker. Raised in the refined and convivial environs of Matoax and Williamsburg where books, music, and sociable conversation dominated, Henry felt isolated and badly out of place. "Well," he soon wrote to his fa-

ther, "here I am . . . quite alone; seated in the parlour by a good fire, but
without one soul even to speak to. How different from some evenings
past! . . . You would laugh to see my little arrangements, and to behold me
seated with one plate and no companion."[32] Henry's refined upbringing
made it difficult for him to adjust to this situation. An older cousin named
George Tucker, who had come to Virginia from Bermuda and stayed in
Williamsburg during the previous decade, likewise found life in western
Virginia a culture shock. After George earned his law license under St.
George's tutelage, he moved west to Pittsylvania County to open a practice.
He later remarked that "the greatest change" he found "was in the society."
George's neighbors and clients were "extremely plain and unpolished . . .
and quite untutored in the ways of the world."[33]

Unexpectedly stiff competition at the bar only exacerbated Henry's
loneliness and isolation in the Shenandoah Valley. In the autumn of 1802,
he rode from county to county throughout northwestern Virginia, attending court sessions in Staunton and the counties of Jefferson, Hampshire,
and Berkeley. Confident in his own abilities, he expected to pick up some
business. But in September he wrote home, "I am yet without business,"
and declared that prospects for success anytime soon "are indeed dreary."
Little business materialized in the months that followed, although many
knew of Henry's family and his educational background. Good social connections proved of little use. He maintained friendly contacts with Hugh
Holmes, but Henry told his father that the prominent attorney "has on no
occasion given me an opportunity of coming forward at the bar."[34]

Henry's disappointments only mounted the following year. "Not an instance has occurred," he told his father in 1803, "in which I have had an opportunity of opening my mouth in public." In the spring he abandoned all
hopes of mustering up business in Berkeley. That court "holds out no prospects of business to me. . . . no man however attentive, however learned and
however blessed with talents has been able to make his way at that bar unless he lived in the County." After a year west of the Blue Ridge Mountains,
Henry had painfully learned what many of St. George's other law students
already had discovered. The law by the early 1800s, though potentially lucrative, had "become a difficult theater in which to obtain success."[35]

Anxious about his future, lonely in his town house, and cut off from
friends and family, Henry grew despondent, particularly because his initial
expectations had been so high. "Like most young people," he admitted, "I
have . . . perhaps flattered myself too highly, and expiate by disappointment

the folly of having done so." Amid rough-hewn, ill-mannered farmers in the state's western section, Henry grew especially nostalgic for his home in the tidewater. Although he assured his father that "when I go abroad I wear the face of chearfulness," more often than not "my thoughts will stray to W[illiamsbur]g to the remembrance of 'departed Joys.'"[36] Obedient and realistic, however, he understood that such laments solved nothing. Therefore, he refused to dwell on his homesickness, at least not in letters to his father.

Henry realized, though, that he had to abandon all thoughts of ever living on the previous generation's genteel scale. He instead conscientiously set his sights lower: "What my success may be I cannot say with certainty—but even moderate success in a society like this will be equivalent to the most brilliant progress elsewhere." Yet "even moderate success" now required that one's nose be constantly kept to the grindstone. After winning several minor cases in the spring of 1803, Henry explained: "My greatest anxiety at present is to maintain every inch that I gain. . . . In order to fit myself for the stand . . . I have resolved to apply myself very closely to my books."[37]

The keen competition and local prejudices Henry met in the western courts were all the more difficult to endure because he had so thoroughly imbibed the elder Tucker's stern lessons concerning self-reliance and industry. Taught that only personal diligence made a gentleman truly "independent," Henry felt an almost desperate need to be free of his father's purse strings and the allowance the judge forwarded monthly to Winchester. In the new Republic dependence on family members for assistance equaled inadequacy and failure. He explained to Tucker, "The impatience which I may sometimes express, proceeds . . . from a wish no longer to abuse a generosity, the benefits of which I have so long experienced." However, with his practice languishing and income "little more than nothing," Henry had no choice but to rely upon this paternal aid month after month. By the fall he was proposing various economizing measures in his own personal life as a way of saving his father money.[38]

He anguished, though, over his diminished lifestyle. In 1806 young Tucker became engaged to and soon married Evelina Hunter, a woman from one of Winchester's better families. Though happy with the match, he found himself financially unable to enlarge the tiny town house he rented, much less purchase a larger home. Ashamed to bring his bride to such a small dwelling, he remarked that perhaps his "education . . . fitted me much better for a large fortune than the narrow resources of a lawyer." He assured his father, however, that he had few illusions about ever achieving a grand lifestyle. "Believe me I am contented—by hard work I shall not fail, I think, of a comfortable support and 'tis all I do or dare aspire to."[39]

A life of toil and reduced expectations came with a price. As Henry remembered his eighteenth-century Virginia ancestors, he grew ever more gloomy about his own meager accomplishments. During these years he also learned from his father about the heroic exploits of his Bermuda cousins. In the early nineteenth century, the sons of his uncle Henry Tucker Jr. served the British Empire across the globe, in India and China, aboard Royal flagships, and "e'en in the Cannon's Mouth" with the duke of Wellington, making Henry's life as an attorney in the hills of western Virginia seem unimportant and without meaning. Attempting to explain his depression, Henry turned on himself. He lamented to his father:

> The virtues of my connections, the exalted stations they have filled and the high and unimpeached integrity of their characters while they fill me with pleasure and admiration, bring also the refection that I am as yet unworthy of them, and of their greatness. . . . I feel myself unworthy to be called [your] son. Abroad the name of your family is not less respectable and no tongue dares sully its purity. Believe me, when I hear of these things I feel the responsibility of my situation, the weight of the task which is imposed on me. . . . Three years have I been at the bar, and tho' the exertions of my friends have forced me into business, yet have I done nothing that was worthy of being done. I look around me and hear of my contemporaries carrying off the palm of honour in their respective circles. . . . My greatest success has been to gain a trivial county Ct. cause. My only reputation is that of being somewhat attentive to business. What a falling off my dear Sir is here.[40]

A year or so later, Henry's law practice at last began to prosper. In 1807 the General Assembly named Hugh Holmes to fill a seat on the Virginia bench, and many of his clients gravitated to young Tucker.[41] Although the new business provided him with a competent living, Henry realized that he would never be able to achieve the opulent lifestyle of his parents' generation and that his material expectations still needed to be tempered.

As Henry struggled in western Virginia, his brother Beverley continued to work toward his law license in Williamsburg. Although they were pursuing success in the same profession, Henry and Beverley maintained few contacts throughout the years. Henry could do little to assist his younger brother tangibly, and from boyhood the two men had vastly different personalities. Henry usually sought to please those in authority, while Beverley possessed a more mercurial temperament. As early as 1790 this had become apparent to all for St. George then noted that his five-year-old son "is not without his freaks and eccentricities."[42]

Beverley's stubbornness and obstinacy only increased during adolescence. In 1803 the elder Tucker complained once more about his son's "eccentricities" as well as about his growing "heedlessness." Yet there never seemed any doubt that the youngest Tucker would also pursue a career in the law. Like Henry, Beverley had few material resources at his disposal. Most of the family's lands had been sold off, and their father greatly depended upon his investments in Virginia banks to support his household. Although less than diligent in poring over the required volumes of Coke, Puffendorf, William Sheppard, and his father's "American edition" of *Blackstone's Commentaries,* Beverley managed to learn enough to obtain a license in the summer of 1806.[43]

Convinced that he knew how best to negotiate Virginia's changing landscape, St. George Tucker took firm control of his younger son's career plans. Remaining in the tidewater was impossible, he told Beverley. The region continued to stagnate economically and still had too many attorneys; a new lawyer could count on little business. As with Henry, the judge insisted that Beverley relocate to a more prosperous region of the state where robust commercial activity would generate business for a well-trained attorney. He proposed Fredericksburg, a growing river town in the Northern Neck at the falls of the Rappahannock. But here father and son locked horns. Although Beverley had accepted the professional path chosen by the elder Tucker, he had a vastly different approach to coping with the realities of the early nineteenth century. Whereas the elder Tucker accommodated himself to the individualizing trends he witnessed, Beverley believed that he could overcome them through both a rigid attachment to past values and a keen reliance upon loyal family members. Preoccupied with his own aristocratic past, Beverley recoiled at the thought of leaving the land of his birth for a world of strangers.[44]

Beverley particularly balked at the thought of leaving his half brother, John Randolph. Similar in temperament and outlook, the pair had spent much time together over the years and had grown remarkably close. Not only had Beverley and his siblings spent summer vacations at Bizarre throughout the 1790s, but John periodically stayed at the mansion in Williamsburg. During this period, when so many cherished kin members died, John and Beverley became deeply attached to one another. The loss of their mother especially drew them together. Only three years old when she died, Beverley barely remembered Frances and depended on his half brother to fill in his memories. In 1806 John revealed that he had carefully preserved many of their mother's epistles. "The Letters you mention will be a treasure to me," Beverley wrote in response. "I believe I have never seen any of my mother's."

As the two focused with growing intensity on their deceased mother, they gradually transformed their memory of her into a metaphor for the now-bygone Revolutionary era when their gentry ancestors had dominated the Old Dominion. Beverley revealed to his half brother "that all my pride of family is concentred in my being the son of such a woman." When conflict brewed with his father over Fredericksburg, Beverley turned to Frances's memory for solace. "Had she lived," he wrote, "she *might* have had cause to be proud of me." Although "her loss was irremediable," young Tucker refused to believe that her virtues and guiding principles regarding the Virginia gentry had been lost. "I have been most gratefully sensible," he told his half brother, "that . . . it had been your study to supply her place. Many of those precepts which you learned from her you taught me, and I have cherished them, with the utmost care."[45] John Randolph, possessing his mother's staunch attachment to land, family, and the superiority of the gentry, would provide Beverley with an alternative path to success. Rejecting Henry's example (isolated in the western part of the state and burdened with hard work), Beverley decided to move instead near his half brother's plantation of Roanoke in Charlotte County. There the new lawyer could practice in the surrounding county courts, as his father wished, and he could help Randolph work to enlarge his plantations, as Beverley believed their mother would have wanted. The values of the past—family interdependence, land ownership, and the fundamental right of the gentry to dominate—would continue with the rising generation.

After he learned of this alternative plan, St. George responded severely. He told Beverley that Roanoke lay in the middle of Virginia's declining tobacco country. There were no towns or cities, and decent roads were few and far between. The village of Charlotte Court House, where Beverley proposed to rent a room, was nothing more than a handful of buildings gath-

Nathaniel Beverley Tucker soon after moving to Charlotte County, c. 1810, painted by Joseph Wood. (Courtesy of Erich Kimbrough)

ered around a lonely crossroads.[46] Other "evils" awaited his son, the judge predicted. Despite the rural character of the region, the counties in the Southside already possessed lawyers in abundance. An overcrowded bar and stagnant economic conditions meant little potential business, especially for one from outside the region. Tucker's unspoken message, of course, was that Beverley's emotional attachment to his half brother, no matter how deeply felt, would not advance his professional career. By the early nineteenth century such a kinship bond actually threatened one's success and independence.

After a series of angry and sometimes bitter letters, Beverley defiantly announced that he would not be deterred. In late 1806, with his law license in hand, he set off to be near his half brother. One biographer of Beverley Tucker has asserted, "In deciding on Charlotte Court House over Fredericksburg, Tucker chose feeling over shrewdness."[47] But it was traditional family bonds over individualism that Beverley decided on. Rejecting a life alone surrounded by strangers, Beverley believed that he could assist his half brother in managing his landed properties as well as succeed in the law.

The two years that followed his arrival in the Southside, however, brought only dashed hopes, repeated disappointments, and ample proof that his father's judgments had been sound. Beverley had expected to practice law in the Charlotte, Halifax, and Prince Edward county courts. He also anticipated business from district court sessions held twice annually in Prince Edward County. Despite his high hopes, problems immediately materialized. In 1806 and early 1807, a severe drought caused crop failures throughout the region, which meant fewer commercial cases to litigate. "You will perceive," he bemoaned to his father that March, "I have little to keep alive extravagant hopes." Several months later he reported home, "My own business goes creeping on, 'snail slow in profit.'" After Congress passed the Embargo Act shutting down all American trade with the outside world, Beverley confessed that he saw only "gloomy prospects" before him.[48]

Competition from men he considered inferior added to his woes and deepened his depression. Like his older brother four years earlier, young Tucker had assumed that competition would be mild in the area where he settled, particularly after one prominent local attorney won an appointment to the state bench. But Beverley's expectations did not correspond with reality. Part of the problem lay with his training. After reading and rereading *Blackstone's Commentaries* over the years, he had come to accept the Englishman's vision of an attorney's proper social role. William Blackstone argued in the mid-eighteenth century that a lawyer should not just be a well-educated individual, but he should also be a distinguished, honorable gentleman who paternalistically conveyed laws and constitutional principles to the people "without any derogation."[49] As a highly trained attorney from a distinguished family, Beverley fully expected that he would be seen as far superior in training and manners to his more humble counterparts.

Armed with this outdated conception, Beverley was stunned when he received shockingly little deference as he traveled from county to county. The rules had changed, he wailed. "Every disgusting circumstance" attending the "practice of the Law in Virginia" had "multiplied tenfold" since the Revolution, he told his father. In particular, the Southside seemed overrun with low-birth outsiders, especially Scotch-Irish immigrants who had come down from the North. Because many of these strangers had taken up the law, Tucker viewed them as mean interlopers and unworthy competitors. He had expected a "moderate number of men of character and ability" sharing business and standing above the multitude, but Tucker found himself contending with "a crowd of pettifoggers who start up in every corner of every county." These newcomers, he complained, consumed all the "plain business" that he had counted on to get him started.[50]

Though distinctly unhappy with his son's choices, the elder Tucker urged Beverley to adopt a conciliatory manner with others, confident that his superior training eventually would lead to success. But Beverley could not suppress his elitism and haughtiness. Most of his competitors, he proclaimed, had a "ready knack of saying a great deal they really do not understand." Among young elite attorneys, Beverley's opinions were not unusual. His Bermudian cousin George Tucker also mocked the local lawyers he had to deal with in and around Pittsylvania County. He sarcastically listed the rules of success in a Virginia courtroom. "When you rise at the bar," George advised, "only remember to speak as fast as possible, to shew your fluency. No matter about the choice of words, (tho', to be sure, the longer and rounder the better)." Yet the Bermudian was always circumspect in his opinions, careful not to let them slip beyond a close circle of family and friends. Beverley, on the other hand, wore his contempt and arrogance on his sleeve. He could not resist, he told his father, directing the "bitterness [of] sarcasm" at the "mean and sneering herd" with whom he had to compete every day.[51]

Beverley's imperious manner naturally won him few friends on his circuit. He most often spent days and nights alone, particularly when John

John Randolph's house and outbuildings at Roanoke, Charlotte County. From Henry Howe's *Historical Collections of Virginia* (Charleston, S.C., 1845)

Randolph was away, and he complained, "I feel myself cut adrift by all the world, surrounded as I am by strangers." Unlike his older brother, who blamed himself for his professional disappointments, Beverley lashed out at family members who he felt had forgotten him. He well knew that a generation earlier a strong kinship network would have provided him with both genteel companionship and a distinguished place in society. But the world had changed, and apparently no one now could be bothered with him. Dismissing the "milk and water epistles" occasionally sent by siblings, Tucker told all that he felt "entirely forgotten." Indeed, "Robinson Crusoe was hardly more completely isolated than I am."[52] At the receiving end of most of this correspondence, St. George Tucker misinterpreted his son's dejection. Convinced that only hard work and self-reliance would lead his son to success in the early Republic, the elder Tucker viewed Beverley's complaints as signs of lethargy and indolence. Writing to his daughter in the spring of 1807, he grumbled that Beverley always felt "himself neglected and forlorn." The judge ended, "I hope his mortifications will excite him to industry."[53]

The bitter alienation from his family that Beverley felt led him to reach back to past memories of when his mother had lived and kinship loyalties had been strong and unbreakable. Such bonds had freed young gentlemen from having to compete with inferior "pettifoggers." Beverley hoped they could do so again. The overwhelming reason he had gone to Charlotte Court House was to be near his half brother, and even before he had arrived in the Southside, Tucker solemnly promised to give Randolph "every assistance due to [a] Brother and friend." True to his word, whenever he was between court sessions, Beverley took off for Roanoke. When his half brother was away, Beverley faithfully checked on the performance of managers and overseers. The young lawyer also inspected his brother's crops, slaves, and livestock.[54]

Attached to past ways himself, John Randolph had every intention of reciprocating his half brother's loyalty by giving him a Virginia gentleman's independence. Within a year of Tucker's arrival, Randolph offered him nine slaves and 300 acres of land. Beverley immediately accepted the gift and made plans to build a new brick "cabin" in which to live. The gift reflected not simply the two brothers' love for one another but also their profound attachment to past ways. Land and slaves, not hard work in the law, they believed, would ensure Beverley's place in Virginia society. "From the generosity of my brother I am taught to expect much," he explained to his father, as the proffered land and slaves (and not his law practice) would "insure [me] the immediate necessaries of Life" and "a competent independence."

The property had one more advantage. It would permit Beverley to marry his sweetheart, Mary "Polly" Coalter, the younger sister of his former tutor and now brother-in-law, John Coalter. Beverley had met the young woman several years before when he had stayed for a time on the Coalter plantation near Staunton. An animated girl, Polly had frequently cheered and entertained Beverley when he was studying the law. He informed his father of the couple's "inviolable attachment" to one another and that Randolph's gift would now allow them to take their vows. Proud of his half brother's largesse, Beverley stressed that the land and slaves were "what I expected, what I wished, and what I have received." He finished with a clumsy appeal to his father's self-interest: the gift meant that the judge no longer would have to pay him his monthly allowance.[55] Beverley's underlying meaning, of course, was clear. John Randolph, unlike his father, had fulfilled his familial duty according to the traditions of the past.

The elder Tucker sent a blistering response within days of receiving Beverley's news. In a long and angry letter, he impatiently told his son that he could not build an independent life upon a foundation of family support and property. He pointed out that Randolph "has already to[o] many Calls for . . . his Benevolence" and "if I am not mistaken he is still encumbered with his fathers debts." Aghast that Beverley would add "to his embarrassments," Tucker reminded the novice lawyer that he stood "without a shilling of property" and "without any *certain* hopes . . . of future success" in his career. With regard to Tucker's own ability to assist his son, the judge bluntly reiterated what he had said many times before: beyond a small allowance, there was little he could do to help. "You have from your Inf[anc]y been inform'd that except an Education, some books, . . . and a small annual allowance until you should be enabled to support yourself, you had nothing to expect from me, during my Life, and little, if anything, when I am no more. . . . you can not, *must not,* count upon my Assistance in settling you with a family." Under these circumstances Tucker demanded that Beverley reject Randolph's offer. Furthermore, he must "abandon every Idea of marrying until by Industry and assiduity you have laid an actual foundation for your mutual support."[56] Hard work and diligence were the only paths to independence and happiness.

With his half brother's liberal offer dangling before him, Beverley misconstrued his father's rebukes and calls for self-sufficiency. Unable and unwilling to grasp that such injunctions were the elder Tucker's response to the larger transformations around them, Beverley interpreted his father's demands as signs of individual greed and parsimony: unlike a traditional Virginia father, the judge simply did not want to help launch his son into the world. In an earlier letter home, Beverley had complained of his "painful feeling" at having to call for his monthly allowance and thus "being made to feel myself an *oppressive* burden to you." Following his father's last letter, Beverley agreed to postpone his marriage, but he refused to conceal his bitterness.[57] He especially unburdened himself to his half brother. "There is a void in my heart which the world cannot fill up," he wrote. "I wish my father could see it—he might then learn that the affection of a son ought not to be thrown away."[58]

After another year of struggling alone at the bar, Beverley decided he could wait no longer. In the fall of 1808, he curtly presented his father with a fait accompli: John Randolph had already conveyed to him the promised land and slaves. Beverley defiantly told the elder Tucker that his half brother "has . . . placed me in a situation which secures to me all the necessaries of life, places me above the fear of want." The gift would now permit him to marry Polly. St. George reluctantly gave in. As his part of the wedding settlement, the judge provided Beverley with $500 in cash, 500 acres of land he still owned in Lunenburg County, and two male slaves. His son's monthly allowance, however, would immediately cease.[59] After Henry learned of the paternal gift, he noted that Beverley exhibited "the most buoyant self congratulations."

Unlike his younger brother, Henry eventually grasped his father's larger aims in this dispute. He too had been confused by the elder Tucker's sternness and harsh demands upon Beverley for diligence. Henry at first had urged his father "to place the resources you could afford him within his [Beverley's] own control." Gradually, though, the older son grasped Tucker's motives. In December 1808 he wrote, "I now see what experience should before have taught me: that your delay was prompted by a desire to make him exert himself before he was placed in a situation comparatively independent."[60] By the early nineteenth century, individual effort and industry should be fully displayed before one received even a modest patrimony, because inherited wealth ultimately meant little. The uncertainties of the age made it impossible for any young gentleman to depend on a traditional inheritance of land and slaves. As the elder Tucker had witnessed time and again since the Revolution, long-standing debts and rapidly changing economic circumstances had wiped out many fortunes. Only due diligence and self-reliance would guarantee success.

Beverley and Polly married in February 1809 in a ceremony at John and Fanny Coalter's home near Staunton. St. George Tucker did not attend. The newlyweds afterward moved onto the lands Randolph had given them. They immediately set up housekeeping and began spring planting, while Beverley continued his efforts at the Southside bar.[61]

When the wedding party and guests had left, John and Fanny Coalter resumed their lives on their farm. After they had married seven years earlier, they had settled in Augusta County west of the Blue Ridge Mountains. Renting a 900-acre plantation called Elm Grove, which they eventually hoped to purchase, John and Fanny moved into its small farmhouse along with several domestic slaves and Coalter's mother-in-law from his second marriage, Frances Davenport. Davenport's daughter, Margaret, had died in childbirth several years before, as had Coalter's first wife, the Tucker's former housekeeper, Maria Rind. Although no letters exist regarding John and Fanny's courtship, later correspondence reveals that the couple felt enormous affection for one another. John was undoubtedly attracted to

Fanny's spry sense of humor as well as to her beauty, for it was often re-marked that she looked a great deal like her mother. Coalter once wrote that Fanny was "my best friend." [62] Fanny was likely drawn to John's sensi-tivity, his willingness to work hard and support loved ones, and the over-whelming regard her father had for the young man.

Although much had changed since St. George and Frances Bland Tucker's wedding in 1778, the fundamental expectations guiding young people in marriage remained largely the same. Patriarchal ideals about a husband's dominant role in the household persisted, but in practice mar-riages continued to be built on the twin pillars of emotional companion-ship and joint management responsibilities within the household. John and Fanny had both grown up in homes where the domestic economy involved both spouses. Fanny saw the close cooperation between her parents in the late eighteenth century and, not surprisingly, assumed that to be the norm for Virginia couples. When she traveled west shortly after taking her vows, she fully expected her role as a new wife to mirror her mother's position on Matoax twenty-four years before. [63]

Although the Coalters expected continuity in their marriage, changes unfolded beyond the plantation that would ultimately create enormous tensions between them. Like his new brothers-in-law, John Coalter had trained to become a lawyer, and in the early 1800s his profession shaped his private life. Historians have contended that the nineteenth-century South's agricultural economy allowed it largely to avoid the dramatic transforma-tions associated with the separation of home and work. [64] The Coalters, however, experienced these developments almost every day of their lives. Nor were their experiences unique. William Wirt, a rising Virginia lawyer and an acquaintance of John Coalter, found this reality as well. Wirt mar-ried Elizabeth Gamble the same year John and Fanny wed. Like the Coal-ters, the Wirts also attempted to organize their new household according to traditional customs and ways. But their efforts repeatedly collided with William's ambitions to succeed professionally. The opposite demands of work and family drove the couple apart and created great strains that left each partner dissatisfied. [65]

Such forces also shaped the Coalter household. Soon after Fanny arrived at Elm Grove, she discovered her new husband was gone much of the time, riding his circuit throughout the Shenandoah Valley. Regular attendance at county court meetings was an unavoidable necessity for almost all lawyers. In one year Beverley Tucker attended fifty-six court sessions and spent much of his remaining "free time" on horseback traveling from place to place. The same situation confronted John Coalter. Although his practice surrounding Staunton was a decade old when he wed Fanny, his professional responsibilities consumed enormous amounts of time. Not only did he attend dozens of courts throughout western Virginia, but often when not actually before a judge, he was meeting with clients in his home. Coalter's practice provided the couple with a competent living, but the obligations badly disrupted their marriage. Distressed by his many absences, Fanny started to call Coalter "my wandering husband" and complained that she expected to forget his face entirely. Whenever Coalter stayed at home for any extended period, his wife always called attention to it. She once told her father, "Mr. Coalter dined four times at home since last Sunday week," a record so unusual that it warranted a prominent mention in her letter.[66]

Most of the time, however, Fanny and John endured days and weeks apart. The situation caused practical problems as well as emotional pain. John's professional responsibilities led to great difficulties in managing Elm Grove. When the couple wed, they thought they could direct the plantation in the same fashion St. George and Frances Tucker had managed Bizarre, Roanoke, and Matoax a generation before. Although tobacco markets remained sluggish in the early 1800s, demand for other crops had strengthened. Virginia wheat particularly commanded high prices because of Europe's ongoing Napoleonic Wars. Thus Coalter planned to secure his family's independence as a lawyer-farmer. Just as St. George Tucker had depended on Frances's help to manage their estates, so did Coalter intend to rely on his new bride, and it was a role Fanny at first embraced.[67]

Like her brothers, Fanny Coalter cherished her mother's memory and accomplishments. When she became Elm Grove's mistress, she looked to her mother as her ideal role model. Within months of her wedding, Fanny assumed key responsibilities on the Elm Grove estate. She started to issue orders to the plantation's overseer regarding planting, manuring, and harvesting; she passed along instructions from John when he was on his circuit; she gathered the field hands together almost every morning in order to read to them their daily assignments; and she kept a diligent eye on everyone at their work. Finally, Fanny often forwarded reports to John about how affairs on the estate were progressing. In particular, she and her husband corresponded about their overseer, "Mr. Aircel," evaluating his industry and gauging his execution of Fanny's commands.[68]

Time-consuming duties immediately around the home—household

maintenance, gardening, and cloth and candle production, among other responsibilities—consumed her days as well. Early in their marriage, Fanny assured her husband that she filled her hours with hard work and so contributed significantly to the family economy. "I'm the picture of bustling Notability," she once explained, "having as you know, [been making] our years stock of candles and soap." She also repeatedly had "to fix" her husband's wardrobe for his many court appearances, complaining one spring to her father, "I am up to my eyes in Mr. C—s summer clothes—old stockings &c." Maternal duties also soon filled her days. Nine months after her marriage, Fanny gave birth to a daughter. The couple christened the baby Frances Lelia to honor the child's grandmother and her stepgrandmother. Two years later another little girl was born, soon named Elizabeth after St. George Tucker's sister in Bermuda. In 1809 Fanny had a son whom the proud parents named St. George. By now, raising the children, nursing their frequent illnesses, and guiding them through their early lessons consumed ever greater portions of Fanny's day.[69]

As time passed, these multiple duties and obligations overwhelmed the young woman. The seasonal task of slaughtering Elm Grove's livestock, which fell under her sphere of responsibility, left her exhausted. "I was so overwhelmed with business last week," she wrote her parents two days after Christmas 1809, "that I had not one moment to devote to you, except in thought. . . . we killed *our* Hogs on Monday [Christmas Day]; and all the business of putting away Lard &c: was going forward so that I was completely bewildered." Other family members noticed how Fanny sought to emulate her mother and struggled to make Elm Grove productive. During one stay on the farm, Beverley observed, "Sister Fanny . . . has been acting like a ploughman."[70]

Despite her efforts, though, Elm Grove never prospered under Fanny Coalter's management. Periodic droughts baked crops in the fields, and the Embargo Act of 1807 depressed economic conditions throughout the Valley. Agricultural and market changes in the state created other difficulties. As people increasingly migrated to the western part of the state and as the Old Dominion shifted away from tobacco in favor of wheat, grain, and livestock cultivation, new and complex agrarian practices had to be learned by laborers and landowners alike. "The agricultural routine changed markedly" in the early nineteenth-century Chesapeake, "with more extensive plowing (instead of preparing cropland by hand), penning and winterfeeding of livestock, cultivation of fodder crops, and the wider use of manure for fertilizer."[71] With these and other changes, Fanny became responsible for overseeing an estate that was strikingly different in its daily operation from the ones her mother had managed a generation before.

Transformations in marketing produce and in the relationships between merchants and planters further altered the business of agriculture. When Fanny's father entered the tidewater in 1771, the bonds linking planters, local traders, and British merchants were largely personal and supported by genteel friendships, respectability, and often family ties. As impersonal market forces and conditions grew more crucial, these economic relations changed significantly. The urban areas in the Chesapeake and eastern seaboard were expanding rapidly, with the help of Virginia's Port Bill of 1784. Designed to break up the monopoly held by British merchants and factors over the state's export trade, the statute restricted foreign vessels to only a select number of Old Dominion ports, including Norfolk, Bermuda Hundred, and Alexandria. The effect was to centralize trade and concentrate capital in only a handful of urban locales. At the same time the size of cities outside the state exploded. Between 1790 and 1810 New York City and Baltimore tripled in population while Philadelphia more than doubled.[72]

As trade became concentrated in these ports, planters lost more and more control over economic transactions. Success in obtaining good prices for their produce no longer depended on respectable "friendships." Rather, prices were determined almost solely by, as one merchant put it, "the spur of the market." Thus in the early 1800s John and Fanny Coalter had to sell Elm Grove's crops and purchase needed commodities from traders who wished solely to maximize their profits. The couple also discovered that urban merchants demanded prompt payment for purchased goods instead of providing generous credit as before. No longer did traditional notions of reputation and "independence" carry much weight to men attempting to balance their ledger books. Although Elm Grove's business accounts are sketchy, St. George Tucker's records reveal that he dealt with a number of different merchants by the early nineteenth century, buying and selling commodities from men in Richmond, Norfolk, Philadelphia, Baltimore, and even New York.[73]

The most distressing part of Fanny's efforts was her isolation. She had very few other relatives nearby to assist with work and to relieve her loneliness. In the 1770s and 1780s Frances Bland Tucker frequently had relied upon her father, mother, and brother as well as extended kin in the Randolph and Banister clans. Everyone viewed this broad web of assistance as critical to the overall success of the great gentry families. Fanny Coalter's isolation west of the Blue Ridge, however, meant she had no close kin to summon for help. Most responsibilities for the estate fell on her shoulders alone, and she felt herself overwhelmed. John Coalter anguished at the hardships his wife had to endure. "She is the axis on which all turn and depend," he told his father-in-law, "and [she] really groans under the weight." [74] With his own burdensome professional duties, he could do little to help.

Maintaining discipline among the slaves at Elm Grove proved especially difficult. John Coalter attempted to assert his influence over their twelve adult slaves even while traveling on his circuit. He once instructed Fanny, "To all who love me and shew it by doing their duty give my love and assurances of best services in return." [75] Decent treatment would be their reward for obedience to orders and good behavior. His need to be away so often, however, undermined his authority and weakened discipline. The Coalters' overseer was generally too passive to keep the slaves at their work. This placed the burden on Fanny.

Historians have sometimes argued that nineteenth-century plantation mistresses possessed only limited authority over their slaves in sharp contrast to the great power wielded by their husbands. Elm Grove's operation certainly reflects this reality. John Coalter's absences, Aircel's lax methods, and the lack of nearby male relatives compelled Fanny to struggle on her own. One breakdown in discipline on the estate occurred in 1809 when two field hands, Sam and Charles, got into a serious fight, necessitating Fanny's intervention. "Both were like Demons with rage," she wrote her husband. "I locked Sam over the Office, and Charles in the Smoak-house." Charles then broke out and ran away. Although he soon returned, Fanny regarded the entire affair as a challenge to her authority as mistress. She confronted the slave after he came back and "told him I would not suffer any Member in the family, who would not respect my situation, during yr. absence," she wrote her husband. "You will suppose I was frightened [and] made sick, and the like. Not the least," she declared. [76]

But the pressures of managing Elm Grove alone and without profit steadily eroded Fanny's self-confidence. She increasingly apologized to her husband over the years for "my want of talents . . . but I cannot help it."

She also began to refer to herself as a "goodfornothing" and "perfect Igno-ramus." Not understanding that the problems she confronted lay primarily in the structural changes within Virginia's economy, Fanny chose instead to fixate on her mother's memory. "In truth," she once told John, "I think if I had . . . some of my Mothers talents for Management," she could then keep the estate's slaves at their work and produce earnings that would benefit the entire family. She assured her husband, however, "I am determined to search for some latent sparks, that may possibly yet become brilliant, notwithstanding past appearances against me. I cannot bear to be such a Cypher, and if health is granted, will seriously become your Pupil when [you are] with me."[77]

Though Fanny most often blamed herself for Elm Grove's problems, she periodically aimed her frustrations at her husband and the profession that took him away so often. Pointing to developing strains within the mar-riage, she asked John in 1804, "What do I do without thinking of you my Husband? Could you be more with me and I could be well, the world would not contain a being so happy as your wife." Above all, Fanny wanted the togetherness and partnership in their union that she had expected when they wed. Coalter too wanted to be home more often, once confiding to his father-in-law, "Between ourselves I have serious thoughts of withdrawing considerabl[y] from the County Courts—staying more at home—attend-ing Chancery Business."[78]

Several years later, however, Coalter accepted an appointment on Vir-ginia's General Court bench, a post which only increased his absences, or "banishments" as Fanny had come to call them. As his periods away from home multiplied, his wife grew bitter, and her letters developed a sharper edge. In 1810 she let her husband know the pain everyone felt as a result of his absences. "The day you left us," she explained after he had started one court circuit, "Liz [Frances Lelia] took her seat at dinner, [and] she ex-claimed with a sigh, warm from the heart, Oh My Poor Daddy!!! not an-other word—but how much was expressed in those few." Fanny then added: "St. George [the couple's nine-month-old baby] looks all over the bed for you. These things wring my heart, but I will not repine and make those around me unhappy." Two days later, however, she informed him that "your wife [is] sick and in all respects weak." The following month Fanny went to Williamsburg with the children to wait for John's circuit to end. From the college town she wrote: "Your friend Mr. [William] Wirt was in town. . . . I did not see him, but heard that he met your Son in the street, and caressed Him, Aga [the Coalters' domestic slave] says she is sure the child took him for you—He clung to him, and was with difficulty taken from his neck. Blessed Angel! at his age *he must* lose all recollections of you in this long—grievously long absence." [79] Fanny's pain may well have jarred Coalter's memory of the letter he had received twenty years before from Maria Rind noting that St. George Tucker's younger daughter mistook him for her father, then traveling the circuit himself. [80] With children not recognizing their fathers, it is clear that the legal profession, westward expansion, and economic change had all fundamentally altered early republican families both inside and outside their households.

In this changed environment the Tucker women increasingly looked to one another for support and comfort. Frances Bland Tucker had largely shunned sex-specific kin and friendship networks, preferring instead the companionship of neighbors and family members of both sexes. The growing separation of home and work changed this situation. Whenever John traveled his circuit, Fanny immediately turned to Frances Davenport for friendship, support, and sympathy. Fanny once unburdened herself to John's former mother-in-law, writing, "The idea of parting with my dear Husband [has] so wholly engrossed me for some days previous to his departure that I was unfit for any employment." She briefly attempted moderation, dutifully saying, "I hope I shall submit with patience to whatever else it is the will of Divine wisdom to inflict," but then she cried that parting with her spouse was a "hard trial." Her sister-in-law Polly Coalter Tucker, frequently alone in Charlotte County while Beverley rode from court to court, also looked to female kin for comfort. "I am quite alone," she wrote Fanny in 1810, "and have sent phil to the post office in hopes of a little comfort from some of you." [81]

As life on Elm Grove became ever more difficult and lonely, Fanny Coalter retreated from her management responsibilities whenever she could. She purposely kept herself uninformed about Elm Grove's finances and profitability. Unlike her mother who kept closely abreast of such matters, Fanny believed herself incompetent and thus had nothing worthwhile to contribute. She once wrote her father: "Mr. Coalter has given you a set of his plans [about the possible purchase of Elm Grove]. he has consulted me on the subject but I confess I do not sufficiently understand business to give an opinion—at all events I feel willing to abide by his and your judgement." [82]

At the same time Fanny began to embrace life inside the home. Like other Chesapeake parents of the early nineteenth century, she increasingly doted upon her children and wrote long tender letters explaining their words and actions. Several months after giving birth to their son, she wrote her husband: "Good St. George is a pattern of sweetness. . . . He laughs quite aloud . . . and promises fair to make a jovial companion for you." A year later she tenderly wrote, "Our dear Boy . . . is quite weaned but still asks to look at my bosom; will spit at, and kiss it by turns—and is as fond of being with me and caressed by me, as when he sucked." Fanny wrote lovingly about her daughters as well. Frances Lelia's school activities filled one of her letters to John: "Fancilea has been head of her class for two days. but the bane of her *Celibrity* inattention, occasioned her to give place to Miss Sally Tazewell who spelt the word she missed. Dear Mortal! She had a dreadful cry about it and promises to try hard and regain her place, that I may tell her dear Father the good news."[83]

Fanny Coalter, however, appeared the happiest and most contented when she visited her father's house where she had grown up. Under St. George's protective eye, she felt safe, secure, and far away from the burdens of Elm Grove. Whenever she could, she traveled east across the mountains to relax and enjoy herself. Staying with her father and stepmother in Williamsburg, Fanny cheerfully detailed their crowded social calendar to Frances Davenport. "We have been continually on the go," she explained, "and now I am obliged to avail myself of a leisure hour (I mean from company) to have my letter ready for Tuesday, as we are to have a pretty large [group] to tea this Evening and are to dine at Coll: Carys tomorrow. and the days unfortunately are of the same length here."[84]

Like many Jeffersonian Virginians, Fanny Coalter had come to idealize life inside the home. Before the family hearth, away from outside pressures and intractable difficulties, close friends and loving kin could be comfortably gathered. Her father articulated the concept of a separate private sphere away from public responsibilities, indicating that the Tucker family as a whole was thinking along new lines. In 1807 St. George wrote to Joseph C. Cabell during a visit to Elm Grove: "We are here as retired as if we were in the midst of a Desert. My heart enjoys the release from . . . the bustle of the World. I would willingly turn Hermit, were I permitted to have my family always around me, and to receive the visits of my friends." If Fanny Coalter had looked over her father's shoulder and seen these words, she would have agreed with them.[85]

The experiences of the Tucker clan's rising generation illustrate the breadth and depth of the changes that had swept Virginia following the Revolution. St. George Tucker's children had to cope with new, more competitive professional realities, market alterations, lower living standards and expectations, and a decline in the power and usefulness of kinship ties. These transformations not only altered their efforts to succeed in the world but also changed their relationships with one another. Separated by growing distances, the Tuckers grew isolated, with the kin interdependencies of the past becoming but fading memories. As a result, the bonds between them were forever altered.

Amid these broad changes, emotional ties within nuclear families shifted as well. Virginia spouses found their home and workplace separating in the Old Dominion. Learning to survive in this new environment proved both difficult and stressful. St. George Tucker had promised his children that the legal profession would provide them with security from their uncertain times. Yet the law proved competitive, time-consuming, and ultimately divisive. As husbands and wives coped with long separations, strains within their marriages emerged. The Tuckers increasingly turned to their children for solace and comfort in a difficult world, hoping that their innocence and affection somehow would mitigate the difficulties they faced. The home was becoming an island of refuge from their turbulent times. Changes in the landscape also led the Tuckers to begin questioning the wisdom of the nation's Revolutionary experiment. As the rising generation entered public life, politics, and elective office, they came to doubt the capacity of their countrymen to manage liberty and to govern themselves.

Five

Disillusion and Reaction

In November 1803 St. George Tucker traveled to Richmond to attend the fall meeting of the General Court. Soon after he arrived, his former law student and then-state attorney general, Philip Norborne Nicholas, showed the judge two letters written by Robert Bailey of Augusta County. Tucker immediately recognized the name. During the autumn court circuit held several weeks earlier, he had convicted Bailey for gambling. Addressed to Philip Grymes Jr., a member of the governor's council, Bailey's letters accused the judge of demanding a bribe in return for leniency. Bailey claimed that before his trial Tucker had "told me he would not give judgment against me . . . if I would give him 100 guineas." Because he had refused, the Augusta County man said, Tucker unjustly convicted him.[1]

The charge came at an awkward moment. That fall Virginia's venerable jurist and state Court of Appeals judge Edmund Pendleton had died. Because of Tucker's experience and reputation, he quickly emerged as the leading candidate to fill the vacancy on the Old Dominion's highest court. Other candidates soon arose, however, including his fellow General Court judge Archibald Stuart.[2] Because Stuart was from Augusta County, he gained the support of many prominent men west of the Blue Ridge who believed the post should go to a Shenandoah man, a region ignored in previous appointments to the court.

Tucker took Bailey's charge very seriously not merely because of Stuart's challenge but also because the accusation threatened his reputation as a gentleman and man of honor. Although Bailey was well known as "a Gamester" and as "destitute of moral principles," the House of Delegates ordered a "deliberate" investigation. Many thought Tucker's high rank and close ties to the state's elite required such a probe. One house member privately explained that delegates feared charges of "gross partiality and injustice" if they let the matter drop. Thus Tucker found himself confronted with a legislative inquiry into his fitness for office. He immediately turned to two trusted kin for help: his son-in-law, John Coalter, and his cousin George Tucker. With their assistance the judge assembled a long petition designed to undercut Bailey's credibility and to restore his own reputation, which Tucker noted, "he had hoped and still hopes, to carry with him, to the Grave."[3] In December the House investigation began, and it lasted several days. Members soon found Bailey's attack without merit and exonerated the judge. Several weeks later the assembly selected Tucker to fill Pendleton's seat on the state's high court.[4]

St. George Tucker's ordeal in gaining a seat on the Court of Appeals illustrates much about early republican Virginia. Bailey's charge and the widespread attention it gained stand in stark contrast to the deferential treatment the gentry received in the previous century. No comparable investigations of the elite occurred in the Old Dominion throughout the 1700s. In the colonial era burgesses drawn from the planter class would never have seriously investigated charges made by a low-birth gambler from outside the tidewater. By 1803, however, the state's social and political environment had shifted in a democratic direction. No longer could the elite automatically count on deference from the population, and no more could the opinions of the lower classes be cavalierly dismissed. Bailey's accusations, though, stunned the Tuckers and shook their faith in the wisdom of popular sovereignty. An angry and perplexed John Randolph best summed up the affair for the entire clan, asking, "Can the character of St. George Tucker be sullied by the breath of this man?"[5] How could such an individual, who in the family's opinion had been drawn from the dregs of society, challenge the reputation of a gentleman who moved in Virginia's highest circles?

The Bailey affair and the Tuckers' reaction to it point to their growing disillusionment with the nation's Revolutionary experiment. This chapter explores the family's involvement in the public sphere in the decade before the War of 1812 as a means to explain both changes in early national politics and the growing conservatism of Virginia's political elite. As their countrymen embraced and seemingly abused those liberties won in the Revolution, the family saw themselves facing a rising tide of disorder, corruption, and instability. Disheartened by what they witnessed, the Tuckers and other elites gradually retreated from the war's liberal principles and tacked in the opposite direction. Eventually they reinterpreted the conflict against Great Britain itself. No longer did they view it as the triumph of enlightened reason over ignorance, nor was it a victory of freedom-loving people over a diabolical tyrant. Rather the Revolution became in the Tuckers' minds an event meant solely to preserve Virginia's plantation culture and to protect the interests of its landed elite. Pessimism about the present, furthermore, led the family to begin looking to the past with ever-increasing nostalgia. Eighteenth-century Virginia became for them an idealized world—a glittering time and place—when the old gentry class had ruled benevolently while secure in its position of authority. At a time when the state's traditional elite continued to lose power, the Tuckers looked sentimentally back to the previous century as their society's ideal time.

Finally, the War of 1812 spawned within the family and its circle grave doubts about their northern brethren. The Tuckers took note of the North's early nineteenth-century commercialization and urbanization and its lack of support for the second war against Great Britain. They concluded that the section's people lacked the proper morals and way of life needed to sustain the Republic honorably into the future. The intellectual and social values that would later characterize the antebellum South—rigid conservatism, nostalgia for the past, animosity toward the North—had begun to emerge.

Like many elite Revolutionaries, St. George Tucker had believed that the Republic established after the war would be politically and socially stable as well as dominated by America's propertied classes. Once educated about their rights and responsibilities, yeomen voters would select wise and wealthy statesmen to govern over them. Tucker once noted that only well-educated gentlemen had the cultivation of mind to practice "immaculate *Virtue*" and to recognize "the best Interests of [the] Country."[6] Throughout the 1790s, as the planter class declined in power, Tucker had hoped that well-trained members of the judiciary would fill this governing role. Such hopes, however, proved illusionary. By the early 1800s college-educated lawyers were struggling and competing with largely untrained newcomers. Elections, instead of ratifying the existing social hierarchy, had become ve-

hicles for middling-class voters to challenge the wealthy's traditional position. Indeed, yeomen and lower-class Virginians had taken up the ideology
of the American Revolution with a determination that their specific interests be respected. The elite could not help but notice, for instance, that a
Baptist minister from Albemarle County won a seat in the House of Delegates from Thomas Jefferson's son-in-law by loudly proclaiming himself
"the poor man's candidate" and emphasizing the "difference of interest between the poor and the rich."[7]

Tucker's own experiences on the bench revealed these transformations
at work. His many contacts with jurors drawn from the yeomen classes had
left him especially grim. Tucker found such men callous about their public duties and disrespectful toward those gentlemen justices in authority,
exactly the reverse of what he had observed when he arrived in the colony
decades before. Before the Revolution yeomen farmers had sought jury service eagerly and almost always deferred to planter justices in order to build
ties to the local elite. By the 1790s, however, as the traditional order began
to crumble, this practice broke down. County and district court judges
found it increasingly difficult to locate responsible freeholders willing to
sacrifice the time and effort in order to serve. Tucker learned through hard
experience that after several days of a court's session, juries came to be composed almost entirely of "idle loitereres about the court, who contrive to get
themselves summoned as jurors, that they may have their expenses borne."
Such men lacked the intelligence to understand the law's complexities and
the moral strength to decide cases dispassionately. Such individuals, Tucker
believed, had brought the state's entire system of justice into sad "disre-
pute." "If the consciences of Jurors were not hardened against the sin of per-
jury," he complained to John Page in 1806, "I am at a loss to guess how so
many offenders could escape." Unless something changed, the judge
glumly predicted, "*we* may live to lament that the order of things among
us was ever changed."[8]

George Wythe's murder that same year seemed to epitomize the anarchy into which Virginia was sinking. Shortly after Wythe's poisoning by
arsenic, Tucker and Page exchanged letters. The former governor ascribed
the crime to the rising immorality he witnessed in general among the
people. Tucker reluctantly agreed. Wythe's grandnephew, who had killed
the old man for an inheritance, was "one of these monsters of depravity that
of late have too often appeared in this Country." The source of Virginia's
moral crisis, Tucker speculated, might be the ideas he and Page had em-

braced years before. Because Virginians now practiced "that affectation of superior refinement, and Philosophical Discernment," they had abandoned their belief in "supreme Wisdom, and Power" and thus had lost their fear of divine punishment. "We have refined upon the words philosophy, philanthropy, and the Rights of Man," Tucker concluded, "until we are in real danger of that system of Anarchy with which the adversaries of a republican government reproach it."[9]

The social "Anarchy" that spun out of the Revolution even worked its way into the Court of Appeals. Although pleased with his appointment to the high court, Tucker almost immediately came into conflict with fellow justice Spencer Roane, precipitating a battle between the two men which St. George saw as rooted in the general turmoil that followed independence. As the court's most respected legal theorist, Tucker always viewed himself as Edmund Pendleton's intellectual heir and as the three-member court's de facto leader. He quickly forged a close alliance with William Fleming, the court's official president. Although younger in age than Tucker, Roane was the more senior judge. Isolated and forced to dissent on many cases, he came to resent Tucker's influence bitterly.[10] Legal scholars have attributed the disagreements between these two jurists to their differing views about the state court's proper role within the national judiciary.[11] Though conflicting visions of the law did cause friction, their disputes more importantly evolved out of the changing nature of public service and officeholding in the new Republic.

St. George Tucker had learned as a youth that an officeholder's carriage and demeanor told the world much about his birth, education, and rank. It was thought in the late colonial age that a genteel bearing and temperament before the public helped secure respect for government magistrates. After the Revolutionary War, Tucker and others within the planter class believed that the need for proper and dignified public officers had only increased, given the historical instability of republics. Throughout the decades Tucker's conduct from the bench was always rigidly mannered, strict, and formal in order to convey the authority of his office physically. By the early nineteenth century, however, his demeanor seemed wholly out of step with the times. In 1800 one of Tucker's law students noted that his teacher's "hauteur and austerity" were notorious throughout Virginia. The judge's insistence on proper decorum inside the courtroom also appeared antiquated. In 1801 Garritt Minor, another former student, saw Tucker jail a Fredericksburg man for an offhand remark that only the judge thought dis-

St. George Tucker in 1807, while he served on the Virginia Court of Appeals, engraving by Charles B. J. F. de Saint-Mémin. (Courtesy of the Tucker-Coleman Papers, Swem Library, College of William and Mary)

respectful. After a local jury found the offender innocent, all the lawyers involved laughed and mocked Tucker for his "disgusting" conduct.[12]

Tucker's formalism stood in distinct contrast to Spencer Roane. Born into a modest Essex County family, Roane had developed a blunt and direct personal manner as a young man. During his youth he fell under the spell of Virginia's hero of the yeomanry, Patrick Henry. Roane married Henry's daughter Anne in 1786, cementing the two men's personal and political relationship. Until Henry's death in 1799, the old Revolutionary exerted considerable influence over the rising lawyer's views and conduct. "Under the sway of Henry, Roane developed a fiery sense of partisanship and pride" that made him "unafraid to lash out against those who posed a threat to the be-liefs he held dear."[13] Tucker felt distinctly uncomfortable with such men gaining power and influence, believing their humble origins and lack of refinement meant only trouble. Tucker revealed (perhaps unwittingly) his own deep-seated uneasiness with such individuals when he once discussed Patrick Henry with William Wirt, who was compiling material for a biog-raphy of the old firebrand. Tucker's recollections, though, proved less than flattering. Henry's "pronunciation," he remembered, "was sometimes in-correct and even vicious. . . . Some . . . words have at times grated my ears." Tucker explained that he found Henry's public manner and speeches crude and coarse. Even Henry's clothes showed the man's lack of refinement and gentility. Tucker concluded that Patrick Henry "was certainly in appear-ance *awkward,* . . . it was the awkwardness of a *modest Gentleman.*"[14]

Tucker doubtlessly saw this same "awkward" appearance in his Court of Appeals colleague. Tucker's own stiff and overbearing manner could not have helped the situation. In late April 1809 the tensions between the two men finally exploded. During a private judicial conference in Richmond, Roane accosted Tucker as he outlined a case the three members of the court were examining. Grabbing Tucker's notes from his hands, Roane angrily threw the papers to the floor and shouted that Tucker wished "to direct the whole business of the court." Roane declared that he would no longer sub-mit to such behavior even "at the risk and peril of his office, and his life." Stunned by the assault as well as at the "very harsh and indecorous lan-guage" used against him, Tucker told Fleming that he would cease to at-tend court sessions until he received an "unqualified" apology. Refusing to apologize, Henry's protégé instead called for the General Assembly to ex-amine "the *whole* ground of controversy." The business of the high court came to a halt.[15]

The Tucker-Roane conflict arose in part because of a professional rivalry between two ambitious men who held different views about the role of the state and federal judiciary. But the dispute also emerged out of the enor-mous cultural and social changes then reshaping Jeffersonian Virginia. Tal-ented and forceful men like Spencer Roane who lacked ties to the state's an-cient families had gained considerable influence since the Revolution. They increasingly refused to buckle to elites like Tucker who still flaunted their "hauteur." Such manners beforehand had set the elite far above the "com-mon herd," but no more. By the 1800s individuals such as Roane demanded power, respect, and attention. Most importantly, they refused to play second fiddle to members of the old guard.

For the Tucker family the changes pointed only to growing disorder. George Tucker learned from one of Roane's acquaintances that he had attacked St. George in order "to be independent." Astounded by this answer, the young Bermudian reflected upon the unintended lengths this adjective—once so vital to the old planter class's lexicon—had been taken in the early Republic. "Is thus [Roane's] independence incompatible with other people's," he asked, "or is nobody to be 'independent' but himself? Strange abuse of words! as if the mild unassuming claim of independence authorized the insolence of a Bashaw or the ferocity of a Tartar." Did independence, George further inquired, also mean that one should be free "of decency, of self respect, and of the approbation of every one who calls himself a gentleman." He tried to reassure his older cousin that those who "take sides against you" in this dispute were low men of vile "appetites," who preferred "putrid meat to sound." [16]

Yet the entrance of such men into the political arena could not be dismissed. Henry Tucker confessed to his father that it seemed almost impossible now for a true gentleman to serve the public. The problem seemed to lie with republicanism itself: "It is a melancholy circumstance that in the formations of institutions like ones [we have] we are always carrying every thing to extremes." Echoing George Tucker, Henry wrote, "How else can we account for the disgraceful conduct of public officers . . . [which] is justified as the effect of independence of spirit." From Washington, D.C., John Randolph wrote what all in the family thought. Although he sympathized with his stepfather, he knew that the conflict with Roane was part of the broader democratic trends then sweeping the nation. With men such as Roane now regularly challenging the traditional elite, "God help" the country, Randolph concluded. "In another generation we shall be a people of blackguards exclusively." [17]

Confronted with such a situation, St. George Tucker only wished to retreat from public life and bury himself inside his home. He cried to Fanny in the autumn of 1809 that he now viewed his judicial duties with "horror" and dreaded returning to them. [18] His frustrations mirrored a general disenchantment with public service among surviving members of the Revolutionary generation. The lack of appreciation for his republican services confounded Thomas Jefferson during the early nineteenth century. As a more combative public sphere emerged, Jefferson turned inward to his family for support and fulfillment.[19] St. George Tucker moved in the same direction at the same time. "No man in public Life can promise himself any portion of *real* happiness," he told his daughter, "and I am not patriot enough to sacrifice *that*."[20] As the attractions of public service declined, the virtues of the private sphere rose in proportion.

Even before he broke with Roane, Tucker had begun to idealize domestic life. In 1807 he told Joseph C. Cabell, who had recently married the judge's stepdaughter, Polly Carter, that when he had his "family" around him, "all the . . . great and little Events of the World affect me not." Two years later he continued to romanticize the private hearth. The same month that Roane accosted him, Tucker sent Henry several poems "on domestic scenes of tenderness and bliss." Several weeks later he wrote John Coalter. The letter was supposed to be a congratulatory one on the birth of Coalter's first son. But it quickly turned into a heartfelt plea that the infant never sully himself by entering public life. The judge proclaimed that government service offered honest upright men only disappointment, frustration, and bitterness. "If my prayers for him may be heard," Tucker finished, "[he] will never descend from the happy dignity of a private station." Although he apologized for these "melancholy reflections," Tucker asked, "Kiss my Grandson for me, and give him my paternal blessing, praying God to make him a *Good* Man, but never a great one."[21]

Tucker's disillusionment with public service reached the breaking point the following year. In 1810 a committee in the House of Delegates censured the Court of Appeals for its lengthening delays in rendering opinions. At the same time the legislature extended the court's sessions with no corresponding increase in salary. Tucker submitted a petition to the assembly in December defending his conduct on the bench and the following April sent a long and angry letter to Governor James Monroe quitting the post.[22] Already in his sixtieth year, Tucker had grown tired of public office. In the early Republic such service had become time-consuming, burdensome, and wholly unappreciated. "I wish," he told Cabell, "for nothing but peace, repose, and a fair name."[23]

Although the elder Tucker withdrew from public life in disgust, his children entered politics as they came of age, seeking important positions for themselves and struggling to make sense of the new order of things. John Randolph was the first of the judge's children to enter political life. Despite Randolph's eccentric personality and diminutive stature, freeholders from the Southside elected him to Congress in 1799. The Randolph family name still commanded attention in the late eighteenth century, and voters were enthralled by John's forceful, cutting, and incisive speeches from the hustings. Earning their respect with his passion and eloquence, Randolph soon held a secure seat.[24]

Voted into office during the bitter debates over the Alien and Sedition Acts, Randolph brought a sharp ideological edge to the Capitol. Old enough to remember the Revolutionary age when landed estates and family-based gentry hierarchies brought order to society, Randolph sought to preserve this past through a staunch commitment to the "Country" principles articulated by England's Augustan writers. Although never a consistent thinker, Randolph revealed his debt to these essayists when once asked about his political principles. "What are they?" he answered. "Love of peace, hatred of offensive war, jealously of the state governments toward the general government; a dread of standing armies; a loathing of public debt, taxes and excises; tenderness for the liberty of the citizen; jealousy, Argus-eyed jealousy, of the patronage of the President."[25] Randolph wanted to protect local authority, curb federal power, and preserve citizens' liberty from ambitious, power-hungry individuals.

Like many Virginians, he saw Jefferson's 1801 inauguration as the triumph of the "Principles of '98." The Virginia and Kentucky Resolutions of that year articulated Jeffersonian pleas for decentralized power, agricultural over commercial interests, real property over paper money, and a strict interpretation of the Constitution. During the president's first term, Randolph closely and successfully worked with the administration as chairman of the powerful House Ways and Means Committee. Many goals dear to the heart of Republicans became legislative realities. Between 1801 and 1804 internal taxes in the United States were abolished, the national debt was partially retired, the standing army was reduced, and the Alien and Sedition Acts expired.[26]

Despite these successes, however, Randolph came to doubt the president's commitment to their shared values. He eventually realized that Jefferson meant only to trim and not to destroy the Federalist edifice constructed by Hamilton, Washington, and Adams during the previous decade. Convinced that only a rigid attachment to "Country" precepts would ensure the Republic's longevity, Randolph tolerated no backsliding. His uncertainty about the administration's ideological purity escalated to open conflict in 1805 over the "Yazoo Compromise." Although the president was attempting to set a past wrong right when he agreed to compensate defrauded land purchasers in Georgia, Randolph believed that the federal government's involvement would taint it with the scandal. His fierce opposition nearly derailed the compensation package the administration supported in the House of Representatives. A week later Randolph's relationship with the administration further deteriorated at Samuel Chase's impeachment trial. Randolph headed the House prosecution of the Federalist Supreme Court justice, who had been charged with improper conduct. Unwell and unprepared because of the Yazoo controversy, Randolph presented a confused and rambling case, leading to Chase's acquittal on all counts by the Senate. The trial's outcome damaged Randolph's authority and position in the party. The following year Tucker's stepson discovered that Jefferson intended to purchase West Florida from Spain secretly, without Congress's approval. Appalled at what he considered to be a grossly unconstitutional act, Randolph announced his formal opposition to the administration.[27]

As his opposition hardened, Randolph grew convinced that the federal government was spiraling toward corruption and collapse. Increasingly pessimistic, he turned to loyal kin for support and comfort. He unburdened himself to his stepfather: "The contest, in which you bore a part, for independence, was a bloodless struggle, compared with that in which, ere long, we must engage. We have a masked monarchy. . . . the servility [to Jefferson] which now prevails surpasses any thing that Jonathan Pindar ever dreamt of." Sister Fanny worried that her half brother had become too "absorbed in politics" and urged him to visit Elm Grove in order to relax. His sister-in-law Judith also sent messages of concern and encouragement, assuring him that his "well earned fame" would not be eclipsed by "despicable" political enemies.[28]

Randolph's staunchest supporters were his two half brothers. During the nineteenth century's first decade, Henry and John corresponded nearly every week while Beverley moved to Charlotte County almost solely to be near his half brother. As John's political influence in the Capitol waned, both Tuckers grew ever more concerned about his well-being. "His constitution," a worried Henry once told St. George, "I fear is much injured by his course of life. He speaks of never ceasing aches and pains, gout and rheumatism." When Republican leaders forced Randolph from the party's leadership in 1807, Henry reacted with fierce loyalty, declaring, "Really the circumstances of my brothers being named on no important Committees countenances his suspicions that he is a denounced man."[29]

Henry Tucker's close relationship with Randolph eventually pulled him into politics. In early 1807, after years of writing to his half brother about public affairs, Henry decided to run for a seat in the state's House of Delegates.[30] Tucker entered public life at a time when his legal practice had finally started to prosper. After Hugh Holmes gained a seat on the Virginia bench, Tucker picked up many of his clients. Henry still could not embark upon a lavish lifestyle, but he at least earned a competent living. Although formal party structures had begun to emerge by this time and more non-gentry candidates were appearing, Virginia freeholders still considered a candidate's personal characteristics when casting their ballots. Henry's manners and education undoubtedly helped him stand out in Winchester. More importantly, his mild temper, modest ways, and especially his respectful treatment of all citizens in the town impressed voters throughout the upper Valley. Tucker's profession also came to his aid. Although some nineteenth-century observers argued that "being a lawyer was . . . a fatal objection" to political ambitions, others recognized that the profession molded superior candidates. In the post-Revolutionary period the number of elections grew with the number of political offices, including some multicounty contests involving thousands of freeholders. Thus a lawyer's monthly circuit provided him a keen knowledge of regional issues and a close familiarity with the area's leading men. As Henry's cousin George later pointed out, "It is no wonder . . . that this class [i.e., lawyers] has obtained such an ascendancy in our country. Their talents, their activity, and their intimate knowledge of men and their concerns, must give them infinite advantages over every other class." With these assets, Henry easily won his contest.[31]

During Tucker's single term in the state legislature, politics brought him closer to his half brother. In 1807–8 the two men focused on advancing James Monroe's long-shot presidential candidacy in Virginia. In view of Jefferson's descent from republican doctrine and his ill-treatment of Randolph, they both rejected the president's handpicked successor, Secretary of State James Madison. Monroe seemed an attractive alternative. Not only was he an unswerving advocate of "Country" principles, but Monroe had also gained the family's affection when he served overseas in London. In the British capital to negotiate American grievances over trade and impressment, Monroe also found time to oversee the education of St. George Randolph, Richard and Judith Randolph's deaf-mute son. Despite John's efforts to lure him into the race, however, Monroe wrote from London that he had no intention of running.[32] He told one friend that he would "rather be constable" than oppose the president's wishes on Madison. In late 1806, however, Madison greatly embarrassed Monroe by sending the Federalist William Pinkney to England with new negotiating instructions, an action Monroe took as a public rebuke of his conduct. The following year the secretary further humiliated Monroe by refusing even to submit the treaty he and Pinkney had hammered out to the Senate. Monroe then decided to throw his hat in the ring to demonstrate his political clout and influence.[33]

At that point Randolph and Tucker swung into action and worked tirelessly to advance Monroe's chances. John canvassed state leaders seeking their support and votes. By December 1807 he and other supporters boasted that Monroe had the backing of a majority of the state legislature. Henry meanwhile took to the floor of the Virginia Assembly to attack both Jefferson and Madison. In early January 1808 he took particular aim at the administration's Embargo Act, explaining to delegates how the measure would devastate planters and farmers in all parts of the Old Dominion. That same month, the brothers sought to demonstrate Monroe's strength. On 23 January 1808 they and other backers held a pro-Monroe rally in Richmond. The meeting proved a disaster. Only 57 state legislators showed up, whereas that same evening 123 General Assembly members attended a pro-Madison gathering at the city's Bell Tavern. The competing rallies revealed the secretary of state's overwhelming power, and Monroe wisely pulled out of the contest shortly afterwards.[34]

Furious because he believed the administration had twisted arms behind the scenes, Henry soon afterwards denounced his fellow legislators. "I never believed there was much public virtue . . . in the legislative bodies," he cried to his father. Indeed, "*there is no independence in the Virginia legislature.* They follow their file leader with all the scrupulous exactness of a prussian recruit." Therefore, Henry's faith in Virginia's republican order began to crumble. More and more, he said, officeholders were inferior men who "'grasp' at office if not 'at power.'" "God help us!" he later concluded, "If with . . . such public bodies we are not ruined." As for himself, Henry announced that he was "disgusted with public life" and would not run for another term.[35]

As the younger Tuckers and Randolph surveyed their situation, the reason for the growing number of worthless officeholders became abundantly clear. Citizens of the Old Dominion not only had lost their respect for their betters, but they had also abandoned their traditional veneration for land, place, and community. In a republic constantly on the move (most often to the West), the locality of one's birth and the community where one lived no longer seemed to matter. Beverley particularly lashed out at this development at the time of Monroe's candidacy. "We lead the lives of Tartars," he wrote. Too many "of my fellow citizens" were "selling the bones of their ancestors, and moving off to another country [i.e., state] that they may lag up a few more dollars to bury their own."[36] This sort of geographical mobility not only led Virginians to shun their past but also had so disrupted the old order that it allowed unworthy men to rise up, men who a generation before would have been cast aside.

At the same time immigration further disrupted things. Although the foreign influx into the Old Dominion had never been strong as in the northern states, Virginia's ethnic diversity grew rapidly during the second half of the eighteenth century with Scots, Welshmen, Scotch-Irish, and Germans all settling in various counties. Those who lacked the pure blood of Englishmen brought few positive traits to America, the Tuckers believed. George Tucker, for instance, noted how the Scotch-Irish in Virginia fully retained their proclivity for violence, poor husbandry, and clannishness.[37] Beverley heaped scorn upon these outsiders. Confronting them in the Southside—mostly as competitors at the bar—he labeled them "the filthy sweepings of the other quarters of the globe." Their crude manners, habits, and customs had so debased "our national character" that they had created a "misbegotten mongrel patriotism." In particular, these interlopers voted for "Blackguards" and "shoe blacks" in elections, giving the state legislators of inferior worth and integrity. In an age when birth, place, and tradition now counted for little, Beverley wondered how Virginia could survive. "Republicanism," he concluded, "appears to me to be nothing but a heterogeneous compound of servility, and insubordination."[38]

These developments in public life not only frustrated family members but thoroughly disillusioned them as well. They had hoped for a rational republic led only by well-educated and well-born men. But these expectations collapsed amid challenges from below. As their pessimism grew, the Tuckers began to reconceptualize their memories of the American Revolution and to reinterpret its ultimate aims. In light of their current experiences, the family reprocessed the War for Independence in a manner that led them to question and doubt its ideological foundations. Indeed, the liberal beliefs that had once motivated so many Americans to fight seemingly by the early nineteenth century had led to political and social chaos. In

Washington, D.C., self-government had spawned corruption and personal aggrandizement in political leaders; in Virginia, Revolutionary ideals had taught the lower classes that freedom only meant liberty from all restraints, including the traditional responsibility to defer to men of rank, breeding, and education. Surely, the Tuckers thought, the founders had not intended their enlightened beliefs to unbalance and destroy society's equilibrium, yet disorder at home and abroad seemed only to grow worse.

Beverley initially questioned the Revolution's philosophic traditions. While a student at William and Mary, he had read the Enlightenment's leading champions, including Jean-Jacques Rousseau, Thomas Paine, and the English philosopher William Godwin. But their ideas had left him emotionally and spiritually empty. In particular, Godwin's precept that man was a creature governed solely by his intellect disgusted the younger Tucker. This "rationalism," he cried, left no room for such feelings as affection for friends, pride in family, and love of country. He mocked in letters to Randolph "the Philosophers of the day who laugh at everything they can not find a reason for." Believing them to be champions of "cold speculative calculation," Beverley argued that "the heart" is "weighty enough to over-balance volumes of reason." Henry chimed in with his brother. Struggling with inferior men at the bar and in the General Assembly, Henry told his father they all lived in times when "every man is at sea without chart or star, or compass." Therefore, "I do not admire the discussion of speculative opinion."[39]

As younger family members moved away from "reason," they gravitated toward a romantic conservatism which viewed the past as manifestly superior to the present. They particularly came to embrace the ideas of Edmund Burke. Unlike proponents of the Enlightenment, Burke argued that immemorial traditions and customs deeply mattered. His indictment of the upheavals in France, *Reflections on the French Revolution,* especially resonated with the Tucker brothers and John Randolph. Downplaying human reasonableness, Burke argued that man's basic instincts largely determined his actions. Therefore, ancient institutions had to be preserved in order to contain the instabilities that had grown in tandem with revolutionary freedoms. Reading and rereading Burke closely during the nineteenth century's first decade, Tucker family members came to doubt the ideological thrust of America's Revolution. Beverley later noted that after his half brother closely read Burke, he began "to suspect that there may be something in the enjoyment of liberty which soon disqualifies a people for self-government."[40] Beverley himself found great solace in Burke's enchantment with the past and used his arguments to attack "the pernicious doctrines of Godwin" and "the sublime doctrine of perfectibility."[41]

Because of such doubts, the younger generation now questioned every change that had materialized since the Revolution. They increasingly idealized Virginia's glorious colonial age in order to contrast it with a dismal present. "Before the revolution," Randolph wrote in 1814, "the lower country of Virginia . . . was inhabited by a race of planters, of English descent, who dwelt on their principal estates. . . . Their habitations and establishments . . . were the seats of hospitality. The possessors were gentlemen [and] better bond men were not to be found in the British Dominions." By the early nineteenth century, however, this idyllic world was gone, and the landscape had fundamentally changed. "The old mansions . . . are fast falling to decay," Randolph continued. "The families, with a few exceptions, are dispersed from St. Mary's to St. Louis. Such as remain here have sunk into obscurity. They whose fathers rode in coaches and drank the choicest wine, now ride on saddlebags and drink grog."[42]

Henry agreed with his half brother's sentiments regarding past and present. He told his father that Virginians must reject all further "change if it can ever be avoided" in order for their society to regain its stability. "The spirit of innovation will be the rock in which we shall split," he warned. "As Church says, 'Tis the germ of mischief and first spawn of hell.'" Unwilling to condemn independence from Great Britain (and hence directly reproach his father's generation), Henry transformed the Revolution into a profoundly conservative event. "Since I have grown up," he finished one letter to the elder Tucker, "I have been induced to think the greatest praise of the American patriots (particularly Virginian) was their aversion to change: and the avoiding of all laceration in the system of things in existence at the commencement of the revolution."[43] In the younger generation's mind the War for Independence became a struggle to preserve the Old Dominion's traditional customs and old power structure. All subsequent transformations represented nothing more than a series of painful and wholly unintended consequences.

As Henry, Beverley, and John Randolph reinterpreted the Revolution, they also reached back nostalgically to their own family's past. Younger members found themselves increasingly enraptured (indeed haunted) by stories of their ancestors' former domination of the Old Dominion. Beverley Tucker and John Randolph continued to cherish the memory of their deceased mother and to commiserate about her early death. The pair started to visit the old Bland family seat of Cawsons regularly, hoping somehow to bridge the widening gap between an unbearable present and a wonderful past. In the fall of 1805, John wrote his half sister, Fanny, "Tomorrow I go to the place of my birth—the birth place of our angel mother—where I have not been for eighteen years!" "How many painful recollections," he continued, "sweetly painful will the sight of that place recall." The family's current situation was particularly distressing compared to the past when the clan as a whole had been close-knit, loyal to one another, and powerful. "It seems but yesterday," Randolph finished, "that I saw our aged Grandfather surrounded by his descendants." Four months later Beverley returned as well to his grandfather's plantation. "I crossed the river one morning to Cawsons," he reported to his half brother. "You may conceive the pleasure which I felt at finding myself on the domains of my ancestors." Like John, however, Beverley's nostalgic memories were bittersweet. During his visit he met the estate's current owner, whom Beverley labeled that "insignificant interloper whose unhallowed feet seemed to profane the ruins he trod on."[44]

The rising generation's obsession with the past also led them to clutch with growing zeal those elements of the old order which had beforehand promised status and wealth. Younger family members all embraced landownership despite their father's pronouncements. Not only did John Randolph and the Coalters maintain and add to their estates during these years, but even the more obedient Henry saw owning land as essential. Although he once wrote that "I am so much of a Tucker that Land and negroes are only incumbrances," he owned both types of property throughout his adulthood. At the time of his marriage, St. George gave Henry title to undeveloped lands in Kanawha County and in eastern Ohio. Several years later he purchased a small estate outside Winchester, and he also owned a small cabin at Sulphur Springs, Virginia.[45] Like most early nineteenth-century lawyers, Henry viewed farming as an important part of his family's economic life. Because tobacco did not grow in the Shenandoah Valley, he and ten slaves he owned cultivated mainly wheat, annually producing between 800 and 900 bushels for market. Agricultural work, moreover, was vital to Henry's identity of himself as a respected freeholder. He told his father in 1810: "I have been obliged to unite the two characters of lawyer and farmer in no small degree. The last ten days of June and the first ten of July I spent in the harvest field. . . . I was [then] obliged to put off the farmer and play lawyer at Staunton long before the crop was in." Although Henry embraced the persona of the diligent farmer-lawyer rather than that of the leisured planter, he never abandoned the eighteenth-century dream that the land (and not the law) would bring him true independence. He once speculated, "If I could make use of the [landed] property I have acquired, as other people would, I should be able to quit the bar after a few years."[46]

Beverley also continued to see the land, and not his profession, as the true source of independence in Virginia. After his marriage to Polly Coalter in 1809, Tucker energetically started to work his 300 acres in Charlotte County. As "the sole and indisputable Lord of the soil," Beverley grandly viewed the farm as the source of his family's every need. He methodically laid out a detailed "agricultural system" through which to prosper: he and Polly rose every day "with the Lark" to begin their labors. After breakfast, while Polly worked around their cabin, Beverley rode to his tobacco and wheat fields to "take a peep at my people," the nine male field hands conveyed to him by his half brother. At the day's end Beverley would return to check upon the slaves' accomplishments. After practicing this "system" for several years, Beverley chortled that the land had indeed granted him his independence. In addition to growing tobacco for the market, "we make almost every thing within ourselves. My orchard supplies my little stock of liquor, my own clothes and those of negroes come from our cotton field and our Sheep, my fields and my stock supply every coarser article of food, insomuch that I have never bought a barrel of Corn and but a single Beef." Even though Beverley's 300 acres and handful of slaves were a far cry from the grand estates of the past, he confessed to John Coalter, "I hope my heart will not repine that the luxuries of life are not added to [my] other blessings."[47] Still, he anticipated greater things in the future.

Members of the Tucker family also collectively decided to maintain slavery both in their households and throughout the state. Years before, St. George Tucker had called upon fellow Virginians to live up to the ideals of the Revolution and to embrace emancipation. Yet his own concurrent dealings with slave traders reveal that the judge would not sacrifice his family's interests when they conflicted with his beliefs. In subsequent years the Tucker family (like most white citizens of the Old Dominion) retreated from even discussing freedom for blacks and gradually drifted toward proslavery ideas.

The Tuckers' journey away from emancipation has many sources, all rooted in their growing reaction against change and their nostalgia for the past. One development that particularly disturbed the family concerned demographic changes within the state's slave quarters. From the Revolution's conclusion to 1810, slave owners saw the number of African Americans throughout the Old Dominion nearly double. Although such growth added to estate valuations, it also fueled fears that one day whites would become a distinct minority in the state, making slave insurrections more likely.[48] Amid this demographic explosion St. George Tucker's own apprehensions mounted. During the Quasi-War of 1798, he had heard rumors that the French had raised "an Army of Negroes, from St. D[omingue]," led by "military Officers of the same Complexion," to be landed along America's southern coast. If such an invasion occurred, he predicted that it would "produce a general Insurrection of Slaves" and result "perhaps in the Subjugation of the Southern part of the Union."[49]

Two years later the Tuckers and other Virginia planters discovered the slave Gabriel's massive conspiracy to overthrow the institution. Although the insurrection was thwarted by a series of summer thunderstorms, the passionate expressions of slaves captured and heading for the gibbet revealed with exceptional force that African Americans had imbibed the Revolution's ideological thrust and were keenly aware of the injustices perpetrated against them. John Randolph attended some of the interrogations and was aghast. The slaves "exhibited a spirit, which, if it becomes general, must deluge the Southern country in blood. . . . They manifested a sense of their rights, and contempt of danger, a thirst for revenge which portend the most unhappy consequences."[50] Family members briefly hoped that the conspiracy might spur white Virginians toward tangible action. Shaken by the near uprising, George Tucker drafted a pamphlet entitled *Letter to a Member of the General Assembly of Virginia.* Published in 1801, it restated many of his older cousin's ideas about gradually emancipating slaves and colonizing them in western lands.[51]

Though George Tucker's piece sold well in Richmond, the state legislature took no action. In fact, after the failed rebellion, the forces against freedom grew more powerful. To many observers Virginia's slaves seemed increasingly numerous, ill disciplined, and rebellious. The threat of chaos made many whites conclude that emancipation and even its open discussion would cause only further dissension and danger. The Virginia legislature began tightening controls over slaves and free African Americans. In this setting the Tucker family as a whole made its peace with slavery. Even as members continued to hope vaguely for emancipation, they soon resigned themselves to the institution's permanence. By 1803 St. George looked upon his *Dissertation on Slavery* as a "Utopian idea" and confessed that he was "without any sanguine hope, that it will receive countenance." [52]

Reconciled to slavery's continuation, the Tuckers still had to contend with the institution on a daily basis in both their households and their professional lives. During the first decade of the nineteenth century, their resignation became open complicity. Indeed, with freedom for African Americans increasingly remote and the potential for social chaos apparently growing, the Tuckers retreated on all fronts. St. George Tucker grew increasingly conservative from the bench, issuing decisions that closed off legal avenues of freedom for slaves while strengthening the authority of the planter class. [53]

The judge's children also moved toward proslavery beliefs and practices. Because they all struggled with difficult careers and economic changes, the younger Tuckers could not help but remember how slavery beforehand seemingly had guaranteed the old gentry's traditional way of life and economic hegemony. Owning slaves had been one of the ways the great planters had asserted their power. Thus, the amount of capital the younger Tuckers had invested in such individuals and their growing nostalgia for the past caused them to accept and even embrace the institution.

As they came to understand slavery's permanence, the nature and character of slaveholding within the Tuckers' homes noticeably changed. Before the Revolution slaveholding in general lacked "sentiment [and] sentimentality." Most planters, including the Tuckers, took little pride in and gave meager attention to the living arrangements and physical needs of their bondpeople. [54] In short, slavery was not yet domesticated. Changes spread, however, soon after white Virginians retreated from reform. When the Tuckers started to consider their family's economic position above all else, they had to explain to themselves and to the outside world why natural rights and freedom no longer applied to African Americans. They tried to do it in a way that would also allow them to escape the obvious charge of hypocrisy. In essence, the Tuckers sought new rationalizations to justify chattel slavery. Like many southern planters of the early Republic, they eventually redefined blacks downward on the scale of humanity and portrayed them as individuals inherently unfit for liberty. Above all, they came to consider African Americans as inferior souls who needed white benevolence to survive the harsh cruelties of their age.

Such sentimental attitudes emerged within the Tucker clan soon after the judge's children married and scattered themselves across the state.

Fanny Coalter insisted that some of her slaves be brought into the family circle soon after her arrival at Elm Grove. On her wedding day Fanny had received six slaves from the Williamsburg household as a gift from her father. Thus African Americans she had probably grown up with accompanied her to Augusta County. Away from her parents for the first time and with her husband often from home traveling on his court circuit, Fanny started to mention her slaves affectionately in letters back home, ostensibly so that the bondpeople at the tidewater house would have news of their kin in western Virginia. But Fanny clearly felt an emotional attachment to her African-American slaves, sparked perhaps by their mutual isolation in the Valley. Fanny also requested to be remembered fondly to those slaves she had left in eastern Virginia. In January 1804 she wrote, "Do give my love to all the servants my good Granny particularly—tell Isabel her Child is very well." By the following year news about household slaves took up the better part of some of her letters.[55] At roughly the same time other women within the family began to include in notes and letters similar expressions of affection for their favorite servants.[56]

When Fanny and other women began to draw slaves into the family circle, their men did not protest. Adjusting to the failure of emancipation and increasingly committed to slavery's permanence, the Tucker men embraced the idea that at least some slaves should be regarded as affectionate (yet distinctly inferior) friends. In 1804 St. George Tucker began granting his "Kind Love and Service" to selected African Americans in his letters. Henry eventually referred to his slaves as members of "our family." Beverley also explained that he now tried "to feel and to act toward these poor creatures as to humble and dependent friends."[57]

In addition to sentimentalism before the hearth, the Tuckers increasingly recognized and respected the formation of African-American families in the quarters, as a way both to rationalize slavery's continuation and to induce blacks to accept the permanence of their condition. Before 1800, Virginia planters only granted a "superficial acknowledgment" to slave families.[58] The Tuckers barely acknowledged black kin networks on their plantations. Once the nineteenth century commenced, however, the family started to discuss and monitor their slaves' kin connections closely. In the 1810s John Randolph listed in his commonplace book over one hundred slaves at Roanoke. In his inventory he demonstrated an intimate awareness of the African-American families around him, carefully noting their relationships to one another, their children's names, and ultimate fates. The lists are organized not by sex, occupation, or monetary value but rather by the specific familial ties the slaves had to each other.[59] The Tuckers' correspondence throughout the period also illustrates a growing knowledge of their slaves' connections to one another. At one level the Tuckers respected these bonds, possibly because they concluded that in any well-ordered society all human beings belong inside domesticated family units. But they must also have realized, once they themselves had made peace with slavery, that these accommodations improved their control by making their human chattel fearful that loved ones could be sold away.

As the Tuckers domesticated slavery, they increasingly prided themselves on the role they played as "good" masters. With talk of emancipation fading, family members came to view themselves not so much as masters but as compassionate teachers who nurtured these "dependent friends" toward proper behavior through persuasion and not the whip. Beverley Tucker told his father how he had brought one formerly difficult slave into line: "Jemmy with the help of good example, has proved himself hitherto very expert and industrious, and seems possessed of an ambition to acquit himself with credit in every thing he undertakes. I have set him as a model one of Essex's children, who is a second edition of his father, and you may therefore conceive well calculated to excite emulation without inspiring envy or ill-will." From Louisiana, Lelia Tucker's kinsman Fulwar Skipwith boasted that he motivated his "gang" of twenty slaves using only the gentlest of means. Although his people were initially "stiff laborers" and "awkward pickers," Skipwith explained, "I have succeeded in bringing them to a sense of duty and subordination, surpassed by none, and with less severity, than I have ever witnesed elsewhere." Here were the paternalistic masters of the post-Revolutionary era at work, those who put "an emphasis on education, on affection, on maintaining order through a minimum of punishment and a maximum of persuasion."[60] No wonder St. George Tucker cheered in 1814 that no longer was slavery the "vale of death" it had once been; rather, in his mind "the treatment of Slaves is infinitely more humane than before the revolution."[61]

As their belief in paternalism grew, the Tuckers found it essential to dehumanize those African Americans they now professed to love. With social flux and disorder everywhere, slavery seemed a comforting affirmation of the old social order. In 1804 Henry wrote his father about a young slave named Bob. The year before, Henry had sold Johnny, his house slave in Winchester, because of his lax habits and disrespect toward white authority. St. George Tucker immediately sent ten-year-old Bob as a replacement, separating the boy from his mother, who worked in the Williamsburg mansion. Although Bob labored dutifully for his new master, the separation tortured him and led to repeated nightmares. Henry told his father that at first he had regarded "this child as insensible when compared with those of our complexion," but Bob's pitiful lamentations led him to question his assumption. Nonetheless, after briefly pondering the issue, Henry concluded that he would not and could not recognize this young child as his "fellow man." To do so would force him to admit that he and his family had inflicted gross injustices on African Americans, something none of the Tuckers were now willing to do. He resolved his dilemma with the simple conclusion that inherent differences existed between "the American and African," differences that he likened as being between "the civilized and savage; . . . nay the man and the brute." Because of Bob's inborn inferiority, he would have to cope with the loss of his mother. Henry likely comforted himself that his servant's pain would be fleeting and wear off soon. In a later letter Henry stressed that Bob possessed an inordinate "simplicity of mind" and was generally "very docile." Surely such a being could not feel emotions as deeply and intensely as whites.[62]

Other family members adopted similar views during these years, disclosing not only a growing belief in the innate inferiority of blacks but also a willingness to sacrifice sentiment when it was inconvenient. In 1809 Fanny Coalter urged her husband to part with their slave Sam, whom she labeled "very deficient." Selling him would remove a troublesome laborer from the farm as well as allow John Coalter "to pay some of y[ou]r debts." Although the transaction meant that Sam's wife would lose her mate, "she would," Fanny assumed, "be happier after the first struggle was over." Her stepmother, Lelia, dehumanized the twelve or so African Americans working in her Williamsburg house to the point of referring to them as *living things* that "must eat and must be clad." Her husband's aggressive management of the Corotoman plantation also reflects the way white interests always superseded the family's supposed concern for their slaves. Tucker experienced few pangs of guilt in 1808, and for many years thereafter, when he employed a cruel manager on the Lancaster County estate. Although this brutish man introduced a harsh work regime which once spawned a "Mutiny" in the slave quarters, the judge employed him year after year, pragmatically realizing that in difficult times such heartless men kept tobacco, corn, and wheat flowing to market. Tucker also felt few qualms about separating slave families and selling them.[63]

By the early nineteenth century, the belief in the natural inferiority of African Americans combined with slavery's domestication made emancipation a moot issue. The Tuckers, like other Virginians, believed that blacks obviously lacked the necessary skills to survive in a difficult and competitive world. They could prosper only inside the institution where white masters would provide them with faithful assistance. "True humanity to the slaves," John Randolph now pointed out, "was to make him do a fair day's work. . . . By that means, the master could afford to clothe and feed him well, and take care of him in sickness and old age." The "morbid sentimentalist" who urged freedom for blacks "could not do this."[64]

Even when limited opportunities for manumission became possible, the Tuckers now rejected them. Particularly revealing is the elder Tucker's derailment of an emancipation plan that would have freed a significant number of his wife's slaves. In 1812 Tucker's stepson Charles Carter decided that he wished to free those bondpeople he eventually would inherit from his mother. St. George opposed the scheme, claiming that the slaves were incapable of surviving on their own. Tucker's friend Dr. Philip Barraud promised to set the youth straight, noting that while Carter's sympathies were among "the best feelings of Humanity, . . . I think it may be proved to Him that He can do much more for these people than they can do for themselves." Such conclusions, Barraud stressed, were not based on romantic "Doctrine" but rather were grounded in "Sound Experience."[65]

The following year Carter again proposed to manumit those slaves who one day would come to him. Tucker once more stepped in and pointedly dissuaded his wife from accepting the plan. In an extended "memo" to her, he explained that he was thinking only of the "poor Ignorant Creatures" involved. If they knew that their emancipation depended upon the death of their mistress, they might be led "by the vicious Counsels of others" to poison her. Upon gaining their liberty, moreover, they would be banished from all "friends and Connexions" and possibly subjected to the worst kinds of exploitation. Tucker speculated that once freed they would "encounter every hardship that poverty, ignorance, [and] a want of friends" could inflict. He concluded that emancipation offered blacks nothing but a life a "hundred times harder than that to which they have been . . . accustomed." Their continued enslavement thus was not only realistic but benevolent.[66]

As the Tuckers embraced proslavery beliefs, the nation lurched toward
its second conflict with Great Britain. The empire's continued impressment
of United States sailors and interference with American trade on the high
seas led President Madison to ask Congress for a declaration of war in
June 1812. Some historians have argued that the War of 1812 served as a
unifying event for the United States and especially allowed the rising generation to show its mettle.[67] In actuality, the conflict divided American citizens and engendered within Virginians particularly a nascent sectionalism
based on a vision of a morally superior South struggling to preserve national unity in the face of a grasping and selfish North. For the Tuckers the
military contest proved a crystallizing event. Although the family initially
was divided over the wisdom of fighting, the war caused all of its members
to doubt the virtue of their northern brethren. At the same time the war
engendered within them a growing pride in the South and the noble values they thought the region exemplified.

As diplomatic tensions brewed before 1812, the Tuckers viewed the
crisis from strikingly different perspectives. Members of the younger generation interpreted the international conflict through the prism of domestic politics. Randolph and his half brothers feared the Madison administration was using the dispute to increase its own power. Henry bitterly labeled
the president and his cohorts "federalists in disguise." "Do not suppose my
dear father," he wrote soon after the war's declaration, "that the evils I an-
ticipate are from [Great Britain]. She can inflict but trivial injuries on
us. . . . I am concerned at our danger from within. We are in danger from
ourselves." John Randolph even asked his fellow congressmen how they
could go to war against the old mother country. With social instability
growing at home and his own mind focused on the Old Dominion's glorious past, he reminded House members that the "blood" of England "runs
in our veins" and that "we claim Shakespeare, and Newton, and Chatham
for our countrymen." This sentimental attachment for Britain even led the
younger family members to excuse the Royal Navy's seizure of American
sailors on the high seas. "As to the impressment of our seamen," Beverley
sniffed, "who are they[?] Scotch and Irishmen with American protection."
He concluded that if British officers abducted United States sailors, it was
"because the American character is so prostituted. . . . And here we are to
squabble for a set of foreigners who are Americans in nothing but name."[68]

In stark contrast to his children, the elder Tucker viewed the crisis as
unmistakable evidence of a sinister Great Britain wishing to reconquer its

former colonies. Reflecting an enmity toward the empire that stretched back to his youth, Tucker wrote in 1787, "Britain is the natural enemy of our liberty and independence, she must necessarily be the same to our political advancement in every instance." Over the decades his opinion about the old mother country changed little. He remained quick to blame the government in London for any and all quarrels that arose between the nations.[69]

Frustrated by his children's blindness to such perils, Tucker wrote a short theatrical piece in late 1811 designed to alert his sons (and other young men) about British treachery and to prepare them for the "just war" he saw coming.[70] Entitled *The Times; or The Patriot Rous'd,* the play centered around the experiences of an aging Revolutionary veteran, "Colonel Trueman," who had fought valiantly in the War for Independence and then in later years kept a vigilant eye on the empire, always fearful of recolonization. In the course of the melodrama, Colonel Trueman's son is impressed aboard a British frigate patrolling off the Chesapeake coast. On board, the young American is taunted and abused by the ship's malicious crew. After the youth makes a dramatic escape, the play comes to a rousing conclusion. In the final scene, after his son's return, Trueman dons his old Revolutionary War uniform and ushers onto the stage the "Washington Volunteers," a corps of fellow veterans. At center stage the elderly warriors turn "to the young men of the Village" and sing:

> Be not blind to Freedom's charms!
> Be not deaf to War's Alarms!
> Rouse ye! Quick to Arms!
>   Rouse! and drive your foes away!

The Patriot Rous'd was Judge Tucker's none-too-subtle call to "young men" throughout the country to unite in order to humble America's ancient foe. Although Tucker's attempts to have his play produced on stage were unsuccessful, the drama points to his long-held belief that the British Empire—not Jefferson, Madison, and scheming Republicans—posed the greatest danger to the Republic.[71]

When the war began in mid-1812, these prewar positions quickly faded, and different viewpoints began to emerge. Despite St. George Tucker's confidence that the conflict would unite the nation's political factions, he and others saw divisions only deepened. Not only did the New England states remain uncooperative throughout the conflict, but ill-equipped United States forces performed miserably due largely to budget cuts proposed by Jefferson and Madison and enacted by Congress.[72]

Despite their animus for the administration, both Henry and Beverley served in the ranks of the Virginia militia. In the spring of 1813, Henry raised a company of cavalry composed of Frederick County's "most respectable" young men. Almost immediately, Governor James Barbour dispatched the unit to the state's Northern Neck near Fredericksburg to help repel British raiders advancing up the Chesapeake Bay. Although the expedition ended "without an Event of any importance," Tucker's men again took to the field the following summer when another invasion fleet appeared. Joining General William Winder's army near Baltimore two weeks after Washington's burning, the cavalrymen shadowed British forces as they left the region. Once more, however, the Frederick County unit saw no major action.[73]

Beverley Tucker also served throughout the war. In early 1813 he enlisted in the Charlotte County militia as an infantry lieutenant and soon marched off to Norfolk to defend the town against a possible assault.[74] Although Tucker's encampment was sickly and the British fleet soon disappeared, Beverley thoroughly enjoyed military life. Unlike civilian society, the army recognized and respected everyone's rank within a precise and orderly hierarchy. With no invaders to repulse, however, military planners sent the Charlotte militia home in January 1814. Although briefly recalled following Washington's capture, Beverley watched the war end from the sidelines. Preferring the military to the law, he had briefly hoped for a permanent position within the army. But when hostilities ended, officer commissions evaporated. Thus the war left the thirty-year-old lawyer further disappointed and disillusioned. As in his legal career, his talents and breeding went unrecognized.[75]

For St. George Tucker as well, the war years proved discouraging. Not only did he fear for his sons' safety, but the elder Tucker also encountered problems of his own. British ships operating in the Chesapeake raided the Corotoman plantation. Although damage to the main house and outbuildings appeared minimal, the enemy carried off over forty slaves.[76] When the British invaded the tidewater again in 1814, Tucker and his wife had to flee Williamsburg westward to the Blue Ridge foothills. John Coalter meanwhile arranged for the Tuckers' furniture to be moved to safer grounds.[77]

Washington's capture represented the war's nadir for family members. St. George's brother Thomas, then the treasurer of the United States, re-

Henry St. George Tucker shortly after the War of 1812, painted by Charles Bird King. (Collection of the Museum of Early Southern Decorative Arts, Winston-Salem, N.C.)

mained inside the city until the British were nearly upon him. On 24 August, the day the Capitol fell, Thomas wrote that he saw "confusion and distress" everywhere and concluded, "Whatever be our fate in this world, it is a comfort that we have a better to retreat to." Thomas then disappeared amid the chaos with no word heard from him for several weeks. Finally, a letter dated 9 September arrived in Williamsburg. Writing near the shat-

Thomas Tudor Tucker, treasurer of the United States, c. 1807, engraving by Charles B. J. F. de Saint-Mémin. (Courtesy of the Tucker-Coleman Papers, Swem Library, College of William and Mary)

tered Capitol, a dismal Thomas explained that he had become "a wanderer without a casting place" soon after the British had seized the city. He eventually returned but upon seeing the destruction felt "humbled and degraded." "I have no longer a country or a Government," he lamented, "that I can speak of with pride." [78]

Washington's fall not only proved personally traumatic for the Tuckers but served as a harbinger of America's future sectionalism. From the war's start bitter regional divisions unseen in earlier years had begun to emerge. Before the conflict Virginians (and southerners in general) had viewed northern members of the Federalist Party as political opponents, politicians who wished to create an overweening, overpowerful central government. During the war perceptions subtly but significantly changed. By the conflict's end northern politicians were seen as belonging to a society which had collectively abandoned traditional republican virtues in favor of greed, avarice, and selfishness. The fall of Washington took place, the Tuckers and other Virginians believed, only because of inadequate support from the North's population. Five months later the Hartford Convention with its "mad" and "frantic idea of dissolution" not only infuriated the Tuckers but affirmed their belief that New Englanders always put profits ahead of the nation's interests. Tucker immediately wrote a pamphlet to express his disgust about the events in Hartford, but William Wirt dissuaded him from publishing it, and the work has not survived.[79]

A coherent southern identity also emerged at the same time, with Virginians and other southerners seeing themselves as the true defenders of republicanism and Revolutionary principles. Andrew Jackson's victory at New Orleans, following on the heels of the Hartford meeting, particularly was interpreted through this prism of burgeoning sectionalism. When news of the battle arrived, Virginians immediately cheered the event as a triumph of southern honor. Dr. Barraud wrote from Norfolk to toast the victory. He claimed it proved without a doubt the superiority of "the Southern portion of this Empire." "The people of the East," on the other hand, were "a sett of vulgar and upstart Northern Mushrooms," whom Barraud hoped would "no longer dare to charge . . . the [southern] states [with] the foul Calumny of seeking Wars without the speech to maintain them with valor, or with their Blood." "None" but southerners, he continued, "have ever exhibited a deeper Love to the Blessings of the Republic. None have ever shewn the true Marks and characteristic of their Revolutionary Fathers." The battle of New Orleans's "Relation to the Southern States . . . seems Gigantic," he concluded. "It fixes the[ir] power and ability to protect the Firesides and to punish their Enemies without Yankee aid."[80] The War of 1812's conclusion had unmasked the American people's divided nature. While northerners had drifted astray toward greed, corruption, and disloyalty, southerners held true to the virtues of 1776.

St. George Tucker himself embraced such views. By the war's end his long-standing animosity for Great Britain had been replaced by bitter doubts about the fidelity and morality of the North. In the spring of 1815, as news of peace spread throughout the country, Tucker wrote another play, entitling this one *The Patriot Cool'd*. A companion piece to *The Patriot*

Rous'd, it celebrated the War of 1812's triumphant conclusion. Instead of aiming scorn at the British, Tucker lambasted treasonous northerners who had undermined the war effort merely to protect their economic interests. The drama opened in a small cabin west of the Blue Ridge Mountains, where "Colonel Trueman," his daughter, and a fellow Revolutionary War veteran named "Major Friendly" had taken refuge because of the British depredations across the tidewater. Beside himself with anger at American misfortunes, Trueman blamed northern treachery for the disasters. "Are not the Yankees quietly looking on," he raged, "whilst our Invaders have possessed themselves of a large portion of their Country?" How different from the last time America found itself confronting British arms. "Was it thus, when Gage took possession of Boston?" he asked. A downcast Major Friendly confessed that the American people were no longer "united in our hearts." Rather "we are now a divided people."[81]

A northern peddler soon afterwards stumbles upon the cabin and requests a night's lodging. The conversations between the characters are filled with cultural meaning and ominous for the Republic's future. Not only did the peddler's profession—viewed by many Virginians as mean, grasping, acquisitive—set him off from these virtuous gentlemen of the Old Dominion, but early nineteenth-century southerners in general believed that Yankee peddlers encouraged slaves to resist white authority. Thus they were greatly despised and mistrusted.[82] Even the terms of traditional hospitality had become a source of sectional conflict. In the course of the evening, the peddler brought news about a recent string of American defeats, causing Trueman to lose his temper and to order the northerner out of his sight. Quickly composing himself, Trueman apologizes: "Stay Friend. I was wrong to impute to *you,* the misconduct of your Countrymen. Stay and take up your Quarters here to night." "Well, so I will," the peddler responds, "but you must let me pay you for my Entertainment." Furious at what he saw as an insult to his liberality, Trueman angrily orders the peddler, "Begone!" The uncomprehending and money-obsessed Yankee replies: "I vow you're a strange Man, you will neither let me go, or stay. Though I offer'd to pay for my Entertainment, I did'nt tell you in what sort of Currency I meant to do it." Like the proverbial man unable to see beyond his nose, a nineteenth-century Yankee could not see beyond money.

The play concludes when news arrives of the victory at New Orleans and the signing of the Treaty of Ghent. Moments later, Trueman's two sons return from the war. Having nobly fought for their country rather than pursuing filthy lucre, they tell their father that both of them have been promoted to captain for gallantry in the field. Beside himself with joy, Trueman cries: "Now my Boys, my Cup of Happiness is full. It can hold no more—come to your Fathers Arms!" As the young heroes rush to the old man's embrace, the peddler observes to the audience: "I guess I may make a dozen trips to Castine before I see such another sight. I vow now, we Yankees don't seem to know what sort of people these Buck'ins are. I begin to wish we were better acquainted."[83]

Tucker's *The Patriot Cool'd* and Philip Barraud's letter reveal that the end of the War of 1812 brought no period of national unity and no "era of good feelings." Rather they demonstrate that the conflict caused regional attitudes and perceptions to shift. The Tuckers and their circle now transferred deeply held doubts about the nation's republican experiment to the North. After the war the younger generation no longer complained about the corruptions of the Madison administration. St. George Tucker no longer expressed fears of Great Britain as a vice-ridden land bent on America's recolonization. Rather the family redirected its misgivings about republicanism's ultimate success to their northern countrymen who had selfishly protected their own commerce and threatened the United States with disunion at its darkest hour. By contrast, southern planters and farmers had successfully defended the nation by adhering to the traditional republican virtues of honor, patriotism, and self-sacrifice. A worldview had emerged of a land divided not just by geography but also by morality, honesty, and character.

This bifurcated picture of a virtuous South adhering to traditional principles in the face of a corrupt North grew only stronger in the years following the Treaty of Ghent. After 1815 John Randolph reemerged as a significant political figure almost solely because of his increasingly intense attacks upon the North. Randolph had spent the war largely alone at Roanoke. Because of his vehement opposition to the conflict, he had lost his congressional seat in the spring of 1813. His time in the political wilderness, however, was short. The sack of Washington led him to tender his services to the governor, scout along the shores of the Middle Peninsula for another invasion force, and warn publicly that Mount Vernon and the first president's body needed protection.[84] He stood for election several months after the war ended and won an overwhelming victory. Once back in Congress, Randolph launched into fresh attacks against President Madison. This time he denounced the president's postwar legislative measures such as the establishment of a Second Bank of the United States and new federal tariffs designed to encourage domestic manufacturing. Such proposals, he spewed, would only help Yankee manufacturers while burdening the "poor men, and . . . slaveholders" within the South. Randolph concurrently waxed nostalgic about the great Virginia planters of old whose principles, character, and wealth were largely responsible for the Old Dominion's onetime power and greatness. Attacks upon Yankees and nostalgia for the past won Randolph wide support throughout the state. In the postwar climate he found his fame and popularity growing for the first time in over a decade. In 1817 a friend wrote him, "*You* were actually toasted lately at a public meeting in Prince George where there were some men present who, but a few short years before, would probably have seen you *roasted* almost as soon as drink [to] your health." [85] After the War of 1812, Virginians saw both northerners and themselves in a new light, one in which northern values were condemned while southern virtues of honor, loyalty, and self-sacrifice were celebrated.

By the conclusion of the War of 1812, the Tuckers without realizing it had rejected the values and beliefs of the Revolutionary era. Deeply pessimistic about the present and future, they no longer believed in universal freedom, popular sovereignty, and the capacity of many of their fellow Virginians to participate in public affairs. Moreover, the Union that had been so heroically stitched together during the Revolution seemed imperiled. In the North a society had emerged which cherished money, commerce, and little else. With Virginia under assault from both within and beyond, the Tuckers reacted strongly, moving in a profoundly conservative direction. The Old Dominion's colonial past became the measure of all things, and the family's energies concentrated on preventing any further alterations. Despite their conviction that they were the stalwart practitioners of past values, however, the Tuckers' family life, social customs, and gender practices illustrate that private life and relationships changed just as significantly as public life. Indeed, during the last years of his own life, St. George Tucker confronted a private world that had become inward-looking, sentimental, and narrowly focused.

Six

Twilight

In the summer of 1813, Fanny Coalter lay near death, her body racked by tuberculosis. Her husband took her to the Warm Springs spa in the Allegheny Mountains hoping that its waters would work some miracle and restore her health. Within days of arriving, however, John Coalter saw his wife's condition worsen, and he realized that she would soon die. With somber resignation he wrote to her father and stepmother to inform them. Although heartbreaking, Fanny's demise came as no shock, for her health had been deteriorating for years. Of slight build like her mother, she had lost a significant amount of weight after the birth of her second daughter in 1805. She developed a persistent and painful cough four years later, indicating to everyone that she had consumption. Her physical condition continued to deteriorate. The pressures of managing Elm Grove and her "continual" illnesses left her "in all respects weak," as she herself once admitted.[1]

St. George and Lelia Tucker immediately wrote back to Warm Springs, desperately hoping that their letters would bring some final comfort to their dying daughter. St. George assured his child that their separation would be only temporary and that he would soon join her in the afterlife. Lelia promised Fanny that she was about to enter "those Mansions where pain and sickness and sorrow will never find entrance." Tucker's wife stated that she even envied her stepdaughter's fate, confessing, "My Soul [has] longed to flee away and be at rest—to throw off a covering of flesh."[2]

Fanny died at the spa on 12 September 1813. In the following weeks family members cheered themselves by admiring the pious way in which she left earthly existence and telling themselves that in heaven her soul had reached a level of perfection unattainable on earth. Moreover, Fanny most assuredly had been reunited with her mother and other deceased relatives. "I . . . see her waking in Heaven," St. George wrote, "surrounded by her dear Mother, and other beloved friends, who have gone before her." The family concluded that to wish Fanny to remain trapped in an earthly sphere of pain and anguish was wrong. "Can I be so selfish, so cruel," Lelia cried to Coalter, "as even to wish a continuance of suffering Life." Instead, Fanny had been "taken to the Bliss of Heaven" to find eternal health, love, and happiness. Solace and sympathy should be reserved for the living and not the dead.[3]

The events surrounding Fanny Coalter's death reveal the transformations that swept elite family life in the early nineteenth century. Members of the Virginia gentry increasingly saw a world they believed had turned against them. Although the great planter class had embraced the Revolution, believing it would establish a republic of liberty and reason, neither success nor happiness had materialized for them. In the decades following 1776, the living standards and estate values of the tidewater planters declined, while democratic challenges from below grew only more intense. In an atmosphere of economic decay and social upheaval, death itself seemed a liberating escape. Death too had become a means through which to be reunited with departed loved ones and to recapture the glorious and happier times of the past.

As Virginians grew increasingly pessimistic, they turned away from public life and retreated inward to domestic affairs. Only inside the home, surrounded by affectionate spouses and children, could they find safety and comfort. Yet the process of withdrawal fundamentally changed the patterns and customs of gentry family life. Women took more control of the household on the eve of the antebellum era, even as they withdrew from life beyond its boundaries. Recognized as more emotional, loving, and caring than their menfolk, they grew determined to set the home's moral tone as well as guide its daily activities. Elite women were also the first to embrace sentimental religion, an uncomplicated Christian dogma that emphasized the Lord's love and a heavenly afterlife with family and friends.

Yet the narrowed focus on the hearth alone and the nuclear kin within the home also points to the breakdown of the Revolutionary age's great extended clans. Family unity and loyalty steadily eroded during the early nineteenth century amid economic change, expansion to the West, and decline in eastern Virginia. Within the Tucker family these transformations led to significant shifts in how members interacted with and related to one another. Throughout these years the Tuckers bitterly quarreled among themselves, some moved far away, and many steadily lost touch with others. As its aging patriarch, St. George Tucker attempted to hold the extended clan together. But his own dwindling resources, changed circumstances, and the growing maturity of the rising generation undermined his efforts. Younger family members saw little practical use in their extended kin ties. Promising few tangible rewards and time-consuming in terms of maintenance, they had become a burden. In the early Republic's hurly-burly, it seemed best to concentrate on loved ones immediately before the hearth and to let all other bonds fade away.

In the winter of 1808, St. George Tucker sat in his Williamsburg study and lamented to his daughter, "I wish there was any such thing as stability in this Country: but it appears vain to hope for it."[4] After nearly four decades in Virginia, Tucker had seen a great deal—political and social revolution, rapid commercial development, and the steep decline of the great planter class—developments that swept away the old world he had found when he arrived in the colony in 1771. As a result, Tucker over time had completely altered his outlook on life. Individuals, he now realized, could no longer depend upon a broadly defined, interdependent family network to achieve success. Rather, men had to enter the public arena alone, dependent solely on their talents, energy, and determination to survive.

As Tucker bemoaned such changes to Fanny, he likely recalled the friends and family of his youth, who like him had embraced the Revolution with great alacrity only to find themselves badly bruised in its wake. His deceased brothers-in-law John Banister and Theodorick Bland Jr. had watched helplessly after the war as extensive debts and structural market changes forced them into poverty. By the eighteenth century's end, the once-powerful Nelson clan was a shadow of its former self. When the struggling family lost most of its extensive properties because of vast liabilities, Tucker loaned them money in the 1790s and provided additional cash to Judith Nelson for her proposed boardinghouse in 1808. The same year John Page died at the now-dilapidated Rosewell.

Economic decline affected other loved ones as well. At Bizarre, Tucker's stepdaughter-in-law Judith Randolph felt the outside world collapsing in on her. The extensive debts Richard had left in 1796 prevented her from carrying out his will's instructions to emancipate their slaves. The slaves, knowing that they should have been freed, grew increasingly angry, surly, and unwilling to work as their emancipation was delayed for twelve long years. Judith had to cut back on her slaves' clothing; she rarely left Bizarre and almost never had company visit the plantation. Her days, she complained, were filled only with caring for her two sons and performing daily chores inside the house. "I . . . spin and weave and spend nothing in order to keep out of debt," she once explained.[5]

As economic woes mounted and as difficult-to-comprehend social changes transformed life, the Tuckers came to view the exterior portion of their existence as unbearable. St. George once told family members that he considered "the Courts, and the bustle of the World" like a "Desert" and that "no man in public Life can promise himself any portion of *real* happiness."[6] Thus in the early nineteenth century, he and others turned inward. Only the home, loving spouses, and innocent children guaranteed happiness in their unstable world. Tucker even came to look upon the household as "my Paradise," a harmonious refuge from the dismal "Events of the World" beyond.[7]

The judge's turn toward the private hearth was replicated throughout the Old Dominion, especially among those who beforehand had held power and authority. Before his death John Page and his second wife, Margaret, exchanged numerous poems with Tucker celebrating not the Revolution but home, marriage, and children.[8] William Nelson Jr., an old college chum of St. George, also viewed the private realm as life's true source of joy. Nelson and Tucker had worked alongside one another first as lawyers and then as General Court judges. Throughout the years, however, Nelson always saw his professional life as secondary to his family. When raised to the bench in 1791, he rejoiced to acquaintances that the post would leave him "more time" than his work at the bar "to read, & enjoy domestick tranquillity." Although some observers thought Nelson without ambition, his aspirations simply differed from earlier times. Satisfaction and contentment, he concluded, no longer came from public work and achievements. He instead found "perfect happiness" with his first wife, Polly Taliaferro Nelson, and after her death in childbirth, with his second spouse, Abigail Byrd Nelson. When not on his court circuit, Nelson lived with Abby and her mother in the Byrd mansion of Westover. Although financially unable to maintain the great house in its eighteenth-century splendor, the judge delighted in the family members it sheltered, especially his five daughters, whom he watched grow into "a group of sweet interesting girls."[9]

As the Tuckers and other clans focused their energies inward, the nature of domestic life fundamentally changed. The market revolution and the professionalization of the law separated the home and the workplace in many areas of Virginia as well as in the industrializing North. As such changes unfolded, definitions of work and where it took place shifted. Many men of the North and South increasingly saw "their own income-producing work as paramount" and viewed their wives' labor in the home as less essential to the family.[10] With the household losing its economic position, the division between public and private life grew significantly more pronounced.

This process, though, allowed women to gain control and autonomy over domestic affairs. Away from home much of the time on court business, St. George ceded authority over the internal workings of his Williamsburg house to Lelia Skipwith Tucker. Lelia ruled over their mansion in a number of ways, arranging dinners, teas, and other entertainments. During the 1770s and 1780s, on the other hand, St. George had managed a very different dwelling. He had participated in planning and organizing social events at Matoax, helping Frances to arrange meals and other types of get-togethers for nearby members of the gentry. Such activities had filled a quasi-public function in demonstrating the hosts' gentility, status, and wealth. A generation later, however, as the great families grew more private, women such as Lelia Tucker gained more responsibility over the hearth. One afternoon in 1804 St. George noted that his wife had spent the "whole morning as busy as twenty bees . . . for we are to have the Amblers, the Madisons, and the Skipwiths to dine with us to day." Another time when the house was "full of company," Tucker explained to his daughter that although he could sit down and compose a letter, "Your Mama of *course* can not find time to write."[11]

Lelia directed other aspects of the household. She orchestrated vacations away from Williamsburg and oversaw the couple's packing and other preparations. One year St. George wrote Fanny that the pair had not yet departed on their annual summer retreat to western Virginia because of his wife's plodding deliberations. Obviously wishing to be off, Tucker

Lelia Skipwith Tucker, likely painted
in the 1810s or 1820s, artist unknown. (Courtesy of the
University Museums, University of Mississippi
Cultural Center)

helplessly wrote: "When we are set off, or whether we are to set out at all, are questions beyond my capacity to answer. Your Mama is as absolute as ever Catherine of Russia was, in these matters."[12]

Lelia thrived on her household responsibilities. Unlike Frances Bland Tucker, who rarely discussed ordinary tasks within the home in her letters, Lelia constantly and happily wrote about such work. She once described the joys of making butter. A sizable plate of it "comes on the Table" every day, she declared, largely because of "the pains" she herself took to care for two milk cows in the backyard. "It is impossible to say how much pleasure I feel every morning when the making of the day before" is placed in front of the family. Lelia also managed the mansion's garden, a task that brought her additional pleasure. One March afternoon she explained to her stepdaughter that she had to "tear myself from the Garden, this first real Spring day that I may not disappoint you." Indeed, she sighed, "I live in the Garden when the weather is mild." Several weeks earlier William Nelson Jr. told an absent St. George, "The earth is too wet for Mrs. T[ucker] to go into the garden, but she is delighted with observing from the door how beautifully her favorite shrubs are budding." Lelia's authority over the household's garden stands in direct contrast to the previous century. At the time of the Revolution, members of the gentry saw the garden as an extension of the mansion's parlor where much public entertainment took place. Because gardens reflected an owner's gentility and refinement, eighteenth-century gentlemen often designed and worked within them. St. George's father even purchased a male slave solely to assist him with the garden at The Grove. During the early nineteenth century, however, gardens increasingly became private retreats. Like households in general, they functioned as protected spaces where husbands, wives, and children could find happiness in each other's presence away from a harsh world.[13]

In addition to home maintenance, Lelia and other women built strong networks of female friends throughout Virginia. Historians have long recognized that a new semiautonomous female sphere emerged during the early Republic.[14] With husbands absent much of the time, elite women drew together amid the changes they witnessed and looked to one another for support and comfort. Judith Randolph and Fanny Coalter became very close friends after the latter's marriage in 1802. Although they rarely saw one another because of distance and work, both women recognized that they confronted similar challenges in their everyday lives: they each managed farms without a constant male presence, dealt with unhappy slaves, and raised children who were frequently unwell. In one letter Judith complained that she recently had had to care for thirty sick slaves at Bizarre while she herself fought off "a bilious fever." As unperformed tasks on the plantation mounted, she unburdened herself to Fanny that "my life has been one uninterrupted series of suffering." Four months later, after receiving no letters from Elm Grove—an unusually long silence—Judith pined to her friend, "I begin to fear you do not care a button for me." [15]

Unlike her stepdaughters, Lelia Tucker focused great amounts of energy on constructing face-to-face bonds with women in her neighborhood surrounding Williamsburg. In the early nineteenth century, she built a strong network of female friends whom she regularly entertained and visited. Maintaining these ties became an important part of her daily routine. She once told Fanny, "Visiting, house-keeping and writing to him [St. George] and you take up the whole of my time." Calling upon and conversing specifically with women also became a significant emotional outlet. During one particular week Lelia explained: "We have been dining and drinking tea abroad since our female company left us. Yesterday we had a party at Mr. Prentis's, exactly to my tastes. About fifteen Ladies of my particular acquaintance, and not a gentleman, except a few little boys. You know I like now and then an assembly of petticoats, all quite at their ease." [16]

Although Lelia enjoyed her life and responsibilities within the household, she wanted nothing to do with affairs beyond it. She particularly shied away from financial matters and management tasks associated with the land. Once again in contrast to Frances Bland Tucker, Lelia pointedly refused to help oversee her children's plantation. After her marriage to Tucker, she immediately handed complete control of Corotoman to her new husband. In surviving letters, moreover, the couple never discussed this 5,000-acre estate with one another. Either Lelia lacked interest in such matters, or the tidewater's economic malaise convinced her that only hardship came with managing a plantation. The difficulties her stepdaughter experienced at Elm Grove and Judith Randolph's woes at Bizarre likely provided her with additional proof that work beyond the home brought women not pride and self-worth but only self-doubt and depression.

With the emergence of gender-segregated spheres by the early nineteenth century, perceptions about women and their character changed. They viewed themselves and were increasingly judged by their menfolk as unable to cope with difficult circumstances beyond the household. [17] At the same time, though, females began to see themselves as inherently superior to men in morals and virtue. The transformation occurred because of the complex array of changes that swept the early Republic. Not only did Virginians and other Americans lose faith in the rationalism that had guided the Revolution, but many concurrently gravitated toward religious evangelicalism. At the time of the war with Great Britain, several radical sects—the Baptists, Methodists, and Presbyterians—had had great success with yeomen farmers in the Virginia backcountry. Although the gentry initially had feared these religious groups, all three sects eventually accepted the planter class's fundamental beliefs regarding rank, gender, and race. As this shift occurred, the pious emotionalism behind evangelicalism grew more acceptable and entered into the gentry's spiritual lives. Elite women particularly embraced these religious trends and exerted growing influence within the Old Dominion's congregations. Finding the evangelical message of spiritual rebirth comforting at a time of general decline, females enthusiastically supported itinerant preachers and found great merit in their call upon the faithful to focus on the kingdom to come.[18]

Amid these changes, attitudes about women evolved accordingly. Ideal females came to be regarded not so much as full-blooded human beings but as delicate and angelic creatures whose pious virtue now made them almost too pure for a sullied and difficult world. In 1805 Henry Tucker criticized Elizabeth Merry, the wife of the British minister to the United States, for being "free, unreserved, and what is commonly called *plain-spoken*" in public. Three years later John Randolph told a recently married friend, "To attempt to descant on [the bride's] value is to expatiate on the whiteness of snow." Dr. Philip Barraud repeatedly wrote about the celestial qualities of his daughter, Nancy, declaring, "In my Life I have never seen such an angel in Spirit and appearance." Her piety and innocence "'fore God" convinced Barraud that "she has not enough of the Devil in her to fit her for our World."[19]

Yet these devout women were increasingly important as the moral arbiters and spiritual guides for families. Eighteenth-century notions that religious values should be orderly and moderately expressed disappeared from the Old Dominion. Instead, nineteenth-century women (and some men) emotionally prayed for reassurances that a universe of eternal bliss existed beyond "this transitory World."[20] When Fanny Coalter died in 1813, the family members' greatest consolation lay in the conviction that their separation would only be temporary. They repeatedly predicted to one another that after human existence they would all gather in heaven to enjoy each other's love and companionship forever.

In addition to finding solace in religion, elite Virginians of both sexes looked to their children for comfort. Eighteenth-century parents certainly delighted in their offspring. Yet perceptions about and the treatment of young children did change over the years, particularly as families turned inward. At the time of the Revolution, adolescent children usually were brought into the family circle, but largely to contribute to the household's sociability and conviviality. At their parent's feet youngsters learned the merits and techniques of polite conversation, wit, and manners. But parents of the Revolutionary age placed their infants in a different category, purposefully keeping them emotionally at arm's length. During the 1770s and 1780s, the Tuckers and others in their circle took only slight notice of their babies, likely because of high mortality rates for children under five. When young ones might be swept away at any moment, why invest love and affection in them? Short and cursory letters usually heralded the arrival of eighteenth-century infants, with the health of the mother almost always the epistle's main focus.[21] In subsequent letters newborns remained background figures, never discussed as individuals and always viewed with detachment. This tendency to look at infants in an aloof manner was especially apparent when young babies died or were born dead. Sir Peyton Skipwith stiffly refused to allow such a tragedy to unbalance him. At the end of one letter to St. George, he scribbled, "P.S. . . . My dearest Wife was delivered last night of a dead Child; she desires to be particularly remembered to yourself and family."[22]

By the early nineteenth century, however, as the world around them changed, so too did perceptions about children and especially infants. No longer ignored or treated with indifference, the arrival of newborns instead became cause for celebration. Between 1803 and 1809, when Fanny Coalter gave birth to two daughters and a son, she and John barely contained their joy. After the arrival of their second daughter in 1805, John wrote his father-in-law: "Be it known that on Tuesday morning last Miss Elizth. Tucker Coalter made her appearance in this world. . . . She is a charming accomplished Girl . . . of a most amiable temper and enjoying manners." Several years later, Henry Tucker sent a happy letter to Williamsburg, announcing, "Evelina . . . present[ed] me with a fine son; the stoutest mountaineer that has ever made his appearance." So great had sentimental pride in infants become that when Beverley's first son arrived stillborn, he could not resist admiring (and even measuring) the dead boy's features. "A finer child was never born," he wrote. Noting that the infant was twenty-two inches in length, he concluded, "How natural is the pride of a father's heart!" Several years later Polly gave birth to a son whom the couple named John. Then in 1812 a daughter arrived who was named Frances. Beverley and Polly prized and adored both children.[23]

The willingness among the rising generation to bestow such emotions upon newborn infants extended beyond the Tucker family. Fanny saw how a new baby's arrival had transformed a neighbor's household. "The Johnsons are happy beyond measure . . . [with] the arrival of a daughter," she reported. "I rode up yesterday to see Mary and the child. . . . her husband is so happy and thinks her so well, that he cannot compose himself." As their newborns grew, parents viewed them as sweet innocents as yet unsullied by the larger world. Being separated from such unblemished creatures now seemed heartbreaking. John Coalter, who labeled his first daughter "the finest child in the world," once asked St. George, "How can you have pleasure and not be where Frances Lelia is?" Several years later Fanny judged her second daughter, Elizabeth, "the most grateful and perfectly good tempered being I ever knew."[24]

As the Tucker family members wrote these words, they fully realized that their sentiments had dramatically changed. St. George's older sister, Frances, seems to have first noticed it. Raised at The Grove upon eighteenth-century principles of balance and moderation, she understood that parents should ideally "resign [their children's fate] to that wise disposer of all things." But by the early 1800s she scoffed at the notion, asking "who can bring themselves to that state of mind." She concluded, "I often think . . . that our griefs, fears[,] anxieties about our Children destroy every comfort that we may derive from them."[25] A parent's love for his or her offspring now ruined that restraint and self-control which the Revolutionary gentry had once thought so vital to happiness.

Members of the rising generation found themselves even more beleaguered when they tried to raise their children according to past standards. At Elm Grove, Fanny initially attempted to moderate her emotions toward her children in concurrence with the norms she had learned while growing up. Yet she soon found herself overwhelmed by the effort. She explained to her father that she did try "not to love [Frances Lelia] too much," but she admitted the attempt was "a very feeble one." When Fanny contemplated her hopes and fears for the child, she confessed, "My heart feels ready to burst." Judith Randolph concluded that the heart had simply triumphed over the head in this new age. When parents now contemplated their children, she asserted, "the feelings of nature cannot be silenced," and "the arguments of reason and propriety are heard in vain."[26]

As the Tuckers contemplated these increasingly powerful "feelings of nature," they realized that their sentiments were somehow linked to the changed public sphere, where hard work, talent, and family connections promised neither success nor happiness. A year after the birth of his first son, Henry wrote his father a long letter in which he tried to understand the overpowering, almost baffling, love he felt for his child. Like his sister, Henry realized from his upbringing that he should be moderate in his sentiments. But this no longer seemed possible, especially given the frustrations he repeatedly met in his legal and political career. "What can be the prospects of a man," he asked, "who after having reached that point of fortune and success beyond which he cannot expect to go, . . . if he has no children?" When a man's professional life had crested and begun to recede, children and the joy they brought must fill the resulting void. At the end of his epistle, Henry remembered "a good song" which expressed what he had been "hammering" to say:

> The days spring of life yet unclouded by sorrow,
> Alone on itself for enjoyment depends,
> But dear is the twilight of age if it borrow,
> No warmth from the smiles of *Wife, Children and friends.*[27]

In the nation's more individualized market and political economies, Henry looked to the nuclear family, filled with affectionate children and a loving spouse, to restore the happiness that the outside world had drained away.

Like many Virginians, Henry also drew stark and protective boundaries around his household designed to keep the harsh public world at bay. Many contemporary observers noticed the change. The "open homes" of the Revolutionary era did not survive into the nineteenth century, as elite Virginians no longer welcomed passing gentlemen, ladies, and other visitors into their mansions with food, drink, and entertainment. Respectable passersby still received polite treatment if they insisted, but they essentially had become intruders into a more secluded private sphere.[28] The number of balls in the Old Dominion significantly dropped during the early Republic because of strained finances and the general desire for more solitude. An old

Chesterfield County neighbor who had regularly visited Matoax throughout the 1770s and 1780s wrote Tucker about these changes: "I suppose you
were all very merry at Christmas [in Williamsburg]. Petersburg was extremely dull, indeed, no dinners, no hops, no balls. every person staid at
home, and ate his own meat." [29]

Tucker himself was of two minds about sociability's decline. He often
waxed nostalgic about the conviviality he had enjoyed as a youth and frequently would "extoll" to his children the "old Virginia spirit of hospitality." Yet by the early nineteenth century, he scrupulously avoided contact
with those outside an increasingly small circle of family and friends. Socializing with acquaintances, professional colleagues, and strangers might
lead to conversations on politics, eastern Virginia's economic decline, and
other painful topics. Best to avoid them altogether. "I hate formal invitations to dinner," he told Fanny in 1808, and "I receive no other except from
our friend[s] the Amblers." Lelia Tucker also avoided socializing with those
outside the couple's modest network of friends. She told one granddaughter that in such times one ought to consider "Solitude . . . a blessing" and
not a "hardship." Toward this end, the couple constructed a private summer cottage in 1820 in Warminster, adjacent to the Nelson County plantation house of their children Joseph and Polly Carter Cabell. Not coinci-
dentally, St. George began a series of essays in the early nineteenth century
entitled "Nuga: The Hermit of the Mountain." [30]

As the Tuckers reconstructed their households along these more secluded lines, even their ties to one another started to fray. During the eighteenth century necessity demanded close cooperative bonds between members of the great families, but the realities of the nineteenth century worked
against these connections. Amid the era's market and legal changes, these
ties were no longer of much use. As these transformations unfolded, most
broad familial associations tapered off. With the Old Dominion's economy
increasingly strained, some bonds shattered altogether.

For the Tuckers, the breakdown of their extended family began during
the War of 1812. The catalyst was Fanny Coalter's long-expected death.
Throughout her latter years St. George's daughter had worked to keep her
siblings on good terms with each other. The farm at Elm Grove periodically hosted family reunions where members gathered to enjoy meals and
conversation and to share their memories of earlier times. Fanny also kept
up a regular correspondence with both her brothers and their Randolph
kin. She wrote inquiring letters to her half brother, asking him about his

health and public activities. She drafted regular missives to Judith Randolph as well, providing words of comfort for all of her woes.[31] Family members lost a linchpin when Fanny died in September 1813. The whole familial structure did not hold together for very long afterwards.

The first relationship to disintegrate was between John Randolph and St. George Tucker. Although the two had rarely seen one another during the previous decade, their mutual affection had continued unabated. After receiving one letter from his stepson filled with expressions of love, Tucker responded in kind, writing him, "Years have not done away the tender recollections of the days, when it was my joy and pride to cultivate the Affections of your infant heart, and to attach it to me through Life."[32] After 1810, however, letters between the pair dwindled and then ended altogether once Fanny died.

The problem lay with Randolph. During these years, as he grew intensely nostalgic for eighteenth-century Virginia, he desperately wished for his family to recapture its former power, wealth, and influence. By 1813, however, one dismal event after another revealed the folly of such dreams. First, Randolph suffered repeated crop failures at Roanoke that severely strained his purse. In addition to Fanny's death, Randolph also learned that year that his twenty-year-old nephew Tudor had grown alarmingly ill and likely would not reach manhood. John had pinned his future hopes for his branch of the Randolph clan on this youth's shoulders, but now the boy would die. Then, in April 1813 the plantation house at Bizarre went up in flames after chimney sparks ignited the roof. The fire also destroyed all the furniture, books, and papers within. That same month Randolph lost his cherished Southside congressional seat because of his opposition to the war with Great Britain.[33]

As all these disasters came down on him, Randolph retreated further into his nostalgic vision of the Old Dominion. In 1813–14 he closely reread the works of Edmund Burke. Like England's great conservative, Randolph longed for a stable and hierarchical landed society and for a political system grounded in sound experience, not speculative ideas and innovations. "What a treasure, what a mine of eloquence, sagacity and political wisdom!" Randolph exclaimed to one correspondent in the spring of 1814. Burke, he concluded, "is the Newton of political philosophy." At the same time he ached for his family's past greatness. He began to carry his father's miniature portrait and three locks of his hair with him everywhere, ascribing to John Randolph of Matoax all the glorious virtues the old gentry had at one time possessed. When he once forgot these items on a trip to Richmond, he immediately had them forwarded. Finally, in March 1814 he returned again to Cawsons, the plantation near the confluence of the James and Appomattox Rivers that had once been his grandfather's. To his dismay he discovered that the great house, where his mother and father had married almost a half century before, had fallen into a state of mournful dilapidation.[34]

At some point during these months, Randolph merged the horrors of his own life with the larger crises of the great planter class. Undoubtedly groping for explanations regarding the unraveling of his world, Randolph soon fixated on his stepfather—a man who for years had urged a strategy of individualism and self-reliance. In the process Randolph convinced himself that Tucker stood against him and was the source of all the decline he saw. Randolph's sentiments came into the open in mid-April 1814, three weeks after his melancholy visit to Cawsons, when both men lodged in Richmond on business. Tucker asked John Coalter to inquire why Randolph had "estranged" himself from the man who had been his "father for thirty years." In his reply Randolph lashed out that while "cold and heartless men" (like Tucker perhaps) could "simulate regard," he could not. Indeed, Randolph cried, "I know not how to avenge a wrong received from a friend."[35]

Aghast at what he read, Tucker immediately sought an explanation. The next day Randolph wrote another more detailed letter explaining that it was St. George who had "estranged" himself from his stepson by "*his* [Tucker's] *treatment* of his mother's *children.*" As Randolph warmed to the subject, his true concerns became clear. Tucker's management of John's patrimony while executor of Frances Tucker's will lay at the source of his anger. When his mother died in 1788, John asserted, "she left funds in hand and clear accounts." Yet Tucker had blatantly "disregarded" her final wishes by his insistence that the Matoax plantation be sold for cash. Thus "the ashes of my parents were conveyed out of the family." When Randolph assumed control of the remaining properties upon reaching adulthood, "I found myself burthened with claims from overseers, blacksmiths, sheriffs, store keepers &c: of long standing! without a cent to discharge them." Where had the money gone? Not toward his education, which Randolph snidely labeled "an inexpensive one." Ignoring his father's debts and Judith and Richard's excessive spending during their marriage, John implied that Tucker must have embezzled the cash.[36]

Worst of all were the fates of those loyal slaves who had been part of his mother's dowry when she married his father. Having romanticized the institution by this point, he saw the slaves as the living vestiges of his family's glorious past. But under Tucker's management his mother's bondpeople had been selfishly scattered and/or worked until they were useless. John noted that his stepfather had "converted" many Randolph slaves "into funds" by selling them off while others labored through their prime years inside the judge's Williamsburg mansion, which benefited no one in the Randolph family. John even accused his stepfather of sending his female slaves to Randolph's overcrowded Roanoke plantation merely to breed and "to encrease for your benefit." John declared that he never immediately returned them because "I loved them too well to ask whether they were Tuckers or Randolphs." [37]

With unmistakable clarity John Randolph had bundled his fears about his own family's descent with his anxieties about the tidewater gentry's overall decline. From his earliest years he had been taught that family loyalty, land, and slaves represented the central elements of the old elite's power and authority. Whereas Randolph viewed his life as dedicated to preserving the circumstances of the past, his stepfather had desecrated the customs and values of old. Since the Revolution, St. George had advocated the principles of individual ambition and self-sufficiency, not family enterprise and fidelity. Tucker had abandoned land and agriculture and urged the rising generation to pursue professional careers, a development that Randolph believed had overturned Virginia's old order and had left its social "fabrick uprooted." St. George Tucker personified all the vile forces that had destroyed the shimmering world of his father's generation. Thus Randolph demanded that their relationship end. It was, he concluded, too "painful to keep up." John Randolph later considered legal action against his stepfather for Tucker's management of his mother's estate, but he never followed up. [38]

Although distraught by his stepson's accusations, Tucker did not comprehend the larger fears that gave shape to Randolph's bitterness. Understanding only that his honor had been challenged, he answered that if Randolph felt cheated, he could seek compensation through the courts. Beyond that, "no reply is necessary." Tucker then ordered John Coalter to tell no one about the rupture. Understanding the "evil consequences" associated with "family breaches," the judge desperately sought to avoid any further dissolution. [39]

But events soon moved beyond his control. The following year Henry

Tucker won a congressional seat from the northern Shenandoah Valley in the wake of the War of 1812. Evelina and the children stayed in Winchester while Henry lived in Washington during sessions. Able to afford only a cramped set of rooms, he initially spent much of his time with his half brother. Unable to contain his bitterness, however, Randolph soon confronted Henry with his accusations concerning the elder Tucker. Distraught at what he heard, Henry quickly wrote his father, "Have you in your possession any part of my mothers Dower property to which Mr. John Randolph had a title?"[40] Horrified that his son had been drawn into the rupture, the judge ordered Henry "to struggle against" any and all animosity he might feel. Henry must "cultivate and preserve . . . [the] brotherly love" he still had for Randolph.

When Tucker turned to the dispute itself, he insisted, "My heart acquits me of ever having given any just cause for this estrangement." In a long and frank letter, he carefully described his marriage settlement with his first wife, the financial decisions he made regarding the Randolph estates during his stepsons' minority, and his management of Randolph and Tucker slaves, a kind of property which "had continually brought me in debt" and which he did sell off whenever possible. Even though Tucker's conscience was clear regarding his actions, he concluded his letter to Henry, "My heart bleeds with the wounds it has received, and is still receiving, and I pray to the Father of mercies that I may soon be relieved from my sufferings."[41]

Although St. George urged peace between the two brothers, Henry soon broke off his personal contacts with Randolph, initiating a kind of cold war between them. Trying to be optimistic, at least in letters to other family members, Henry explained that his half brother now "finds it impossible to Controul me" regarding to public matters "and therefore treat[s] me with more respect and attention." Nevertheless, the personal relationship had been shattered beyond repair. Like the elder Tucker, Henry never grasped John's underlying social fears regarding his family's decline and the social changes throughout Virginia. Henry simply ascribed his brother's actions to greed. "I have long suspected," he later wrote, "that an inordinate love of riches was becoming the primary vice of that unfortunate man."[42]

In the months before their final break, at a time when the elder Tucker was anxious to know why his stepson had ceased all communication, Beverley wrote his father that Randolph was then "under the influence of one of those fits of gloom," during which he "does not know his friends."

Beverley knew firsthand how destructive these spells could be. Two years earlier, in the autumn of 1811, the younger Tucker himself had experienced a painful break with his half brother in another dispute over money and property. Since her husband's death in 1796, their sister-in-law Judith Randolph not only had to struggle during hard economic times, but she also fought bitterly and repeatedly with her sister, Nancy. Tensions between the two women had percolated ever since the "Bizarre scandal" of 1792–93. Though the courts exonerated Richard, the sisters apparently were unable to place the affair behind them. By late 1806 their resentments had escalated so much that Nancy left Bizarre. That winter she wandered from one Randolph plantation to another to escape what she said was Judith's unmitigated hatred. In the spring of 1807, Nancy found herself living alone in a Richmond boardinghouse, but even that was not far enough away from her sister. She soon traveled alone to New England. Judith always insisted that she had never given Nancy any reason to leave but rather always sought reconciliation.[43]

Although Judith claimed family harmony mattered most to her, financial concerns increasingly dominated her thinking. Judith had surrendered all hopes of living on a grand scale, but worries about her children consumed her. Nancy earlier had told the elder Tucker that her sister was "insolvent" following Richard's death and feared "that her boys wou'd not get a sliver" of property upon her death.[44] Their only hope, it seemed, was a future inheritance from their uncle John. Therefore, Judith watched closely as her brother-in-law grew closer and more attached to Beverley. In 1809, as she struggled to make ends meet, her concerns mounted significantly when Randolph gave the younger Tucker both land and slaves. Then astonishing news arrived that Nancy had married the wealthy New York politician Gouverneur Morris. The match gave Nancy access to Morris's lordly estate and may well have been the final straw. Judith began quietly denigrating John Randolph to other family members, including Beverley. Launching into "cavils" at how Richard's estate had declined over the years, she condemned John for his lack of attention and care.

Beverley unwisely informed his half brother of the accusations, which immediately led Judith to turn on him. She labeled Beverley's affection for John "hollow and insincere," merely "a design on his purse and property." The two brothers began to grow hostile to one another. By the autumn of 1810, their suspicions had escalated to the point that, as Beverley explained to his father, Randolph "wished me to return him the land he had given me offering to purchase for me a place as good or better any where I chose." Indignantly rejecting this offer, Beverley left his land and cabin and moved into a tiny house four miles away.[45]

He wished, however, to go much farther. Families just could not hold together in these changed times, he concluded. Soon after he left his half brother's estate, Beverley pointed out to his father that the tidewater's dismal economy "drove me from you" in Williamsburg. A "similarity of professional pursuits" prevented the young attorney from relocating near "my brother Henry" in Winchester and "my sister's husband" in Staunton. Jealousy over land and property "now drive me from" Roanoke. The "disgusting circumstance[s]" that still attended the law in Virginia made Beverley wonder where he should go.[46]

As he cast his eyes around for a new locale in which to settle, Beverley began to look beyond the Old Dominion and toward America's "Western Country." Perhaps he could find success and happiness somewhere west of the Appalachians. Like Randolph, Beverley idealized Revolutionary Virginia as the perfect society. It had been, he convinced himself, a land dominated by great gentry families who had governed both freeholders and slaves alike with benevolence, kindness, and generosity. Unfortunately, this magnificent world no longer existed in the Old Dominion. However, with a loyal wife, his two children, and other kinsmen beside him, perhaps he could carve out of the western territories a new and better society based on his glorious vision of the past.[47]

He would not be the first within the family to go beyond the mountains. A number of his stepmother's kin from the Skipwith clan had gone to Louisiana a decade before to grow cotton.[48] Although the War of 1812 temporarily delayed him, Beverley was determined to be off, especially as both his legal career and his relationship with Randolph continued to founder. Eventually choosing the Missouri Territory in which to settle, Beverley spent the spring and summer of 1815 selling his remaining Old Dominion lands, purchasing supplies, and arranging for slaves to go west with him. When their arrangements were at last completed in mid-November, Beverley, Polly, the children, and several servants departed.[49]

As their caravan of four wagons rumbled out of the state, the Tuckers all took stock of the family's situation. Everyone could see now that the era of the great clans had irrevocably passed. Beverley's departure, however, especially grieved Henry. Although he always attempted to deal with life with moderation, the family's scattering caused him tremendous pain. Even before Beverley's migration west, Henry saw that changed circumstances had imposed great barriers between kin members. He and his brother were a distinct example. Busy with legal careers, separated by hundreds of miles, and with family connections of little practical use, the two men rarely corresponded. Usually one letter per year passed between them.[50]

But as Beverley left Virginia altogether, it crystallized for Henry just how much the clan as a whole had deteriorated. His brother's departure coincided with the long-expected death of twenty-three-year-old Tudor Randolph. The youth's passing not only devastated Judith and John Randolph, but it also greatly distressed Henry even though he confessed that he "had scarcely known" his nephew. Tudor's demise and Beverley's emigration, as Henry told his father, had "forcefully brought to my reflection how much our family are dispersing and diminished." Because "the present generation" now lived "scattered abroad," members possessed little "Knowledge of each other." He predicted that they would all most certainly lose touch in the years ahead. Powerless to halt the deterioration, Henry embraced resignation. These many concerns, he conceded, were "unavailing regrets." To compensate, he turned to those closest around him—his nuclear family— for love and comfort. His "amiable partner" and his "tribe of brats" now would have to fill "the void" left by the larger clan's decline.[51]

Beverley himself was not yet ready to give up on this aspect of the past. As his wagons approached the Appalachians, they were joined by a number of Polly's relatives from the Coalter clan in South Carolina. Bad roads, periodic illnesses, and mountain snowstorms slowed everyone, and by the following spring they had only reached Kentucky. Despite the delays Tucker drew strength at being surrounded by so many extended kin all cooperating in a common venture. From the road he wrote his father about "the delectable bustle of a family consisting of sixteen white persons. You may be assured that we have noise enough, but it is all in harmony and . . . every note is in tune." In June 1816 the group finally reached St. Louis where Beverley purchased "a small tract of land" on which he planned to begin his "true Virginia settlement." Although he intended to practice law, Tucker particularly wanted to own a great landed estate that would provide his family with independence, status, and influence. Nearby kin members would give him and Polly all the assistance they would need, just as the great clans of pre-Revolutionary Virginia had always supported one another. Working together, Beverley concluded, they could not help but create a "choice society." Out on the frontier the old order would be reestablished.[52]

Although his hopes for familial greatness were high, tragedy soon struck. During a single week in September, Beverley's two children died suddenly of a "worm-fever" apparently brought on by eating apples from a nearby orchard. Both children—"wonderful" five-year-old Jack and two-year-old "dear little Fan"—had been a constant source of parental pride and happiness as well as Beverley's hope for his family's future. Trying to cope with their loss, he and Polly embraced sentimental religion. Beverley explained that he knew with absolute certainty that his little ones were now supremely "happy" in "the Bosom" of the Lord. Beverley also believed that God had taken Jack and Fan from him because he had been "an unworthy parent."[53]

Nevertheless, his children's deaths did not deter him from his larger mission. The following year, 1817, he and Polly purchased a new farm which they named St. George in order, as Beverley proudly noted, to "record the lineage of its first possessor" and "the stainless purity of my name and race." The estate was only a modest start, several hundred acres with two cabins joined by a dogtrot. Envisioning Virginia's glorious past, the younger Tucker wished for nothing less than to be "the founder of a new dynasty."[54]

The opportunity to build this new "dynasty" came in 1818, soon after Polly's brother David Coalter arrived from South Carolina. Coalter at first stayed in St. Louis with the families of his two sisters from Kentucky, the Naylors and McPheeters, both of whom lived near St. George. Deciding to "pitch our tents together," the group searched for lands upon which to establish themselves. Because rising values had made land in St. Louis prohibitive, the party looked northwest of the city. Eventually they found and purchased 8,000 acres of bottomland along Dardenne Creek, a small Missouri River tributary fifteen miles north of St. Charles, a trading-post town and the capital of the territory. Beverley explained that the land would "give us command of as much vacant prairie as will afford large estates for ten or twelve persons." Proud that only "good and wealthy people" would settle around him, Beverley viewed himself as Moses, leading family members and gentry planters into a promised land where old values and traditional social hierarchies would dominate. That same year Frederick Bates, the territorial governor and a fellow Virginian, appointed Beverley to Missouri's northern circuit court. With great pride Beverley asked John Coalter to spread the news of his judgeship to his friends and family back east.[55] Imagining the impact he would have on the new territory, Beverley mused,

"I came here like the patriarch of old, leaning upon my staff and behold I am become a great nation."[56]

But some had their doubts. Writing to his sister Elizabeth, St. George Tucker sarcastically called Beverley an "enthusiastic" and hinted that his "flourishing colony" probably would soon fail.[57] Many Missourians, themselves recent emigrants from the East, turned against the Dardenne settlers as well. Beverley had noted earlier in a letter sent to Virginia that they had "some Yankees" in the territory. As Tucker labored to establish his model gentry settlement, thousands of northern farmers poured into Missouri determined to scratch out their independence free from the domination of society's "great" men. Thousands of Irish immigrants, moreover, arrived in St. Louis throughout the 1810s. These people not surprisingly resented the haughtiness and elitism of the Dardenne colonists, especially the attitudes of Tucker himself.

In early 1820 this animosity reached the breaking point when a letter Beverley had written to a correspondent in Virginia found its way into St. Louis's *Missouri Gazette and Public Advertiser*. In it the slave-owning Tucker lauded the arrival of propertied men from the South while cheering that "scarcely one Yankee has moved into the country." Beverley proclaimed that Missouri, led by his Dardenne colony, "is becoming more homogeneous" every day, just like the Old Dominion before the Revolution. Tucker's words generated considerable hostility throughout the region. Applauding the "polite and dignified" Tucker, one resident sarcastically asked, "What a big man the Dardenne prairie-man must be. How ought the good people of this territory rejoice at having such a *luminary* among them?" He finished by imagining the aristocratic Tucker traveling through the plains in an ornate and gilded coach with uniformed footmen kicking the surrounding peasant farmers out of his way.[58]

The Missouri Controversy of 1819–20 further undermined Beverley's position in the territory. Like the rest of the Tuckers, he had made his peace with slavery during the nineteenth century's first decade. By the time he reached Missouri, the institution had become in his mind an essential component—a sine qua non—of his larger vision to establish an agrarian society led by genteel and propertied families. Slaves were vital not merely to satisfy a planter's labor needs but also to demonstrate to others his wealth, status, and power. The crisis over the territory began in February 1819 when New York congressman James Tallmadge proposed to prohibit slavery from the territory as a condition of statehood. Like his father and brother back in Virginia, Beverley viewed the measure as constitutionally flawed.[59]

Beginning in the spring of 1819, the younger Tucker crafted five long essays for the *Missouri Gazette* in which he assembled a formidable constitutional case against the Tallmadge amendment based largely on his father's legal theories in *Blackstone's Commentaries*.[60] By so publicly interjecting himself into the debate, however, Beverley further alienated himself and his Dardenne settlement from the general population. Although he avowed that he cared little about slavery and even declared to a friend that "if a pledge were demanded I would emancipate all I have," he insisted on attempting to reconcile the institution with the nation's founding principles.[61] In the 28 April *Missouri Gazette,* he addressed himself to abolitionists who argued that "slavery is incompatible with the constitution and the genius of our government." To such people Tucker smugly declared, "Slaves have been found . . . no where in greater numbers than under governments called republican." As slavery once had strengthened the ancient republics, it now strengthened republicanism in Missouri by enhancing the territory's agrarian system. Slavery helped to create a noble and independent class of genteel planters, while removing an inferior class of people from the political process. "Yankeys" with their calculating values and antislavery sentiments, only threatened to undermine the republican system established by the Revolution. Tucker thus concluded that for both the nation and free government to survive, slavery must expand.[62]

The essays generated a blistering response from surrounding farmers who already despised Tucker's arrogance and condescension. One reader noted that slavery was "a national evil" and reasoned that the House of Representatives had passed the Tallmadge amendment to aid "the poor, honest, industrious and laborious classes," not to assist "opulent slave-holders" like Tucker and the other Dardenne colonists. Another writer lampooned Beverley as the son of St. George Tucker. The piece saluted the "highly distinguished" "Judge Tucker" for his bold and progressive *Dissertation on Slavery.* The author stated the elder Tucker might have failed to "convince his fellow citizens" of the Old Dominion about the wisdom of emancipation, but he most certainly "has convinced me on that point."[63] This barb must have especially wounded Beverley. These letters illustrate both rising social tensions on the frontier and growing resistance to Tucker's vision of Missouri as a traditional agrarian slave society.

As such pressures mounted, Tucker's Dardenne settlement gradually came apart. Migration of the "finest materials" from Virginia and South Carolina into the colony all but stopped during the Missouri crisis. Not only did the political controversy dissuade many southerners from coming, but the panic of 1819 further stanched the flow. The nation's economic downturn began early in the year. Easy credit, excessive land speculation, and a sudden drop in demand for American goods abroad led to a collapse in prices across the country. After the Second Bank of the United States called in many of its outstanding loans, the economy from New York to St. Louis violently contracted. No longer could Beverley's kin and friends afford the journey to the West. Indeed, many Dardenne colonists had to return east amid the hard times in order to rescue those properties they had left behind. Many members of the Coalter clan left for South Carolina, and other settlers headed east as well. Beverley's friend William Campbell Preston left with his wife in 1822, soon followed by another Dardenne neighbor, William Harper. Meanwhile, poorer immigrants continued to stream into the state, including Irish settlers (a "viler flock" Beverley said he could not imagine). As "men of talent and virtue" traveled eastward and as "straggling vagabonds" arrived on St. Louis wharfs, Beverley no longer looked upon his Dardenne lands as a "true Virginia settlement" but rather as a lonely "city of refuge."[64]

Thus he and Polly struggled on the prairie increasingly alone. The childless couple acutely felt their isolation and turned to their bondpeople for support, companionship, and even comfort. Polly once filled an entire letter to Williamsburg with news about several slaves to whom she and Beverley had grown particularly close. Although one old servant named Granny Phillis was confined to bed, she had "a good warm cabin" and a "daughter [who] stays with her constantly." Another female servant refused to be sold to a neighbor even though the proposed sale would reunite her with her husband. "She will not agree to leave us," Polly proudly explained, because of "her attachment to her Master and myself." Beverley had told his father earlier that he had developed "a certain rational regard" for many white individuals in Missouri but concluded that "the heart has little to do" in the West. At the same time he felt great "tenderness" for those "persons of very inferior worth" whom he owned. Because of their "early associations" together, his slaves reminded him of old Virginia and thus possessed a hold on his heart.[65]

Beverley's nostalgic effort to re-create eighteenth-century Virginia in

Missouri can only be regarded as a failure. He had gone west to reestablish his family's social and economic power as well as to recover Revolutionary-era notions of kin interdependency, closeness, and togetherness. In the years following the Missouri crisis, however, he found himself alone, alienated from the surrounding white population and convinced that his only true friends were his slaves. Like others back in Virginia, moreover, Beverley had to rely largely on his talents and professional training in order to survive. Throughout the early 1820s he and Polly lived mainly on his salary as a state judge. More than anything else, his experiment in the West further demonstrated the ongoing decline of Virginia's once-great families.

St. George Tucker took little satisfaction in the fulfillment of his prediction of the failure of Beverley's colony. Problems continued to abound in the Old Dominion as well. While Beverley struggled in Missouri, family ties continued to come apart in the East. In 1816 Judith Randolph died in a Richmond boardinghouse. She moved to "this busy city" after her slaves had been emancipated and the main house at Bizarre was destroyed by fire. From her "solitary chamber" Judith told St. George in her final letter to him that she saw "few friends" now and considered her "life" to be most "unpleasant." She concluded, however, "I am nearly indifferent to it." Tucker noted on this letter that Judith died three weeks later and added, "Blessed be her soul." Surviving family members, meanwhile, clashed bitterly over dwindling property holdings. The status of the Corotoman plantation, for instance, caused tremendous animosity on Lelia Tucker's side of the family. St. George had long disliked managing the 5,000-acre estate.[66] After Joseph C. Cabell married Lelia's daughter, Polly, in 1807, the judge sought to hand over the plantation's management to his stepson Charles Carter and to Cabell. In return, Lelia would receive an annual annuity from the estate's profits. Tucker had expected the arrangement to end his headaches, but the proposal merely added to them. After Carter and Cabell decided to divide the estate between them, Charles demanded both the best lands and the strongest slaves. He also restated his intention eventually to emancipate those bondmen he would receive. As this news spread through the slave quarters, apprehension and discord quickly materialized on the plantation. After several years of fruitlessly trying to arrive at a settlement, Carter and Cabell refused even to speak to one another. Tucker had to hire three local planters for £100 to propose an impartial division everyone could live with. From Williamsburg, he helplessly cried, "Every moment seems pregnant with some new cause of interrupting, and perhaps destroying forever that harmony which it has been the wish of my heart . . . to establish and preserve between members of our family."[67]

Tucker's own personal resources declined as well throughout these years. During the War of 1812, British troops raided Corotoman and carried off over forty slaves. The incursions not only hurt the estate's production but greatly reduced the overall value of these property holdings. Tucker feared, moreover, that Virginia's state banks, where the bulk of his own resources were still invested, might be driven to bankruptcy because of the conflict. So great were his anxieties over money that he reluctantly accepted in 1813 an appointment from President Madison as a federal judge to the district court in Norfolk. Assured that his duties would be light and that cases before the court would focus solely on admiralty law (and not political issues), Tucker took the office in order to secure a regular salary.[68]

Despite these difficulties, St. George Tucker entered his final years determined to maintain his patriarchal position as head of his entire clan. Historians have long debated the evolving role of patriarchalism in America (and especially the South) during the early Republic.[69] Within the Tucker family a complex picture of gradual but unmistakable change emerges. Patriarchal authority most certainly waned in the early 1800s, but its demise was neither complete nor obvious to contemporaries. Tucker recognized more clearly than most that great shifts had taken place within the nation's economy, and he attempted to reposition his family accordingly. But Tucker never fully grasped how these larger changes had fundamentally weakened the traditional power that fathers possessed over their families.

Throughout the late colonial and Revolutionary eras, St. George's own father had never confronted such problems. Confident of his position within the family, Colonel Tucker wielded his authority over the Bermuda clan mildly and always with the expectation of obedience. Family members accepted the Colonel's prerogatives and only rarely challenged them. When St. George became the head of his own family a generation later, he found a dramatically changed situation. Not only were fathers less able to pass down property and status, but families in general had lost their interdependency and interconnectedness. Instead of relying on extended kin for crucial jobs, assistance, and social connections, individuals learned that their households functioned largely as detached and isolated entities.

By the early nineteenth century, St. George realized that in this environment parents could no longer count on automatic obedience from their children. Rather offspring (no matter their age) now had to be constantly reminded of their duties to parents, and parental authority had to be exercised in a much more forceful manner. Tucker explicitly stated this when he advised Nancy Randolph on how to raise the son she and Gouverneur Morris had in 1813. Tucker pointedly told Nancy, "I most sincerely hope that his Education may be conducted in such a manner as to make him feel his obligation to *your* parental Cares, and tenderness far beyond any *other* sublunary Wish, or Sentiment."[70]

Beyond giving advice, the judge took tangible steps to ensure his own children's continued submission to his will, and in the process he acted more like a traditional patriarch than his father had. Until the day he died, Tucker demanded regular and thoughtful letters from his children. Paternal demands for frequent correspondence were not uncommon among eighteenth-century elites. Tucker, though, insisted on constant epistles long after his children had reached maturity and had established households, families, and careers of their own. He once angrily charged then-forty-two-year-old Henry with neglect after several weeks passed with no letters from Winchester. The elder Tucker thundered to his niece Elizabeth Coalter, "Tell your Uncle Henry I am astonished at his Silence, not having received a Line from him since I left home."[71]

The elder Tucker also fully expected his grown children to conduct complex and burdensome errands for him whenever he demanded. John Coalter often had to perform a variety of tasks for his father-in-law as he traveled through Virginia on legal business. One time when in Richmond, Coalter wrote a long and dutiful letter to the judge, explaining that "I have obeyed your orders in all things." Not only had Coalter paid off a number of Tucker's debts to merchants in the city, but he also had to supervise the construction of a carriage the judge had ordered built and delivered to Williamsburg. Earlier Tucker had bluntly informed his son-in-law that despite the time-consuming nature of these chores, "I make no apologies for asking you to do these things for you are my Son."[72] Such work was part of a child's ongoing duty to a father, and thus no gratitude should or would be forthcoming.

The most revealing aspect of St. George Tucker's patriarchalism involved his continued insistence that his adult children make no major decisions in their lives without first obtaining his explicit blessing. In the spring of 1811, soon after Tucker resigned from the Virginia bench, the state legislature expanded the Court of Appeals from three to five judges and appointed Coalter to fill one of the vacancies.[73] Because of his dispute with Spencer Roane, Tucker made no secret that he did not want his son-in-law to take the post. Coalter, though, desperately wished to accept the position. Not only was he "awe-struck" at the honor, but the high court's winter session in Richmond would permit him to lodge his family in the city for several months and hence be with them for a long uninterrupted period. When Coalter hinted he would take the judgeship, Tucker grew particularly angry. He initially ordered Henry to compose a letter to dissuade Coalter. Tucker then wrote a scathing epistle himself chastising his son-in-law for disobedience. The letter drew a pained and emotional reaction. "I call upon you," Coalter cried in reply, "my Father my best of Friends with eyes overflowing with tears, and in heart rent asunder between filial piety and love to you [and] duty to myself and family . . . to pity me, to console me, not to despise me." Although reduced to wretchedness, Coalter took the post shortly afterwards. Tucker reluctantly accepted Coalter's decision and wrote to smooth over ruffled feelings.[74] This incident reveals that Tucker's emotional hold on his children remained strong throughout his life. But his patriarchal authority—that is, his manifest ability to make his children do as he expressly wished—had declined. This became a recurring pattern by the 1810s. Tucker's children expressed deep respect for their father's views, but they always did what they thought best for themselves and their individual households.

As Tucker's paternal authority deteriorated with the passing years, the extended family ties that had so greatly influenced the previous age faded as well. Because they had been so crucial to his success and happiness as a youth, St. George never forgot his roots and always strove until his death to keep in touch with his surviving kin. Tucker and his brother Thomas maintained a regular correspondence, exchanging personal and political news every month or so. The two brothers also keenly felt the traditional responsibility to help all kin members in need. The pair annually sent money to their English sister-in-law, Jane Wood Tucker, widow of their brother Nathaniel. The couple had lived in Hull, outside York, where Nathaniel built a modest medical practice and worked in a local hospital. After his death in 1807, Jane moved to London where she supported herself and their six children almost solely on the charity of her two brothers-in-law. Although St. George once had to borrow money to keep up his gift, neither he nor Thomas ever complained about this responsibility. Both brothers believed they were fulfilling the customary obligations owed to loved ones beyond the nuclear family.[75]

St. George and Thomas also sent food and money to their sister Elizabeth in Bermuda.[76] Because she had never married, both brothers sought assurances from other island kin that they kept a close eye on her. There was little cause for concern. One nephew, Robert Tucker, the son of Frances and Henry Tucker of Somerset, wrote to Thomas in 1822 to assure him that family members throughout the island remained "very much attach'd to" their aunt, and that the elderly spinster's grandnieces and grandnephews "are a good deal about her."[77] St. George also worked to develop lasting ties to the rising generation of Bermuda family members, many of whom were born after he left the island. Over the years he wrote seeking news about relatives, children, and careers. His Bermuda kin often reciprocated with news about the island, the passing of friends and family, and the arrival of newborn Tuckers. A kinsman named Richard J. Tucker replied to one letter by sending the judge his warmest regards along with detailed descriptions of his growing children. Richard concluded with the heartening assurance, "To them all Sir, your name is quite familiar."[78]

Passing this deep sense of familial duty to the rising generation in America, however, proved impossible. Yet it was not through a want of trying. The elder Tucker attempted for years to interest his sons in their Bermuda kin. In 1809, soon after he learned of the deaths of two of his brothers, Henry and Nathaniel, Tucker wrote his boys long letters about their island relations and about the Bermuda family in general. Although he did not order them to begin a correspondence, the judge clearly hoped that this would be the result. Beverley's romanticized view of his family's past meant that he responded first and with the most enthusiasm. Forever longing to reestablish traditional kin ties, he declared, "I can not lose a moment in thanking you." He also wrote that he would cherish forever the copy of his uncle Nathaniel's poem *The Bermudian* that was enclosed with the letter. Beverley explained that he read the 1774 lyric about The Grove with great relish. He already had showed the work to a friend, who commented that it reflected "a sort of family Pride that would insinuate itself into the most republican heart."[79] But with days filled with legal work, court dates, and traveling schedules, Beverley found little time to contact his surviving relatives overseas.

Henry also wrote the elder Tucker to thank him for his recent letter, noting, "I should be much interested in a further notice of our Bermuda Connections and particularly in . . . the younger branches of it." Yet he also told his father that it was unrealistic to expect him to cultivate these distant bonds with the enthusiasm of earlier generations. "At this season of life," Henry explained, when young men pursued their professional careers with a single-minded energy, extended family ties were "of less importance and interest than [they] will be when some part of the hurry and bustle of life is over." In short, because kinship bonds no longer provided ambitious individuals with tangible advantages, they must wait until the autumn of one's life when ease and retirement beckoned.[80]

St. George Tucker never accepted that these ties must collapse amid the changes of the early Republic. While cognizant of the nineteenth-century need for economic self-sufficiency, the judge could not understand why emotional bonds between kin members also must decline. Throughout the years he continued to send his children news about their English and Bermudian relatives, hoping to spark some latent interest. His letters only engendered indifference. As a result, he began to work on the next generation—his grandchildren—realizing that if he did nothing, these broad family ties would forever crumble. In 1822 he wrote his teenaged granddaughter Elizabeth Coalter that "my Brother [Thomas] enclosed me by the last mail one of the sweetest Letters that ever were written by a Lady of seventy-five of age . . . from your dear Aunt Bet." Hoping to pique her interest, Tucker told Elizabeth that he would soon make a copy for her so that she could see what a "Treasure" her great-aunt was. But Elizabeth Coalter never took up her pen to write her aunt.[81]

Two months earlier Tucker had written Henry to explain that it was high time for his son's eldest daughter, the thirteen-year-old Anne, to begin a correspondence with her Bermudian aunt. Once again the judge's efforts came to naught. Henry thanked the elder Tucker for news about Aunt Bet, insisting "we are always deeply interested in her letters." But he added, "I trust you will present us most affectionately to her." He tried to explain as gently as he could: "If I thought Annes letters could give her pleasure I should not hesitate to adopt your suggestion; but she is yet too young for such a correspondence. Letter writing is an awkward matter for young folks at best."[82] Despite Henry's efforts to be diplomatic, the broad family ties that had once stretched between Bermuda and Virginia would cease with the older generation's passing.

Henry's answer may have come as no surprise to the now seventy-two-

year-old Tucker. By 1822 he had come to realize how fragile (and sometimes burdensome) ties to distant relatives could be. His painful experiences with one Bermuda nephew, Henry Tucker of Sandy's Parish, likely
convinced him how significantly kin relationships had changed in his lifetime. Henry's parents were St. George's sister Frances and brother-in-law
Henry Tucker of Somerset. During the Revolutionary War, St. George had
grown very close to the couple, especially Henry of Somerset. Not only had
he partnered with the Colonel and St. George's eldest brother in business,
but Henry had visited The Grove often and kept up a frequent correspondence with St. George once he left for Virginia. But after Henry died in
1796, St. George maintained few direct contacts with his brother-in-law's
children. In 1810, however, Henry Tucker of Somerset's oldest child was a
struggling middle-aged merchant from Bermuda's West End. That year he
wrote his American uncle to request both a cash loan and the use of any "respectable mercantile" connections Tucker might possess in the Chesapeake.
Although the judge pleaded that he had few commercial contacts, he did
offer his nephew a $1,500 loan to be paid back at a later unspecified date.[83]

The money, intended to salvage Henry's business, did not rescue him.
A victim of Bermuda's post-Revolutionary economic decline as well as of
his own ineptitude, the merchant was forced into bankruptcy in 1816. In
1818 the penniless merchant sailed to the United States where he promptly
borrowed money from his uncle Thomas in Washington, D.C. Henry then
used the cash to travel, apparently in high style, up and down the eastern
seaboard, ostensibly to seek out new business opportunities. Finding none
and soon broke once more, he eventually went home.[84]

Henry did not stay in Bermuda for very long, however. In late 1820 the
bankrupt merchant returned to America, this time sailing for Norfolk, determined to request more aid from his Virginia uncle. Landing at the port
in late December, Henry carried a letter from his aunt Bet addressed to St.
George. Clearly writing this missive with great reluctance, she explained
that Henry "wishes, he says to consider you a father, brother, uncle and
friend, on this occasion." Although only thirty miles away in Williamsburg, the elder Tucker now wanted nothing to do with his nephew. Both
embarrassed and angered at his kinsman's forwardness, Tucker explained in
a quickly drafted note that he felt "very great distress" upon learning of
Henry's arrival in the tidewater. Although the two relatives had never met,
the judge further explained that it would serve no purpose for his sister's
son even to visit Williamsburg. To get his nephew to go away, the elder

Tucker offered a $300 "loan," extended solely on the condition that Henry would return straight to Bermuda.[85] Immediately accepting the cash, the merchant caught the next ship for the island, and the two family members never corresponded again. From Washington, D.C., a relieved Thomas wrote to his brother, "It is no small satisfaction to me . . . that the intended visit to you by our unfortunate nephew has been avoided, tho' at a great expence." "My apprehensions," Thomas concluded, "were that you wou'd find it difficult to get rid of him."[86]

As these traditional clan ties declined during the 1820s, St. George Tucker confronted the full emergence of the isolated, emotionally centered nuclear family. Throughout the decade he and Lelia lived alone in Williamsburg while his sons largely ignored their extended relations abroad and one another closer to home. Henry and Beverley made few efforts to keep in touch with each other, instead focusing on domestic concerns in their own households. Henry left the Congress in 1819 largely because of the time-consuming burdens of public life. He explained to St. George upon leaving that his highest ambition in life was now simply to occupy "the honorable station of 'the father of the family.'"[87] After he left the Capitol for what he hoped would be the last time, his joy was palpable. "I need not say how happy we all were made," he wrote when he arrived home. "My little brats . . . were almost beside themselves at meeting with me, and their mother had cause indeed to rejoice," for now the ex-congressman could help with the household. "After all," Henry had earlier reflected, "what is popularity? What is political advancement?" especially when compared to the happiness provided by one's wife and children.[88]

As the years passed Henry's family grew increasingly self-sufficient and exclusive. During the 1820s he put down firmer and deeper roots in the upper Valley. In 1824 he was appointed chancellor of the state's fourth judicial district in Winchester. The following year he opened a law school in the city to supplement his income. However, he never tried to develop his kinship ties beyond the Winchester region. He composed respectful letters to his father but never required his children to write their grandfather, and he seemed particularly uninterested in his kinsmen outside Virginia. John Coalter was remarkably like Henry. Although he wrote letters to Tucker, he did not require his own son, St. George Coalter, to write his grandfather. In fact, only one letter between the two has survived.[89]

By contrast, the aged St. George Tucker seemed to despise both his growing isolation and his lack of control over events. Not only did he fail to convince Henry and Beverley and other family members to write their overseas relatives, but he also attempted and failed to persuade his two sons to move back to Williamsburg to be with him during his twilight years. After Henry left Congress, Tucker proposed that he relocate in the old colonial capital. Henry begged off. The town's gradual economic decline and its long unhealthy summers, he claimed, made such a move unwise. The domestic and professional upheavals that would inevitably ensue during relocation also convinced him to stay put.[90] Several years later the elder Tucker still wanted family members close to him. Once it became clear that Beverley's Dardenne colony would fail, Tucker urged his youngest son to return to Virginia. He even thought Beverley could assume his federal judgeship in Norfolk. Like his brother, Beverley refused. Although he admitted that the federal post would place him "among friends that I love and respect," he and Polly had not yet given up on Missouri. Beverley furthermore explained that his ignorance of admiralty laws as well as his vocal denunciations of the current Adams administration likely would doom such an appointment.[91]

Thus Tucker spent his final years largely removed from those family members whom he had loved and cherished as a younger man. He retired from the federal bench in 1824, and afterwards, he and Lelia routinely spent winters and springs in Williamsburg and then summers and autumns in western Virginia in their small cottage on Joseph Cabell's plantation of Edgewood. In the fall of 1827, while still at Edgewood, Tucker suffered a massive stroke which left him paralyzed and unable to communicate. After lingering for six weeks, he died at the age of seventy-five on 10 November 1827.

Although he had lived to be an old man by contemporary standards, Tucker's death saddened both friends and kin. All acknowledged, though, that he had gone to a better world to be reunited with loved ones gone before.[92] His death also served as a clarifying event of sorts for family members, revealing to them how much their world had changed during Tucker's lifetime. The nation soon would elect Andrew Jackson president, signifying a sharp break with the Jeffersonian era. Attempts by the elite to establish the new Republic upon a foundation of reason, knowledge, and talent had clearly come to an end. Private life too had undergone a profound change by the end of the 1820s. Extended kin no longer depended on one another, or in many cases even knew each other. Self-sufficient nuclear families increasingly focused inward, with spouses, parents, and children finding solace and comfort only in one another's arms. It was a universe that the eighteenth-century Tuckers of The Grove and the great families of Revolutionary Virginia would hardly have recognized.

Beverley Tucker returned to the Old Dominion in early 1828 to help his brother and John Coalter settle their father's estate. He also came home to help overcome his grief over the sudden loss of Polly. The previous fall Beverley's wife of eighteen years died due to complications from an unexpected and difficult pregnancy. Throughout his visit family members pleaded with him to remain in Virginia. He refused, arguing that although he was a Virginian at heart, his life was now centered in the West. The night before his brother's departure for Missouri, Henry lamented, "What his [Beverley's] plans are I know not, but I sometimes fear he will not return to Virginia as a resident."[93] As he left the Old Dominion, Beverley too realized how greatly times had changed now that both his wife and father were dead. He also grasped that his once-united and now deeply fragmented family probably would never all be gathered together again. As he traveled westward away from Virginia, he wrote a poem:

> Farewell to the home of my Heart;
> Farewell to the home of my Youth!
> From the Friends of my childhood I part,
> The Disciples of Honor and Truth.
> Farewell to the gentle and kind,
>   The cheerful the gracious the fair;
> Whose smile chased the cloud from my mind;
>   Whose Song wiled my Heart of it's care.[94]

Afterwards

Three years before St. George's death, his Bermudian cousin George Tucker published *The Valley of Shenandoah.* The first of the so-called Virginia novels, the book reveals the Tucker family's view of their world at the dawn of the antebellum era. Set in 1796, it depicts the Old Dominion in the throes of a profound and irreversible social revolution. Tracing the collapse of the Grayson clan, an old and once-wealthy family of good English stock, Tucker's novel is an exploration of the breakdown of the tidewater gentry and the painful transformations that followed.

Like so many within the planter class, the fictional Graysons succumbed to overwhelming debt. The family's patriarch, the elegant Colonel Grayson, generously but unwisely had signed the promissory notes of a friend who ultimately could not pay. Just as the novel opens, Grayson dies, and his widow and two children, Edward and Louisa, are forced to deal with a host of grasping creditors. Compelled to move to a small cottage in the Shenandoah Valley when their properties in eastern Virginia are seized, family members find themselves thrust into a world of mean, uncouth, and disrespectful German and Scotch-Irish settlers. These low-birth commoners, including one of their former overseers, not only refused to defer to the old James River grandees in this new more democratic age, but they were determined to buy up the exhausted gentry's lands, slaves, and other properties.

Mimicking the survival strategy of the Tuckers themselves, young Edward Grayson pursued a legal career as an alternative path to "fortune and fame." But here too only disappointments awaited. "The law, as an occupation," one character relates, "has little to recommend it." Any well-educated lawyer "must be surrounded by a set of ill-mannered, low-minded people, who are either rapacious, unfeeling creditors, or knavish, fraudulent debtors, seeking to evade their contracts; savage bullies on one side, or contemptible cowards on the other. . . . In short, he is familiar with every form which violence, injustice, meanness, or crime can assume."[1]

Tucker's novel particularly longs for Virginia's noble genteel past. Williamsburg, for instance, is remembered by the Graysons in wistful idyllic terms as a place once dominated by a handful of wise and benevolent families. "For here one saw the advantages of wealth," Tucker wrote, "without parade or rivalship, learning without pedantry or awkwardness, frankness without rusticity, refinement without insincerity or affectation, luxury unattended with gaming or any excess, and a free intercourse between the sexes, with the most perfect innocence and purity of manners." This memory of the former capital was "the sunny spot in the dreary field of [their] existence."[2] For the Grayson family this "dreary" present only became more painful. At the book's end Edward is killed in a duel fought to vindicate his sister's honor after she has been spurned by a roguish suitor from New York. Louisa and her mother find themselves all alone in the world, confronting a troubled and uncertain future.

The Valley of Shenandoah's sentimental nostalgia for the past and its dour pessimism regarding the present reflected the Tucker family's outlook in the years following St. George Tucker's death. Although none collapsed into poverty and some even did well professionally, family members struggled with the new order of things while they continued to drift apart from one another.

After St. George Tucker was buried at Edgewood, his wife soon returned to Williamsburg where she found a "solitary and silent home." Lelia wrote her niece Elizabeth Coalter that she already missed her husband's "tender" hand and "warm" voice. "Alas!" she cried. "Never more will they be extended to me in this world of sin, of care, and of woe."[3] She remained in the big house living alone with only her domestic slaves around her into the 1830s. She continued to travel west every summer, however, to be at Edgewood with her daughter and son-in-law. There she stayed in the small cottage she had shared with St. George. In 1837 Lelia quietly died on the plantation at the age of sixty-nine. Polly and Joseph Cabell buried her next to her second husband.

In the years after 1827, St. George Tucker's own children met with various successes and failures. Hard work and individual effort brought Henry Tucker both financial rewards and prestige. His law school in Winchester grew quite prosperous in the late 1820s and early 1830s. The legislature, moreover, appointed him president of the state's Court of Appeals in 1831. This was soon followed by a request from President Andrew Jackson that he serve as United States attorney general. Not wanting to leave Virginia to become embroiled in national politics, Henry refused the appointment.[4]

After Beverley returned to Missouri, he struggled more often than not. In October 1828 he married his deceased wife's niece Eliza Naylor, who had lived with the Tuckers in their Dardenne homestead. Although twenty years his junior, Eliza was already sick with an advanced case of tuberculosis. Despite a doctor's opinion that marriage would halt her illness, she died just six months after her wedding day. The following year the now-twice widowed Tucker became enthralled by the seventeen-year-old daughter of his friend Thomas Adams Smith. Regarded by all as beautiful and charming, Lucy Ann Smith did not discourage her forty-six-year-old suitor. They wed in April 1830. The marriage briefly rejuvenated Beverley, for neighbors soon saw him "dancing and frolicking" with his new bride at social gatherings. The following year a daughter was born, the first of seven children the couple would have.[5]

Nevertheless, the breakdown of the broader family continued at a rapid pace. Not only did communications with Bermuda cease after St. George's death, but Henry and Beverley wrote few letters to one another during these years. Bonds to other Virginia kin withered as well. Henry lamented in a letter to his nephew St. George Coalter, "I sigh as well as wonder that somehow or other the tie seems to have silently dessolved which bound you to me." Henry explained that he was writing in order "to prevent an entire annihilation of an intercourse between us."[6]

John Randolph's death proved particularly painful, for it revealed the final collapse of family ties. Randolph died in 1833 after a long illness. The year before, he had briefly reconciled with Beverley, who returned to Roanoke to help nurse his sick half brother. The two men apparently put past bitterness behind them and spent many hours during the visit discussing earlier memories as well as the current nullification crisis between South Carolina and the Jackson administration. After Randolph died, however, the Tuckers were shocked by their half brother's will. They learned that they were entirely cut out of Randolph's legacy, and even worse, John repeated in one will (drawn up in 1821) his charge that St. George Tucker had embezzled his patrimony. What had been a closely guarded family dispute was now exposed for all in the state to see. Henry cried to one correspondent about the painful choices now before them. He and Beverley had to admit either that their father was "a fraudulent guardian and plunderer" or that their half brother was "a calumniator and slanderer." In the litigation that followed, the brothers decided to assert before the court that Randolph had been insane when he drafted the will. The legal challenges took years to resolve and, for the Tucker brothers, proved fruitless. Although few Virginians took Randolph's charges against St. George seriously, Henry and Beverley never received any of John's extensive properties.[7]

While the legal challenges to the will plodded on, Henry continued his work on the state's high court, dividing his time between Richmond, where the court sat, and Winchester, where Evelina and the children remained. In 1841 he resigned the post in order to accept the law professorship at the University of Virginia. The appointment proved a satisfying one. Not only did he enjoy his students, but he became reacquainted with his cousin George Tucker, then the school's professor of natural philosophy. As Henry entered his sixties, however, his health began to deteriorate. Because he realized that his memory was also failing, he resigned the professorship in 1844 and retired to Winchester. Four years later one son, St. George Hunter Tucker, wrote an urgent letter to his uncle Beverley begging him to come see Henry, perhaps for the last time. "It seems a pity," the nephew lectured his uncle, "that brothers whose lives have run so smoothly and successfully for sixty years, should not now be together more than you and father are." Beverley soon came to Winchester. On 28 August 1848 he was able to witness his brother's last breath.[8]

Beverley Tucker himself had returned to Virginia during the previous decade. After Randolph's death, he attempted to win a Missouri seat in Congress but lost the race. He then decided to move back to the Old Dominion after learning that William and Mary's Board of Visitors had selected him to fill the law chair once occupied by his father. When his stepmother died three years later, Beverley even moved back into the family mansion.

In addition to preparing his law lectures, Tucker published several novels during the decade. His first novel appeared in 1836, entitled *George Balcombe.* Like Cousin George's *Valley of Shenandoah,* the work examines the fate of the sons of the old elite. The book's narrator, William Napier, belongs to an ancient Virginia clan and has even attended William and Mary before heading to Missouri to seek better opportunities. On the frontier he soon discovers that he has been cheated by a villainous upstart out of an inheritance of his father's tidewater lands. Unlike *Valley of Shenandoah,* however, this story has a happy ending. Napier eventually recovers his Old Dominion properties with the help of an older refined gentleman named George Balcombe. Despite its pleasant conclusion, Tucker's fable explores the social dangers and uncertainties of this new republican age.

Beverley's second novel came out later that same year. Entitled *The Partisan Leader,* it examines the political perils of the 1830s. As "a tale of the future," it predicts that the South one day will secede from the Union because of the growing tyranny of a northern-dominated federal government. Although the book received mixed reviews, it reflected Tucker's growing vision of the South as a separate culture and his belief that the region's future survival depended upon its leaving the United States.[9]

Beverley spent the final years of his life trying to re-create the past he imagined had once existed. In 1850 he attended and addressed the Nashville Convention where he called upon southern delegates to lead the South peacefully out of the United States. Such a move was essential, he claimed, so that the region could protect its agrarian ways, preserve its ancient institutions, and guarantee its prosperity in the years ahead through free trade. He was calling for the creation of the sort of republic he believed his Revolutionary forefathers had wanted.[10]

Beverley also physically lived in the past as much as possible. On a November evening in 1848, a young illustrator named David Hunter Strother visited Tucker's Williamsburg mansion. Upon entering the front door, the artist found himself "steeped in dreamy traditions." As was his habit, Beverley showed his guest the generous open hospitality that had characterized the previous century. An elderly house slave repeatedly filled Strother's silver goblet with the hot whiskey punch Tucker had ordered mixed for the evening. In the candlelight Strother noticed that the old furniture seemed especially "solid, dark and ancient." Family portraits hung everywhere on the walls, with the earlier Tuckers all dressed "in the quaint costumes of past generations." Beverley excitedly regaled Strother and his other guests with tales of old Virginia's glorious past and noted that he was "mortified by the [present] decrepitude of his native State."[11]

Beverley never re-created the gentry-dominated world he longed for. Instead, Virginia only became more individualistic and families more isolated with each passing year. Nonetheless, Tucker's family ties came to his aid at the end of his life. In July 1851 Lucy Tucker set out for Missouri with the couple's five younger children on a long-planned visit to her parents. Late that month Beverley met with his friend William Gilmore Simms in Richmond. Although already ill, Tucker set out with Simms for the spas in the western mountains. Upon reaching Capon Springs, however, Beverley suddenly became "quite sick." Twenty miles west of Winchester, Simms sent word to Henry Tucker's children who still lived in the city. Several of them at once rushed to care for their uncle and even brought him back to the home of one of his nephews. Therefore, on 26 August 1851 Beverley Tucker died not alone but surrounded by loving family members.[12]

Notes

Abbreviations

BCT Coll.	Brown-Coalter-Tucker Collection, Swem Library, College of William and Mary
BP	Bryan Papers, University of Virginia Library, Charlottesville
HSGT	Henry St. George Tucker
JR	John Randolph
LC	Library of Congress, Washington, D.C.
LV	Library of Virginia, Richmond
NBT	Nathaniel Beverley Tucker
SGT	St. George Tucker
VHS	Virginia Historical Society, Richmond
VMHB	*Virginia Magazine of History and Biography*
WMQ	*William and Mary Quarterly*

The vast majority of the Tucker family's letters are in the Tucker-Coleman Papers, Swem Library, College of William and Mary. Unless otherwise indicated, Tucker letters and other manuscript materials are from this collection.

Introduction

1. William Cabell Bruce, *John Randolph of Roanoke, 1773–1833: A Biography Based Largely on New Material,* 2 vols. (New York, 1922), 1:8–9.

2. JR to Josiah Quincy, 1 July 1814, John Randolph Papers, LC.

3. Bruce, *Randolph of Roanoke* 1:8–9.

4. SGT to Alexander Campbell, 7 July 1809.

5. JR to SGT, 14 April 1814.

6. See Gordon S. Wood, *The Radicalism of the American Revolution* (New York, 1992); Richard L. Bushman, *The Refinement of America: Persons, Houses, Cities* (New York, 1992); Robert H. Wiebe, *The Opening of American Society: From the Adoption of the Constitution to the Eve of Disunion* (New York, 1984); Joyce O. Appleby, *Inheriting the Revolution: The First Generation of Americans* (Cambridge, Mass., 2000).

7. See esp. Daniel Jordan, *Political Leadership in Jefferson's Virginia* (Charlottesville, Va.,

1983); William Shade, *Democratizing the Old Dominion: Virginia and the Second Party System, 1824–1861* (Charlottesville, Va., 1998).

8. Among Eugene Genovese's key works regarding the antebellum planter class are *The Political Economy of Slavery: Studies in the Economy and Society of the Slave South* (New York, 1965), *The World the Slaveholders Made: Two Essays in Interpretation* (New York, 1969), esp. pt. 1, and *Roll, Jordan, Roll: The World the Slaves Made* (New York, 1974).

9. See esp. James Oakes, *The Ruling Race: A History of American Slaveholders* (New York, 1982); Robert William Fogel, *Without Consent or Contract: The Rise and Fall of American Slavery* (New York, 1989).

10. See esp. Eugene Genovese, *The Slaveholders' Dilemma: Freedom and Progress in Southern Conservative Thought, 1820–1860* (Columbia, S.C., 1992). See also William W. Freehling, *The Road to Disunion: Secessionists at Bay, 1776–1854* (New York, 1990) and *The Reintegration of American History: Slavery and the Civil War* (New York, 1994).

11. See Elizabeth Fox-Genovese, *Within the Plantation Household: Black and White Women of the Old South* (Chapel Hill, N.C., 1988); Bertram Wyatt-Brown, "The Ideal Typology and Antebellum Southern History: A Testing of a New Hypothesis," *Societas* 5 (1975): 1–29, and *Southern Honor: Ethics and Behavior in the Old South* (New York, 1982).

12. See Daniel Blake Smith, *Inside the Great House: Planter Family Life in Eighteenth Century Society* (Ithaca, N.Y., 1980); Jan Lewis, *The Pursuit of Happiness: Family and Values in Jefferson's Virginia* (Cambridge, Mass., 1983); Jane Turner Censer, *North Carolina Planters and Their Children, 1800–1860* (Baton Rouge, La., 1984); Anya Jabour, *Marriage in the Early Republic: Elizabeth and William Wirt and the Companionate Ideal* (Baltimore, 1998). On the rise of the sentimental nuclear family in Great Britain, see Lawrence Stone, *Family, Sex and Marriage in England, 1500–1800* (New York, 1977); Randolph Trumbach, *The Rise of the Egalitarian Family: Aristocratic Kinship and Domestic Relations in Eighteenth-Century England* (New York, 1978). For this trend in the North's middle class, see Mary P. Ryan, *The Cradle of the Middle Class: The Family in Oneida, New York, 1790–1865* (Cambridge, Mass., 1981). See also Anne Firor Scott, *The Southern Lady: From Pedestal to Politics, 1830–1930* (Chicago, 1970); Catherine Clinton, *The Plantation Mistress: Woman's World in the Old South* (New York, 1982); Suzanne Lebsock, *The Free Women of Petersburg: Status and Culture in a Southern Town, 1784–1860* (New York, 1984); Cynthia A. Kierner, *Beyond the Household: Women's Place in the Early South, 1700–1815* (Ithaca, N.Y., 1998).

On the aims of family scholars, see Tamara K. Hareven, "The History of the Family and the Complexity of Social Change," *American Historical Review* 96 (1991): 95. See also Helena M. Wall, *Fierce Communion: Family and Community in Early America* (Cambridge, Mass., 1990); Carole Shammas, "Anglo-American Household Government in Comparative Perspective," *WMQ*, 3d ser., 52 (1995): 104–44; Steven Mintz and Susan Kellogg, *Domestic Revolutions: A Social History of American Family Life* (New York, 1988); Carl N. Degler, *At Odds: Women and the Family in America from the Revolution to the Present* (New York, 1980); Daniel Blake Smith, "The Study of the Family in Early America: Trends, Problems, and Prospects," *WMQ*, 3d ser., 39 (1982): 3–28; Thomas P. Slaughter, "Family Politics in Revolutionary America," *American Quarterly* 36 (1984): 598–606.

13. The Tuckers have received considerable scholarly attention in the past. On St. George Tucker's early life and legal career, see Charles T. Cullen, *St. George Tucker and Law*

in Virginia, 1772–1804 (Westport, Conn., 1987). Mary Haldane Coleman's *St. George Tucker: Citizen of No Mean City* (Richmond, 1938) is lively but outdated. See also Robert Morton Scott, "St. George Tucker and the Development of American Culture in Early Federal Virginia, 1790–1824" (Ph.D. diss., George Washington Univ., 1991); Christopher Leonard Doyle, "Lord, Master, and Patriot: St. George Tucker and Patriarchy in Republican Virginia, 1772–1851" (Ph.D. diss., Univ. of Connecticut, 1996). See also Robert Brugger's psychological biography of Tucker's youngest son, Nathaniel Beverley Tucker, *Beverley Tucker: Heart over Head in the Old South* (Baltimore, 1978).

For Beverley Tucker's eccentric and brilliant half-brother, John Randolph of Roanoke, see William C. Bruce's 1922 biography; Hugh A. Garland, *The Life of John Randolph of Roanoke* (1850; rept. New York, 1969); Russell Kirk, *John Randolph of Roanoke: A Study in American Politics, with Selected Speeches and Letters* (1964; 4th ed., Indianapolis, 1994); Robert Dawidoff, *The Education of John Randolph* (New York, 1979).

14. The late nineteenth-century German historian Wilhelm Dilthey argued that individuals of a particular generation are integrally linked to one another because of their common experiences. See Julian Marias, "Generations: The Concept," in *International Encyclopedia of the Social Sciences,* ed. David L. Sills (New York, 1968), 6:89.

1. Family Ambitions within the Realm

1. Henry Tucker Jr. to SGT, 3 Dec. 1771.

2. Robert Dennard Tucker, *The Descendants of William Tucker of Throwleigh, Devon* (Spartanburg, S.C., 1991), 31–35; Janet Coleman Kimbrough, *A Brief Outline of the Tucker Family: History and Ancestry of the Branch of Which St. George Tucker of Williamsburg Was a Member* (Williamsburg, Va., 1977), 3. On Daniel Tucker's tenure as Bermuda's governor, see Charles M. Andrews, *The Colonial Period of American History,* 4 vols. (New Haven, 1934), 1:218–21.

3. Tucker, *Descendants of William Tucker,* 17, 48, 167; Beverley Danridge Tucker, *Nathaniel Beverley Tucker: Prophet of the Confederacy, 1784–1851* (Tokyo, Japan, 1979), 2–6.

4. David Hancock, *Citizens of the World: London Merchants and the Integration of the British Atlantic Community, 1735–1785* (New York, 1995), chap. 1, esp. 25–27; Charles Sellers, *The Market Revolution: Jacksonian America* (New York, 1991), 21. See also Neil McKendrick, "The Consumer Revolution of Eighteenth-Century England," in *The Birth of a Consumer Society,* ed. Neil McKendrick et al. (Bloomington, Ind., 1982), 9–34; Paul Langford, *A Polite and Commercial People: England, 1727–1783* (Oxford, 1989); Carole Shammas, *The Pre-Industrial Consumer in England and America* (Oxford, 1990); T. H. Breen, "'Baubles of Britain': The American and Consumer Revolutions of the Eighteenth Century," *Past and Present* 119 (1988): 73–104, and "An Empire of Goods: The Anglicization of Colonial America, 1690–1776," *Journal of British Studies* 25 (1986): 467–99.

5. For Bermuda population estimates, see Terry Tucker, *Bermuda Today and Yesterday, 1503–1973* (London, 1975), 173; Wilfred Brenton Kerr, *Bermuda and the American Revolution* (Princeton, N.J., 1936), 8–9; Lawrence Henry Gipson, *The British Empire before the American Revolution,* 15 vols. (New York, 1936–70), 13:78; Henry C. Wilkinson, *Bermuda in the Old Empire: A History of the Island from the Dissolution of the Somers Island Company until*

the End of the American Revolutionary War, 1684–1784 (London, 1950), 244, 340–42. On Bermuda's trade within the empire, see Ian K. Steele, *The English Atlantic: An Exploration of Communication and Community, 1675–1740* (New York, 1986), 54–56. On smuggling and looting of wrecks at Bermuda, see Gipson, *British Empire before the American Revolution* 13:81, 83.

6. Quoted in *The Complete Poems of Nathaniel Tucker,* ed. Lewis Leary (Delmar, N.Y., 1973), 41.

7. Tucker, *Descendants of William Tucker,* chap. 5; Kerr, *Bermuda and the American Revolution,* 14.

8. Wilkinson, *Bermuda in the Old Empire,* 294. On the lack of records of eighteenth-century businessmen, see Hancock, *Citizens of the World,* 9.

9. On the emergence of the modern family, see esp. Lewis, *Pursuit of Happiness;* Smith, *Inside the Great House;* Censer, *North Carolina Planters and Their Children.*

10. Michael Zuckerman, "William Byrd's Family," *Perspectives in American History* 12 (1979): 255–311; Fox-Genovese, *Within the Plantation House;* Wyatt-Brown, "Ideal Typology and Antebellum Southern History" and *Southern Honor.* Philip Greven argues that issues of class and religion must be kept in mind when analyzing pre–Civil War families (*The Protestant Temperament: Patterns of Child-Rearing, Religious Experience, and the Self in Early America* [New York, 1977]).

11. Wood, *Radicalism of the American Revolution,* 18–19; Wiebe, *Opening of American Society,* 11.

12. Michal J. Rozbicki, *The Complete Colonial Gentleman: Cultural Legitimacy in Plantation America* (Charlottesville, Va., 1995), 120. See also Gordon J. Schochet, *The Authoritarian Family and Political Attitudes in Seventeenth-Century England* (New York, 1975); Kathleen Brown, *Good Wives, Nasty Wenches and Anxious Patriarchs* (Chapel Hill, N.C., 1996), pt. 3.

13. See Lewis, *Pursuit of Happiness,* chap. 1, and "Domestic Tranquillity and the Management of Emotion among the Gentry of Pre-Revolutionary Virginia," *WMQ,* 3d ser., 39 (1982): 135–49.

14. Thomas Tudor Tucker to SGT, 14 Aug. 1771, 10 July 1779, Elizabeth Tucker to SGT, 12 Aug. 1770.

15. For example, see Henry Tucker Jr. to SGT, 16 April 1779.

16. SGT's Journal of His Voyage to Bermuda, entry of 16 Aug. 1773.

17. Mintz and Kellogg, *Domestic Revolutions,* 38–39. On unhealthiness, see Lois Green Carr et al., *Robert Cole's World: Agriculture and Social in Early America* (Chapel Hill, N.C., 1991); Lois Green Carr and Lorena S. Walsh, "The Planter's Wife: The Experience of White Women in Seventeenth-Century Maryland," *WMQ,* 3d ser., 34 (1977): 542–71; Darrett and Anita Rutman, *A Place in Time: Middlesex County, Virginia, 1650–1750* (New York, 1984); Jack P. Greene, *Pursuits of Happiness: The Social Development of Early Modern British Colonies and the Formation of American Culture* (Chapel Hill, N.C., 1988), 15. See Smith, *Inside the Great House,* 176–77, on lengthening life spans and multigenerational households. The Colonel's mother-in-law, "Grandmother Butterfield," lived with the family at The Grove until her death in 1772.

18. On naming patterns, see Tucker, *Descendants of William Tucker,* 191, 255; see also Mary Beth Norton, *Liberty's Daughters: The Revolutionary Experience of American Women,*

1750–1800 (Boston, 1980), 85–86; Mintz and Kellogg, *Domestic Revolutions,* 39; Kulikoff, *Tobacco and Slaves,* 241–42.

19. Henry Hinson to SGT, 31 July 1772, Nathaniel Tucker to SGT, 1 Aug. 1774, Anne Tucker to SGT, 3 Aug. 1772; see also Henry Tucker of Somerset to SGT, 9 Dec. 1771, Donald Campbell to SGT, 11 Oct. 1774.

20. Smith, *Inside the Great House,* 141–43; Wall, *Fierce Communion,* 133–34; Mintz and Kellogg, *Domestic Revolutions,* 45–46; Jay Fliegelman, *Prodigals and Pilgrims: The American Revolution against Patriarchal Authority, 1750–1800* (Cambridge, Mass., 1990), chaps. 5 and 6. On the marriage decision as one affecting the entire family, see Edmund Morgan, *Virginians at Home: Family Life in the Eighteenth Century* (Williamsburg, Va., 1952), 29.

21. Tucker, *Descendants of William Tucker,* 139–40; Kerr, *Bermuda and the American Revolution,* 16–17, 32–33; Wilkinson, *Bermuda in the Old Empire,* 368–69, 361; George James Bruere to SGT, 15 Oct. 1773.

22. Wilkinson, *Bermuda in the Old Empire,* 340–42; Kerr, *Bermuda and the American Revolution,* 8–9.

23. Reid quoted in Rozbicki, *Complete Colonial Gentleman,* 100.

24. Hancock, *Citizens of the World,* 280, 281 (Josiah Tucker quote).

25. Bushman, *Refinement of America,* xiv. See also David Shields, *Civil Tongues and Polite Letters in British America* (Chapel Hill, N.C., 1997).

26. Henry Tucker Sr. to SGT, 1 Aug. 1772; Daniel Calhoun, *The Intelligence of a People* (Princeton, N.J., 1973), 154–55; Bushman, *Refinement of America,* 44; Wood, *Radicalism of the American Revolution,* 149–51.

27. Coleman, *St. George Tucker,* 5–9.

28. Lewis Leary, *The Literary Career of Nathaniel Tucker, 1750–1807* (Durham, N.C., 1951), 9.

29. Thomas Tudor Tucker to SGT, 21 April, 27 Nov. 1773, SGT's Journal of His Voyage to Bermuda, 6 Aug. 1773. For the Tuckers' characterizations of God, see Thomas's letter and Elizabeth Tucker to SGT, 5 Jan. 1773.

30. Nathaniel Tucker quoted in Leary, *Literary Career of Nathaniel Tucker,* 56; Anne Butterfield Tucker to SGT, [Dec. 1771], [March], 3 Aug. 1772.

31. Melvin Yazawa, *From Colonies to Commonwealth: Familial Ideology and the Beginnings of the American Republic* (Baltimore, 1985), 38; Wood, *Radicalism of the American Revolution,* 18–19, 57–58, 64–65, 74–78, 92; Bushman, *Refinement of America,* chap. 1.

32. Henry Tucker Sr. to SGT, [1770?], 1 Aug. 1772, 29 April 1773, 30 Nov. 1771.

33. Nathaniel's *The Bermudian,* quoted in Leary, *Literary Career of Nathaniel Tucker,* 9; SGT's Journal of His Voyage to Bermuda, 10 Aug. 1773.

34. The "how-to" book is Robert Dodsley, *The Preceptor* (London, 1775), quoted in Bruce Redford, *The Converse of the Pen: Acts of Intimacy in the Eighteenth-Century Familiar Letter* (Chicago, 1986), 4. See also Bushman, *Refinement of America,* 90–92; Andrew Burstein, *The Inner Jefferson: Portrait of a Grieving Optimist* (Charlottesville, Va., 1995), chap. 4.

35. Bushman, *Refinement of America,* 92.

36. Wilkinson, *Bermuda in the Old Empire,* 294–95. On British social attitudes about the learned professions, see Wood, *Radicalism of the American Revolution,* 22.

37. Elizabeth Tucker to SGT, 12 Aug. 1770. See also Nathaniel Tucker to SGT, Sept. 1773.

38. Thomas Tudor Tucker to SGT, 4 Feb. 1773.

39. Leary, *Literary Career of Nathaniel Tucker,* 10; Greene, *Pursuits of Happiness,* 50, 147; see also M. Eugene Sirmans, *Colonial South Carolina, 1663–1763* (Chapel Hill, N.C., 1966).

40. Leary, *Literary Career of Nathaniel Tucker,* 11–13; Thomas Tudor Tucker to SGT, 14 Aug. 1771.

41. Letters from Williams and Tucker appeared in the *South Carolina Gazette and Country Journal* on 3 and 9 Aug. 1773, respectively. For the near duel and trial, see Leary, *Literary Career of Nathaniel Tucker,* 20–29. For reputation and dueling, see Wood, *Radicalism of the American Revolution,* 40–41.

42. Henry Tucker Sr. to SGT, 6 Dec. 1773; Leary, *Literary Career of Nathaniel Tucker,* 28, 48; Thomas Tudor Tucker to SGT, 20 May 1774.

43. Thomas Tudor Tucker to SGT, 10 Jan. 1768; Cullen, *Tucker and Law in Virginia,* 5–6; John M. Murrin, "The Legal Transformation: The Bench and Bar of Eighteenth-Century Massachusetts," in *Colonial America: Essays in Politics and Social Development,* ed. Stanley Katz and John M. Murrin (New York, 1983), 555.

44. Elizabeth Tucker to SGT, [1770?], 19 Aug. 1770; Cullen, *Tucker and Law in Virginia,* 5–6; Scott, "St. George Tucker and the Development of American Culture," 26.

45. See Thomas Tudor Tucker to SGT, 22 June 1771.

46. For St. George's first months on the continent, see Cullen, *Tucker and Law in Virginia,* chap. 1; Coleman, *St. George Tucker,* 13–18. On letters of introduction, see Wood, *Radicalism of the American Revolution,* 60.

47. See Rhys Isaac, *The Transformation of Virginia, 1740–1790* (Chapel Hill, N.C., 1982), pt. 1; Allan Kulikoff, *Tobacco and Slaves: The Development of Southern Cultures in the Chesapeake, 1680–1800* (Chapel Hill, N.C., 1986), esp. chap. 4; T. H. Breen, *Tobacco Culture: The Mentality of the Great Tidewater Planters on the Eve of Revolution* (Princeton, N.J., 1985), esp. chap. 2; Rozbicki, *Complete Colonial Gentleman,* chaps. 2–4; Greene, *Pursuits of Happiness,* chap. 4. On the cultural importance of the great homes in America, see Bushman, *Refinement in America,* chap. 4. On Norfolk, see Thomas C. Parramore et al., *Norfolk: The First Four Centuries* (Charlottesville, Va., 1994), chaps. 6–7; Thomas Jefferson Wertenbaker, *Norfolk: Historic Southern Port,* 2d ed. (Durham, N.C., 1962).

48. Henry Tucker Sr. to SGT, 10 April 1772; Coleman, *St. George Tucker,* 21; Cullen, *Tucker and Law in Virginia,* 8; Frank Dewey, *Thomas Jefferson, Lawyer* (Charlottesville, Va., 1986), 58–72. On the social attributes of erudition, see Isaac, *Transformation of Virginia,* 22–23.

49. Henry Tucker Sr. to SGT, Jan. 1772, Henry Tucker Jr. to SGT, 30 July 1772.

50. Henry Tucker Sr. to SGT, 10 April, 1 Aug. 1772, 5 Jan. 1773, Donald Campbell to SGT, 3 April 1772.

51. See Jane Carson, *James Innes and His Brothers of the F.H.C.* (Williamsburg, Va., 1965); Shields, *Civil Tongues and Polite Letters,* chap. 6; Emory G. Evans, *Thomas Nelson of Yorktown: Revolutionary Virginian* (Williamsburg, Va., 1975); entries on the Page family, Land Tax Records and Personal Property Tax Records, Gloucester County, 1782, LV.

52. Henry Tucker Sr. to SGT, 8, 29 April 1773, Henry Tucker Jr. to SGT, 23 April 1773.

53. Cullen, *Tucker and Law in Virginia,* 9; Scott, "St. George Tucker and the Development of American Culture," 36–38.

54. Thomas Nelson to Henry Tucker Sr., 21 Jan. 1774; Henry Tucker Sr. to SGT, 10 April 1774; Cullen, *Tucker and Law in Virginia,* 12–13.

55. On Tucker's planned purchases, see Henry Tucker Sr. to SGT, 19 April 1774; on the importance of appearances, see Isaac, *Transformation of Virginia,* 132; on the importance of fine horses, see Rozbicki, *Complete Colonial Gentleman,* 162–63.

56. Henry Tucker Sr. to SGT, 10 April 1774; Cullen, *Tucker and Law in Virginia,* 14.

57. Carson, *Innes and the F.H.C.,* 23. Tucker may have gone to New York to examine some property claims of his Bermudian kin; see Henry Tucker Sr. to SGT, 31 Jan. 1774.

58. Henry Tucker of Somerset to SGT, 21 March 1774.

59. Nathaniel Tucker to SGT, 23 June 1774.

60. John E. Selby, *The Revolution in Virginia, 1775–1783* (Williamsburg, Va., 1988), 8–9.

61. Henry Tucker Sr. to SGT, 31 July 1774. For pro-American views expressed by other family members, see Henry Tucker of Somerset to SGT, 28 Oct. 1774, Nathaniel Tucker to SGT, 1 Aug. 1774, Henry Tucker Jr. to SGT, 31 Dec. 1775, SGT to John Page, 31 March 1776. On the generally pro-American stance of Bermudians, see Kerr, *Bermuda and the American Revolution.*

62. Henry Tucker Sr. to SGT, 6 March 1775; see also Henry Tucker Sr. to SGT, 26 March, 18 May 1775.

63. Kerr, *Bermuda and the American Revolution,* 42–47; Wilkinson, *Bermuda in the Old Empire,* 379–81. For the growing privations on Bermuda in 1775, see Henry Tucker Sr. to SGT, 18, 29 May 1775. For the midnight raid of 14 Aug. 1775 on the island's powder magazine, see Tucker, *Descendants of William Tucker,* 192–94; Kerr, *Bermuda and the American Revolution,* 47–50.

64. Memoirs of Henry St. George Tucker, quoted in Wilkinson, *Bermuda in the Old Empire,* 380–81; Henry Tucker Sr. to SGT, 26 March 1775; see also Robert Innes to SGT, 8 June 1775.

65. Thomas Tudor Tucker to SGT, 14 June 1775; Cullen, *Tucker and Law in Virginia,* 18; certificate to practice law signed by Governor Bruere, 21 July 1775, copy in the Tucker-Coleman Papers.

66. John Page to SGT, 28 Sept. 1776, Thomas Tudor Tucker to SGT, 8 Dec. 1776.

67. Henry Tucker Jr. to SGT, 13, 18 June 1776, Thomas Tudor Tucker to SGT, 8 Dec. 1776.

68. Hancock, *Citizens of the World,* 104–14; John J. McCusker and Russell R. Menard, *The Economy of British America* (Chapel Hill, N.C., 1985), chap. 4. On the Caribbean, see Sheridan, *Sugar and Slavery,* 389–486. On Henry Tucker of Somerset and the Colonel, see Kerr, *Bermuda and the American Revolution,* 17. On the rivalry between the two firms, see Wilkinson, *Bermuda in the Old Empire,* 423–24. Henry of Somerset's partners in Jennings, Tucker & Company were all family members, among them his brother, John Tucker, and

two of his cousins, Richard and John Jennings, who were considered the wealthiest citizens on the island.

69. Thomas Tudor Tucker to SGT, 6 Aug. 1777, Henry Tucker Sr. to SGT, 5 Nov. 1777, SGT to Maurice Simmons, 6 Feb. 1778, to William Sargeant, 26 April 1778, Anne Butterfield Tucker to SGT, 2 March 1780, St. George Tucker Jr. to SGT, 14 Aug. 1780, bill of lading for the *Porgy*, 23 Dec. 1780; Robert Colin McLean, *George Tucker: Moral Philosopher and Man of Letters* (Chapel Hill, N.C., 1961), 3; Tucker, *Descendants of William Tucker*, 146.

70. SGT to John Page, 24 Oct. 1776, photocopy of the original at the Morristown National Park Library; see also SGT to [John Page], 22 Oct. 1776, St. George Tucker Papers, LC.

71. SGT to Edward and John Black, 16 Nov. 1776, to the Owners of the *Dispatch*, 10 Dec. 1776, Nathaniel Nelson to SGT, 16 Jan. 1777, SGT to Messrs. Tucker and Jennings, 24 March 1777; Cullen, *Tucker and Law in Virginia*, 19.

72. SGT to John Page, 24 Oct. 1776; see also Archibald Campbell to SGT, 11 Aug. 1775, Walker Maury to SGT, 24 Aug. 1775.

73. John Page to SGT, 28 Feb. 1777. See also John Page to SGT, 2 Nov. 1777, 22 Oct. 1779, SGT to John Page, 19 April 1779, William Gooseley to SGT, 4 Sept. 1779.

74. Order of [the Virginia] Council, 18 Feb. 1777; Cullen, *Tucker and Law in Virginia*, 19-20; SGT to Messrs. Tucker and Jennings, 24 March 1777, Henry Tucker Sr. to SGT, 29 June 1777; Tucker, *Descendants of William Tucker*, 256; Henry St. George Tucker, "Patrick Henry and St. George Tucker," Henry Family Papers, VHS.

75. Henry Tucker Sr. to SGT, 5 Nov. 1777, Thomas Tudor Tucker to SGT, 20 Nov. 1777, Henry Tucker, in the name of Henry Tucker & Son and Jennings, Tucker & Company, to SGT, 14, 15 Dec. 1777, Daniel Hylton to SGT, 3 Nov. 1777, SGT to Maurice Simmons, 6 Feb. 1778, S. and J. H. Delap to SGT, 15 Aug. 1778, John Brickwood to SGT, 4 Feb. 1779; Cullen, *Tucker and Law in Virginia*, 20-21. See also SGT to S. and J. H. Delap, 26 April 1778, to Daniel Jennings, 10 May 1780, Henry Tucker Sr. to SGT, 4 Sept. 1778. On the importance of salt, see Jean B. Lee, *The Price of Nationhood: The American Revolution in Charles County* (New York, 1994), 150.

76. Jaquelin Ambler to SGT, 25 Jan. 1778. For Ambler, see Norman Risjord, *Chesapeake Politics, 1781-1800* (New York, 1978), 135.

77. SGT to Maurice Simmons, 15 Jan. 1778, Thomas Tudor Tucker to SGT, 19 April 1778; see also Thomas Tudor Tucker to SGT, 20 Nov. 1777, 8 April 1778.

78. Henry Tucker Sr. to SGT, 29 June 1777, Blakes & Sanyer to SGT, 30 June 1777. See also Thomas Tudor Tucker to SGT, 19 April 1778, Will and John Cowper to Henry Tucker Sr., 7 Dec. 1778.

79. SGT to Pierre Texier, 31 July 1778, Pierre Texier to SGT, 12 May 1779, Henry Tucker Sr. to SGT, 24 Feb. 1779. For the *Sally Van*, see John Peyton to SGT, 27 July 1778, SGT to John Strettel, 25 March 1779, Henry Tucker Sr. to SGT, 1 Feb. 1785.

80. Theodorick Bland Jr. to SGT, 21 Sept. 1779, Thomas Tudor Tucker to SGT, 13 Nov. [Dec.?] 1779, Henry Tucker of Somerset to SGT, 27 Nov. 1779, Benjamin Harrison to SGT, 29 Aug. 1779, Henry Tucker Sr. to SGT, 27 Dec. 1779, 2 Aug. 1783, Henry Tucker Jr. to SGT, 17 Dec. 1783.

81. Henry Tucker Sr. to SGT, 23 Aug. 1778, 15 May 1779, Henry Tucker Jr. to SGT, 13 April 1780.

82. Jaquelin Ambler to SGT, 25 Jan. 1778. For the family's endless problems with insurance on their smuggling vessels, see Edward and John Blake to SGT, 29 Jan. 1777, Thomas Tudor Tucker to SGT, 6 Aug. 1777, Henry Tucker Sr. to SGT, 29 Dec. 1779, 21 Aug. 1784, Henry Armistead to SGT, 20 May 1784, John Pringle to SGT, 6 Aug. 1790.

83. Henry Tucker Jr. to SGT, 4 Feb., 3 March 1780, St. George Tucker Jr. to SGT, 24 Jan. 1781.

84. Henry Tucker Jr. to SGT, 4 Feb., 3 March 1780, Henry Tucker of Somerset to SGT, 9 Aug. 1781. For Henry Tucker Sr.'s mission to London, see Henry Tucker Sr. to SGT, 3 June 1779.

2. Revolutionary Times: War, Marriage, Opportunity

1. SGT to Robert Walsh, 2 Oct. 1812.

2. Carl Bridenbaugh, *Myths and Realities: Societies of the Colonial South* (Baton Rouge, La., 1952), 11; Elizabeth Tucker to SGT, 29 Jan. 1774. See also Rozbicki, *Complete Colonial Gentleman*, 36.

3. Charles Campbell, ed., *The Bland Papers: Being a Selection from the Manuscripts of Colonel Theodorick Bland, Jr. of Prince George County, Virginia, to Which Are Prefixed an Introduction and a Memoir of Colonel Bland*, 2 vols. (Petersburg, Va., 1840), 1:xiv-xv; Dawidoff, *Education of John Randolph*, 68; an indenture confirming Frances Tucker's ownership of slaves brought with her in her marriage, 1 June 1784.

4. Coleman, *St. George Tucker*, 40.

5. William Ewart Stokes, "Randolph of Roanoke: A Virginia Portrait—the Early Career of John Randolph, 1773–1805" (Ph.D. diss., Univ. of Virginia, 1955), 16–18; Bruce, *Randolph of Roanoke* 1:18.

6. Stokes, "Randolph of Roanoke," 14. On the common southern practice of co-signing notes for friends and family, see Kenneth S. Greenberg, *Honor and Slavery: Lies . . . in the Old South* (Princeton, N.J., 1996), 78.

7. Nathaniel Tucker to SGT, 21 Nov. 1772, Esther Evans Tucker to SGT, 7 Sept. 1774; see also Nathaniel Tucker to SGT, 23 May 1774. For Nathaniel's unsuccessful pursuit of an unnamed wealthy Charleston belle, see Nathaniel Tucker, "A Bold Stroke for a Wife," 1774.

8. SGT to Frances Bland Randolph, [1778?]. On the rising importance of affection, intimacy, and love in elite southern marriages, see Smith, *Inside the Great House;* Jabour, *Marriage in the Early Republic,* 1–22; Kierner, *Beyond the Household,* 28–30; Degler, *At Odds,* chap. 1; Linda K. Kerber et al., "Beyond Roles, beyond Spheres: Thinking about Gender in the Early Republic," *WMQ,* 3d ser., 46 (1989): 565–85; Lewis, *Pursuit of Happiness,* chap. 5, and "The Republican Wife: Virtue and Seduction in the Early Republic," *WMQ,* 3d ser., 44 (1987): 689–721.

9. SGT to Frances Randolph, 15 Jan. 1778; Jabour, *Marriage in the Early Republic,* 19–20; Kierner, *Beyond the Household,* 23–24; Lebsock, *Free Women of Petersburg,* chap. 2; Joan R. Gundersen and Gwen Victor Gampel, "Married Women's Legal Status in Eighteenth-Century New York and Virginia," *WMQ,* 3d ser., 39 (1982): 114–34.

10. Frances Bland Randolph to SGT, 10 July 1778. See also Claudia Lamm Wood, "'With Unalterable Tenderness': The Courtship and Marriage of St. George Tucker and Frances Randolph Tucker" (M.A. thesis, College of William and Mary, 1988). On courtship, see Smith, *Inside the Great House,* 132−38; Jabour, *Marriage in the Early Republic,* 13; Censer, *North Carolina Planters,* 65−68, 78−95; Clinton, *Plantation Mistress,* chap. 4; Lorena S. Walsh, "The Experiences and Status of Women in the Chesapeake, 1750−1775," in *The Web of Southern Social Relations: Women, Family, and Education,* ed. Walter J. Fraser Jr., R. Frank Saunders Jr., and Jon L. Wakelyn (Athens, Ga., 1985), 3−4, 9.

11. Frances Bland Tucker to SGT, 3 May 1779, SGT to Frances Bland Tucker, 23 Sept. 1781. For other examples of genuinely passionate love, see John Page to SGT, 12 June 1787; Smith, *Inside the Great House,* 156.

12. Brugger, *Beverley Tucker,* 5; Charles Washington Coleman Jr., "The Southern Campaign, 1781, from Guilford Court House to the Siege of York," *Magazine of American History* 7 (1881): 37. For Matoax, see JR to Elizabeth Coalter Bryan, 1 Nov. 1828, 22 Dec. 1830, BP; Land Tax Records and Personal Property Tax Records, Chesterfield County, 1786, LV.

13. SGT to Theodorick Bland Jr., [1780 or 1781], Bland Papers, VHS.

14. Brent Tarter, ed., *Revolutionary Virginia: The Road to Independence* (Charlottesville, Va., 1983), vol. 7, pt. 2, 449; John Page to SGT, 28 Sept. 1776.

15. *Liberty* was first published in 1788 and is reprinted in Scott, "Tucker and the Development of American Culture," 220−28; see also Brugger, *Beverley Tucker,* 8.

16. Selby, *Revolution in Virginia,* 204−8; SGT to Theodorick Bland Jr., 6 June 1779, *Bland Papers* 2:11.

17. John Banister to Theodorick Bland Jr., 24 Oct. 1780, *Bland Papers* 2:38; Beverley Randolph to SGT, 26 Oct. 1780; Selby, *Revolution in Virginia,* 216−17; SGT almanac, quoted in Coleman, *St. George Tucker,* 52.

18. SGT to Theodorick Bland Jr., 21 Jan. 1781, *Bland Papers* 2:55. For Virginia's "rebellious" slave population, see Sylvia R. Frey, *Water from the Rock: Black Resistance in a Revolutionary Age* (Princeton, N.J., 1990), 167.

19. SGT and Frances Bland Tucker to Theodorick Bland Jr., 7 April 1781, St. George Tucker Papers, VHS; John Hughes to SGT, 23 Jan 1826 (see SGT's endorsement of this letter); Selby, *Revolution in Virginia,* 221−24.

20. SGT to Frances Bland Tucker, 11 Feb. 1781, Frances Bland Tucker to SGT, 14 July 1781; Coleman, *St. George Tucker,* 65−67; SGT to Theodorick Bland Jr., 21 Sept. 1781, John Banister to Theodorick Bland Jr., 16 May, 12 July 1781, *Bland Papers* 2:75, 69−70, 73−74; James Kirby Martin, ed., *Ordinary Courage: The Revolutionary War Adventures of Joseph Plumb Martin* (St. James, N.Y., 1993), 142.

21. SGT to Frances Bland Tucker, 5, 15 Sept. 1781.

22. Thomas Nelson Jr. to SGT, 16 Sept. 1781; SGT to Theodorick Bland Jr., 20 July 1779, Charles Campbell Papers, Perkins Library, Duke Univ. On the impact of the specie shortage, see Risjord, *Chesapeake Politics,* 96−97.

23. SGT to Frances Bland Tucker, 22, 23 Sept. 1781; Selby, *Revolution in Virginia,* 298−99. See also Lee, *Price of Revolution,* 183−84.

24. Quoted in Coleman, *St. George Tucker,* 78.

25. Shade, *Democratizing the Old Dominion,* 17–18; Jackson T. Main, "The One Hundred," *WMQ,* 3d ser., 11 (1954): 354–84 (quote on 364n); resolution of the House of Delegates, 30 Nov. 1781, in *Calendar of Virginia State Papers and Other Manuscripts,* ed. H. W. Flournoy, 10 vols. (Richmond, 1892), 3:41; Benjamin Harrison to SGT, 1 Dec. 1781, J. McClurg to SGT, 25 Dec. 1781, William Pierce Jr. to SGT, 28 Dec. 1781.

26. On patriarchalism as an ideological construct and as it was really practiced, see Jabour, *Marriage in the Early Republic,* 30–31; Walsh, "Experiences and Status of Women in the Chesapeake," 4. For the Revolution's reshaping of the position of wife and mother, see Jabour, *Marriage in the Early Republic;* Linda Kerber, *Women of the Republic: Intellect and Ideology in Revolutionary America* (New York, 1980); Norton, *Liberty's Daughters.* For the Revolution's strengthening of the position of husband, see Kulikoff, *Tobacco and Slaves,* chap. 5; Joan Hoff Wilson, "The Illusion of Change: Women and the American Revolution," in *Our American Sisters: Women in American Life and Thought,* ed. Jean E. Friedman and William G. Shade (Lexington, Mass., 1982), 117–36.

27. Frances Bland Tucker to SGT, 14 Oct., 24 March 1781. See also Theodorick Bland Jr. to SGT, 11 May 1781. For the insecurities felt by Theodorick's wife, Martha Bland, see Martha Bland to Frances Bland Tucker, 30 March 1781.

28. Martha Bland to Frances Bland Tucker, 25 Jan. 1783.

29. Frances Bland Tucker to SGT, 7 Sept. 1781. See also Elizabeth Tucker to SGT, 12 Aug. 1770, for her awareness of her father's business affairs and his difficulties.

30. Joseph F. Kett, *Rites of Passage: Adolescence in America, 1790 to the Present* (New York, 1977), 23; SGT to John Coalter, 2 Aug. 1797.

31. Martha Bland to SGT, 17 March 1786; SGT to Theodorick Bland Jr., 20 July 1779, Charles Campbell Papers, Duke Univ. See also Sally G. McMillen, *Motherhood in the Old South: Pregnancy, Childbirth, and Infant Rearing* (Baton Rouge, La., 1990); Jan Lewis and Kenneth A. Lockridge, "'Sally Has Been Sick': Pregnancy and Family Limitation among Virginia Gentry Women, 1780–1830," *Journal of Social History* 22 (1988): 6; Smith, *Inside the Great House,* 28.

32. Dawidoff, *Education of John Randolph,* 87–88; Beverley Randolph to SGT, 20 June 1778, SGT to Frances Bland Tucker, 6 May 1779.

33. Land Tax Records, Cumberland County, 1782, 1791, Dinwiddie County, 1782, LV; Beverley Randolph to SGT, 18 June 1783, 6 Dec. 1784, James Monroe and Samuel Hardy to SGT, 7 Aug. 1783, SGT to Robert Turnbull, 3 Feb. 1784, Daybook containing accounts of work done for SGT by a blacksmith of Blandford,, 2 May 1785–9 Sept. 1789, Unnumbered Notebooks, no. 6, Guilford Dudley to SGT, 28 March 1786, John Whitlock to Christopher McConnio, 20 Dec. 1789.

34. Quoted in Dawidoff, *Education of John Randolph,* 93–94. For the piety of John Coalter's mother, see "Sketch of John Coalter in His Own Writing" (transcript), John Coalter Papers, VHS.

35. Robert Andrews to SGT, 14 Oct. 1778; see also Rev. James Madison to SGT, 22 Jan. 1779, William Pierce Jr. to SGT, 6 Feb., 10 July 1782.

36. SGT to Frances Bland Tucker, 22 July 1778; Bruce, *Randolph of Roanoke* 1:51. See

also JR to SGT, 25 March 1795, 12 Jan. 1796, Randolph-Macon Woman's College; Richard Randolph to Frances Bland Tucker, 15 July, 28 Oct. 1787; Garland, *Life of Randolph* 1:61−62; Dawidoff, *Education of John Randolph,* 311n.

37. Frances Bland Tucker to SGT, 7 July 1781, and SGT's Journal and Result of the Proceedings in New York, entry of 5 July 1786. See also Frances Bland Tucker to SGT, [April 1787]. For affection between the new siblings, see JR to SGT, 10 July 1781.

38. Norton, *Liberty's Daughters,* 92.

39. Frances Bland Tucker to SGT, [April 1787], Henry Tucker Jr. to SGT, 18 Feb. 1780; SGT to Theodorick Randolph and JR, 11 April 1787, BP.

40. Frances Bland Tucker to SGT, 4 June 1781, SGT to Frances Bland Tucker, 28 June, 11 July, 27 Sept. 1781.

41. Richard Randolph to Frances Bland Tucker, 29 June 1786, to John Banister, 18 Aug. 1786, SGT to Frances Bland Tucker, 29 June 1786.

42. Richard Randolph to Frances Bland Tucker, 4 Oct. 1786, JR to Frances Bland Tucker, 20 June 1786. See also Richard's letter of 18 Aug. 1786.

43. SGT to Frances Bland Tucker, 29 June 1786; Bettina Manzo, "A Virginian in New York: The Diary of St. George Tucker, July−August, 1786," *New York History* 67 (1986): 157. For the prestige of Princeton graduates among Virginians, see Philip Fithian to John Peck, 12 Aug. 1774, in *Journal and Letters of Philip Vickers Fithian, 1773−1774,* ed. Hunter Dickinson Farish (Williamsburg, Va., 1943), 212.

44. Richard Randolph to Frances Bland Tucker, 28 Oct. 1787. For a different interpretation of this letter, see Smith, *Inside the Great House,* 103−4.

45. Rev. James Madison to SGT, 18 June 1778, SGT to David Ross, 29 April 1782, to Frances Bland Tucker, [Nov. 1787?]. See also James Hunter to Theodorick Bland Jr., 20 Sept. 1782, Bland Papers, VHS. For the stereotypes of merchants, see Rozbicki, *Complete Colonial Gentleman,* 64−67, 186−87; Breen, *Tobacco Culture,* chap. 2.

46. May, *Enlightenment in America,* 84. See also Hans C. von Baeyer, "The Universe according to St. George Tucker," *Eighteenth Century Life* 6:1 (1980): 67−79.

47. Weibe, *Opening of American Society,* 14.

48. William Pierce Jr. to SGT, 6 Feb. 1782.

49. Quoted in Coleman, *St. George Tucker,* 46−47. On the importance of versification for polite individuals, see Shields, *Civil Tongues and Polite Letters,* chap. 2.

50. Thomas Tudor Tucker to SGT, 21 April 1785; Personal Property Tax Records, Chesterfield County, 1786, LV; Evans, *Thomas Nelson of Yorktown,* 22−23. On the importance of racing, see Rozbicki, *Complete Colonial Gentleman,* 162−63; Bridenbaugh, *Myth and Realities,* 22; Isaac, *Transformation of Virginia,* 98−101, 118−19.

51. Dudley Digges to SGT, 15 Jan. 1783, Archibald Cary to SGT, 5 March 1785, Edmund Randolph to SGT, 11 June 1786; Cullen, *Tucker and Law in Virginia,* 47.

52. Frances Bland Tucker to SGT, 4 June 1781. On the role hospitality played, see Rozbicki, *Complete Colonial Gentleman,* 159−60; Isaac, *Transformation of Virginia,* 70−79; on its growing restriction, see ibid., 302−3.

53. Frances Bland Tucker to SGT, [April 1787]; see also Frances Bland Tucker to SGT, 9 Oct. 1787, SGT to Frances Bland Tucker, 6 April, 3 Oct. 1787.

54. Neill Buchanan wrote these words in the days following Frances Tucker's death in

January 1788. They were conveyed to St. George Tucker by Buchanan's widow (Mary Buchanan to SGT, May 1794).

55. Quoted in John Randolph Tucker, "The Judges Tucker of the Courts of Appeals in Virginia," *Virginia Law Register* 1 (1896): 797.

56. SGT to Frances Bland Tucker, 6 May 1779, 28 May 1786. On the importance of furnishings, see Bushman, *Refinement of America,* chap. 4, esp. pp. 118–22.

57. Overseer Phil Halcombe's report to St. George Tucker about the crop's production on Bizarre in Halcombe to SGT, 14 June 1785; Frances Tucker quoted in Smith, *Inside the Great House,* 161–62. See Lewis, *Pursuit of Happiness,* 110–11, for the Virginia gentry's longing for "independence."

58. Frances Bolling Bland to Frances Bland Randolph, [1770 or 1771]. On the household duties of women, see Brown, *Good Wives, Nasty Wenches, and Anxious Patriarchs,* 83–88; Gloria Main, *Tobacco Colony,* 167–204; Carr, Menard, and Walsh, *Robert Cole's World,* 51–52, 71–75, 90–117; Carr and Walsh, "Planter's Wife."

59. Account Book of Frances Bland Randolph, 1775–78.

60. Solomon Wilson to SGT, 10 Feb. 1780, Henry Skipwith to SGT, [Aug. 1782], Edward Pegram Jr. to SGT, 21 Feb. 1783, Duncan Rose to SGT, 2 Jan. 1785, John Banister to SGT, 10 July 1787, SGT to Frances Bland Tucker, 3 April 1786, 14 Sept. 1780, Frances Bland Tucker to SGT, 19 July 1781; see also Capt. William Munay to SGT, 20 Jan. 1779.

61. Frances Bland Tucker to SGT, [April], 4 April 1787, to Duncan Rose, 7 April 1787, to Theodorick Bland Jr., 4 June 1781.

62. Phil Halcombe to SGT, 14 June 1785, to Frances Bland Tucker, 21 April 1787, Claiborne Barksdale to Frances Bland Tucker, 10 Sept. 1787, John Banister to Frances Bland Tucker, 29 April 1784, 30 Aug. 1787, Frances Bland Tucker to SGT, 18 April 1787, to John Banister, 12 Nov. 1787, to [?], 14 Nov. 1787.

63. Lewis, *Pursuit of Happiness,* 149–50; see also Norton, *Liberties Daughters,* 7, 26–27; Smith, *Inside the Great House,* 80–81, 237–38, 292.

64. Richard Randolph to Frances Bland Tucker, 25 June 1787. For the "endless work" of running a plantation, see Bridenbaugh, *Myth and Realities,* 17. See also Kulikoff, *Tobacco and Slaves,* 183.

65. Rev. James Madison to SGT, 7 July 1779.

66. Philip D. Morgan, *Slave Counterpoint: Black Culture in the Eighteenth-Century Chesapeake and Lowcountry* (Chapel Hill, N.C., 1998), 278. See also Willie Lee Rose, "The Domestication of Domestic Slavery," in *Slavery and Freedom,* ed. William Freehling (New York, 1982), 22–23.

67. Theodorick Bland Sr. to Theodorick Bland Jr., 4 Aug. 1779, *Bland Papers* 2:18; William Withers to SGT, 20 May, 10 Aug. 1781, 24 Jan., 11 March 1782, SGT to Frances Bland Tucker, [Aug. 1778], Frances Bland Tucker to SGT, 27 Aug. 1778.

68. SGT to Frances Bland Tucker, 13 March 1781, Frances Bland Tucker to SGT, 14 July 1781, Ryland Randolph to SGT, 27 Oct. 1784. On the creation of these black family bonds, see Morgan, *Slave Counterpoint,* chap. 9; Kulikoff, *Tobacco and Slaves,* 364–65; Mary Beth Norton et al., "The Afro-American Family in the Age of Revolution," in *Slavery and Freedom in the Age of the American Revolution,* ed. Ira Berlin and Ronald Hoffman (Charlottesville, Va., 1983), 175–92.

69. Frances Bland Tucker to SGT, [Nov. 1787?]. See Theodorick Bland Jr. to SGT, 13 May 1783, for another example of indifference toward slaves.

70. Theodorick Bland Sr. to John Randolph of Matoax, 12 Oct., 30 Nov. 1772, BP.

71. Theodorick Bland Sr. to John Randolph of Matoax, 12 June 1772, ibid.

72. Theodorick Bland Jr. to SGT, 24 April 1780, Duncan Rose to SGT, 2 Jan. 1785, John Banister to SGT, 27 March 1787.

73. Theodorick Bland Sr. to SGT, 13 April 1784, Theodorick Bland Jr. to SGT, 6 Oct. 1783.

74. Thomas Gordon to SGT, 10, 16 Oct., 1 Dec. 1780, Henry Tucker of Somerset to SGT, 17 Aug. 1780.

75. Elizabeth Colbert to SGT, 15 Oct. 1779, SGT to Capt. Hunter, 20 Oct. 1779, "Statement of SGT regarding His Research in New York City for John Tudor, Esq., of Bermuda," 26 Aug. 1786, Daniel Tucker to SGT, 16 Feb. 1786, Henry Tucker Sr. to SGT, [15 June 1786?], Donald Campbell to SGT, 7 Sept. 1786.

76. Theodorick Bland Jr. to SGT, 5 Aug., 27 Oct. 1780, 14 Aug. 1786, to Richard, Theodorick, and John Randolph, 26 Jan. 1781, Beverley Randolph to SGT, 1, 9 Jan. 1789, 22 Feb. 1788. For relations with Theodorick Bland Sr., see SGT to Theodorick Bland Sr., 14 July 1780, Charles Campbell Papers, Duke Univ.; Frances Bland Tucker to SGT, 4 June 1781, Thomas Tudor Tucker to SGT, 23 Dec. 1784.

77. Elizabeth Tucker to SGT, 20 Oct. 1778, Henry Tucker Jr. to Frances Bland Tucker, 13 April 1780. See also Elizabeth Tucker to Frances Bland Tucker, 25 Nov. 1778 [1779?], Henry Tucker Sr. to SGT, 2 Aug. 1783.

78. Anne Butterfield Tucker to SGT, 2 Nov. 1782. For the ties between the Bermuda and Virginia families, see Henry Tucker Sr. to SGT, 15 May 1779, 2 Aug., 20 Oct. 1783, 21 Aug. 1784, 1 Feb., 1 Dec. 1785, Elizabeth Tucker to Frances Bland Tucker, 3 June 1779, to SGT, 14 Aug. [1780], 8 May 1783, SGT to Frances Bland Tucker, 28 Feb. 1780, Thomas Tudor Tucker to SGT, 26 March 1781, 13 Aug. 1783. For the importance of gift giving, see Smith, *Inside the Great House*, 186.

79. For the Bermuda Tuckers' care of John Randolph, see Elizabeth Tucker to SGT, 24 Aug. 1784, 15 April 1785, Anne Butterfield Tucker to Frances Bland Tucker, 15 April 1785, to SGT, 4 May [1785], Henry Tucker Sr. to SGT, 16 April 1785.

80. John Banister to SGT, 4 Dec. 1785, Beverley Randolph to SGT, [Dec. 1785].

81. Coleman, *St. George Tucker,* 84-86; Elizabeth Tucker to Frances Bland Tucker, April 1786, Henry Tucker Sr. to SGT, 19 April 1786.

82. Henry Tucker Sr. to SGT, 6 April 1779, Elizabeth Tucker to SGT, 3 April 1784.

83. Henry Tucker Jr. to SGT, 15 May 1787, Elizabeth Tucker to SGT, [Oct. 1787]. See also Henry Tucker of Somerset to SGT, 25 July 1787, sister Frances Tucker to SGT, 30 Oct. 1787.

84. Henry Tucker of Sandy's Parish to SGT, 28 Oct. 1787, sister Frances Tucker to SGT, 30 Oct. 1787, Elizabeth Tucker to SGT, 30 Sept. 1788. See also Thomas Tudor Tucker to SGT, 21 Nov. 1787.

85. Donald Campbell to SGT, 23 July 1787, Richard Randolph to Frances Bland Tucker, 10 Sept. 1787.

86. Theodorick Bland Jr. to SGT, 14 Feb. 1788; John Coalter to Michael Coalter, 28

Jan. 1788, BCT Coll.; Thomas Tudor Tucker to SGT, 2 Feb. 1788, Henry Tucker Jr. to SGT, 3 July 1788. See also Thomas Tudor Tucker to SGT, 28 Feb. 1788, John Page to SGT, 25 July 1788. Daniel Blake Smith notes that "by the mid-eighteenth century" people in the Chesapeake were losing their "controlled style of bereavement" (*Inside the Great House,* 265–66).

3. Surviving the New Republic: New Strategies, New Educations

1. SGT to Theodorick Randolph and JR, 29 June 1788, BP.

2. Isaac, *Transformation of Virginia,* 115–38, 247, 251. For the indebtedness of Virginians south of the James River, see Emory Evans, "Private Indebtedness and the Revolution in Virginia, 1776 to 1796," *WMQ,* 3d ser., 28 (1971): 363, 368–69.

3. Frey, *Water from the Rock,* 210–11; SGT to Theodorick Bland Jr., 21 Sept. 1781, John Banister to Theodorick Bland Jr., 12 July 1781, *Bland Papers* 2:75, 73–74.

4. John Banister to SGT, Aug. 1786, Israel Hall to SGT, 20 July 1789. On the economic difficulties of the tidewater, see Herbert E. Sloan, *Principle and Interest: Thomas Jefferson and the Problem of Debt* (New York, 1995), 26–32; Lorena S. Walsh, "Work and Resistance in the New Republic," in *From Chattel Slaves to Wage Slaves: The Dynamics of Labour Bargaining in the Americas,* ed. Mary Turner (Kingston, Jamaica, 1995), 97–98, 105–6; Richard S. Dunn, "Black Society in the Chesapeake, 1776–1810," in Berlin and Hoffman, *Slavery and Freedom in the Age of the Revolution,* 50–52; Kulikoff, *Tobacco and Slaves,* 157–58; Jacob M. Price, *France and the Chesapeake: A History of the French Tobacco Monopoly, 1674–1791, and of Its Relationship to the British and American Tobacco Trades* (Ann Arbor, Mich., 1973), 729–34, 841–42. On the soil exhaustion of the Chesapeake, see Shade, *Democratizing the Old Dominion,* 32–33; Avery O. Craven, *Soil Exhaustion as a Factor in the Agricultural History of Virginia and Maryland, 1606–1860* (Urbana, Ill., 1926); Lewis C. Gray, *History of Agriculture in the Southern United States to 1860,* 2 vols. (1933; rept. Gloucester, Mass., 1958).

5. John Banister to SGT, [1787?], 29 March 1787, Neill Buchanan to SGT, 27 April, 15 May 1789. For John Banister's economic woes before and after his death, see John Banister to Theodorick Bland Jr., 16 May 1781, *Bland Papers* 2:69–70; John Banister to SGT, 6 April 1787, 16 April 1788, St. George Tucker Jr. to SGT, [17 Oct. 1788], Neill Buchanan to SGT, 17 Feb., 27 July 1789. See also SGT to Theodorick Randolph, 2 Oct. 1788, BP; JR to SGT, 25 Jan. 1789, St. George Tucker Papers, LC.

6. Henry Tucker Sr. to SGT, 19 April, 14 Sept., 1 Dec. 1786, Elizabeth Tucker to SGT, 19 April, 27 May 1786, Henry Tucker Jr. to SGT, 8 July 1786, William Nelson to SGT, 1 July 1794, 10 May 1795, 10 Nov. 1800. For this loan, see William Nelson to SGT, 12 Dec. 1792, 17 Jan., 5 April 1794, 15 March 1796, 19 March 1798, HSGT to SGT, 1 Sept. 1799. See Evans, *Thomas Nelson of Yorktown,* 124–38, for the Nelsons' fall.

7. Thomas Tudor Tucker to SGT, 9 Feb. 1783. For Thomas Tudor Tucker's land purchases, see Rachel N. Klein, *Unification of a Slave State: The Rise of the Planter Class in the South Carolina Backcountry* (Chapel Hill, N.C., 1990), 191–92; for his economic woes, which continued until Jefferson named him treasurer of the United States in 1801, see Thomas Tudor Tucker to SGT, 13 April 1784, 21 April, 1 Oct. 1785, 29 May 1786, 8 April 1787, 17 April 1788, 3 March, 14 April 1791, 12 Feb., 4 March 1793, 16 March 1794, 6 Sept. 1798,

23 March 1800, 30 June 1801. For the economic problems of Theodorick Bland Jr., see Theodorick Bland Jr. to SGT, 13 May 1783; Theodorick Bland Sr. to SGT, 13 April 1784; see also SGT to Theodorick Randolph, 30 Aug. 1789, BP. For the difficulties of Archibald Cary, see Carter Page to SGT, 31 Jan. 1788. For the problems of Beverley Randolph, see Beverley Randolph to SGT, 29 Nov. 1784, 8 Jan., 18 Dec 1785. For the economic troubles of John Page, see John Page to SGT, 28 June 1792, 27 June 1793, 3 Dec. 1795, 24 Feb., 23 March 1798, 28 Nov. 1801, 21 May 1804; see also Lelia Skipwith Tucker to Frances Tucker Coalter, Jan. 1806, BCT Coll. For the problems of William Fitzhugh, see William Fitzhugh to SGT, 21 Dec. 1796. Allison is quoted in Evans, "Private Indebtedness and the Revolution," 361–62. For the declining economic power of the planter class, see Breen, *Tobacco Culture,* 124–59; Wood, *Radicalism of the American Revolution,* 113–17, 142–43. For how planters in general dealt with debt following the Revolution, see Sloan, *Principle and Interest,* chap. 1.

    8. St. George Tucker Jr. to SGT, 2 March 1790.

    9. Robert Innes to SGT, 25 March 1783. For Tucker's early legal career, see Cullen, *Tucker and Law in Virginia,* chaps. 3–4.

    10. Cullen, *Tucker and Law in Virginia,* 37–39.

    11. A. G. Roeber, *Faithful Magistrates and Republican Lawyers: Creators of Virginia Legal Culture, 1680–1810* (Chapel Hill, N.C., 1981), 172; Duncan Rose to SGT, 11 Feb. 1784, SGT to Edward Wyatt, 12 Feb. 1784.

    12. Henry Tucker Sr. to SGT, 21 Aug. 1784, SGT to Frances Bland Tucker, 7 April 1787; Smith, *Inside the Great House,* 161–62. For the difficulties St. George Tucker had in getting paid by clients, see Thomas Tudor Tucker to SGT, 21 April 1785.

    13. Thomas Tudor Tucker to SGT, 17 April 1788.

    14. Risjord, *Chesapeake Politics,* chaps. 5–6.

    15. Ibid., 148–56, 177.

    16. James Madison to James Monroe, 22 Jan. 1786, quoted ibid., 263. On Tucker's part in the Annapolis Convention, see Henry Lee to SGT, 14 Oct. 1786. On his support for the new Constitution, see SGT, "Of the Several Forms of Government," *Blackstone's Commentaries with Notes of Reference, to the Constitution and Laws, of the Federal Government of the United States and of the Commonwealth of Virginia,* 5 vols. (1803; rept. South Hackensack, N.J., 1969), 1: 12–13; Cullen, *Tucker and Law in Virginia,* 60; Robert M. Cover, "St. George Tucker, *Blackstone's Commentaries with Notes of Reference to the Constitution and the Laws of the Federal Government of the United States and of the Commonwealth of Virginia,*" *Columbia Law Review* 70 (1970): 1478–79.

    17. Roeber, *Faithful Magistrates and Republican Lawyers,* 220–21.

    18. SGT, "Some Thoughts on the Improvement of the Police &c. in Virginia," [1797], Unnumbered Notebooks, no. 1, 12–13. For the decline in deference shown county justices, see Roeber, *Faithful Magistrates and Republican Lawyers,* 174; Isaac, *Transformation of Virginia,* 318–19.

    19. Theodorick Bland Jr. to SGT, 2 Jan. 1788. The state assembly revamped the judiciary to unclog the backlog of cases in the county courts and to increase efficiency in the resolution of disputes. See Cullen, *Tucker and Law in Virginia,* 72–73.

    20. John Page to SGT, 28 June 1792, 27 June 1793, 3 Dec. 1795, 24 Feb., 23 March

1798; Land Tax Records, Gloucester County, 1782, 1800, LV; SGT, "Concerning Usury," *Blackstone's Commentaries* 3 : 104.

21. For Tucker's sale of lands, see Beverley Randolph to SGT, 19, 20 Nov. 1787, Creed Taylor to SGT, 8 Dec. 1796, William Cowan to SGT, 11 Jan. 1793, Deed of Agreement between SGT and Gilbert Ricks, 15 Nov. 1804, Indenture concerning the Marriage of Frances Tucker and John Coalter, 5 June 1802; Land Tax Records, Dinwiddie County, 1788, 1789, LV. d

22. SGT to HSGT, 10 March 1816.

23. SGT to Richard Rush, 27 Oct. 1813, in Mrs. George P. Coleman, ed., "Randolph and Tucker Letters," *VMHB* 42 (1934): 218–19.

24. Henry Tazewell to SGT, 16 Nov. 1790, Neill Buchanan to SGT, 26 Nov. 1790, John Page to SGT, 31 Dec. 1790, Benjamin Harrison to SGT, 30 Jan. 1791, Donald Campbell to SGT, 1 Feb. 1791, Thomas Tudor Tucker to SGT, 9 March 1791; Coleman, *St. George Tucker,* 104.

25. See Isaac, *Transformation of Virginia,* 311–12; Paul G. E. Clemens, *The Atlantic Economy and Colonial Maryland's Eastern Shore: From Tobacco to Grain* (Ithaca, N.Y., 1980).

26. SGT, *Blackstone's Commentaries* 1:xiv-xv, 3 : 104; SGT, "A Short and Candid View of the Operations and Affects of the Establishment of the Bank of Virginia," [1805], Robert Sanders to SGT, 11 Sept. 1797, James Brown to SGT, 23 Oct. 1797, William Wilson to SGT, 6 Feb. 1798, 24 Jan. 1799, SGT to John Page, 24 Feb. 1798, to William Wilson, 12 June, 1 Dec. 1800. For other Virginians' recognition of the need for banking institutions in the state, see Roeber, *Faithful Magistrates and Republican Lawyers,* 234.

27. Cullen, *Tucker and Law in Virginia,* 117–18; SGT, "Introductory Lecture [to his law students]," 1790; SGT, *A Dissertation on Slavery: With a Proposal for the Gradual Abolition of It, in the State of Virginia* (Philadelphia, 1796), 7–8.

28. Quoted in Robert M. Cover, *Justice Accused: Antislavery and the Judicial Process* (New Haven, 1975), 37–38.

29. On emancipation in the North, see Arthur Zilversmit, *The First Emancipation: The Abolition of Slavery in the North* (Chicago, 1967); Freehling, *Road to Disunion,* 131–34; Duncan J. MacLeod, *Slavery, Race, and the American Revolution* (London, 1974), 98–99. On manumissions in Virginia in the 1780s, see Gary Nash, *Race and Revolution* (New York, 1990), 17–18.

30. James D. Essig, *The Bonds of Wickedness: American Evangelicals against Slavery, 1770–1808* (Philadelphia, 1982), 67. See also Nash, *Race and Revolution,* 11–12, 42–43.

31. Frederika Teute Schmidt and Barbara Ripel Wilhelm, "Early Proslavery Petitions in Virginia," *WMQ,* 3d ser., 30 (1973): 133–46.

32. SGT to Jeremy Belknap, 29 June 1795, quoted in Nash, *Race and Revolution,* 45; SGT, *Dissertation on Slavery,* 2–3.

33. "Letters Relating to Slavery in Massachusetts," *Belknap Papers* (Boston, 1891), 373–431; "Queries respecting Slavery and the Emancipation of Negroes in Massachusetts," *Collection of the Massachusetts Historical Society,* 1st ser., 4 (1795; rept. 1968): 191–211; see also Cover, *Justice Accused,* 38; Donna Stillman Bryman, "St. George Tucker and the Complexities of Antislavery Advocacy in Jeffersonian Virginia" (M.A. thesis, College of William and Mary, 1972), 19–21.

34. SGT, *Dissertation on Slavery,* 80 – 81, 89 – 92. For Tucker's plan, see David Brion Davis, *The Problem of Slavery in the Age of Revolution, 1770 – 1823* (Ithaca, N.Y., 1975), 335 – 36; Winthrop Jordan, *White over Black: American Attitudes toward the Negro, 1550 – 1812* (Chapel Hill, N.C., 1968), 555 – 61. For Pennsylvania's plan, see Zilversmit, *First Emancipation,* 124 – 37.

35. SGT, *Dissertation on Slavery,* 74 – 78, 92, 99 – 100, 102n.

36. SGT to the Virginia Speaker of the House of Delegates, 30 Nov. 1796, George Taylor to SGT, 8 Dec. 1796, SGT to John Coalter, 2 Aug. 1797; SGT to Belknap, quoted in Cover, "Tucker, *Blackstone's Commentaries,*" 1492 – 93.

37. Personal Property Tax Records, Williamsburg, 1796, LV; SGT to William Haxall, 2 Dec. 1796, William Haxall to SGT, 20 Dec. 1796, 10 Feb., 28 June 1797, Robert Sanders to SGT, 11 Sept. 1797. For further slave transactions, see William Haxall to SGT, 31 Aug. 1797, 15 April 1798, SGT to William Haxall, 17 Feb. 1801.

38. Theodorick Bland Jr. to Frances Bland Tucker, 2 April 1781, 26 Sept. 1777; Washington quoted in Wood, *Radicalism of the American Revolution,* 197 – 98. For Bland Jr.'s educational efforts on behalf of his nephews, see also Theodorick Bland Jr. to SGT, 16 April, 17 July 1780, 11 May, 20 Aug. 1781, to Richard, Theodorick, and John Randolph, 26 Jan. 1781, to Frances Bland Tucker, 14 Aug. 1781. See also Samuel Chandler to Theodorick Bland Jr., 2 Oct. 1781, Bland Papers, VHS. On southern anti-intellectualism and preference for sociability over learning, see Wyatt-Brown, *Southern Honor,* 92 – 99.

39. SGT, "Of the Several Forms of Government," *Blackstone's Commentaries* 1 : 28. For the influence of the new nation's republican ideology on Tucker's child-rearing habits, see Brugger, *Beverley Tucker,* 12; Yazawa, *From Colonies to Commonwealth,* 160 – 65, 173, 184 – 85; William R. Taylor, *Cavalier and Yankee: The Old South and American National Character* (New York, 1957), 124 – 27. Others, Daniel Blake Smith in particular, argue that such shifts in education reflected postwar confidence in the society's middle and upper ranks (Smith, *Inside the Great House,* 96 – 98). Still other scholars contend that the Tuckers, along with other Americans, were adopting John Locke's injunctions on child rearing, which urged firm paternal authority directed toward developing "independent self-sufficient individuals"; see Robert N. Bellah et al., *Habits of the Heart: Individualism and Commitment in American Life* (Berkeley, Calif., 1985), 57 – 58.

40. SGT to Alexander Campbell, 7 July 1809.

41. SGT to Theodorick Randolph and JR, 22 April, 12 June 1787, JR to Frances Bland Tucker, 27 Sept. 1787, Theodorick Bland Jr. to SGT, 15 April 1789; Thomas Tudor Tucker to SGT, 14 April 1788, BP; JR to SGT, 7 Dec. 1788, 25 Aug. 1789, St. George Tucker Papers, LC. For other examples of such parental concern, see SGT to Frances Bland Tucker, 22 May 1779, to Theodorick Randolph and JR, 12 June 1787, to Alexander Campbell, 31 May 1811, Charles Carter to SGT, 1 Nov. 1804, Elizabeth Tucker to SGT, 23 Nov. 1804; see also SGT to Theodorick Randolph, 2 Oct. 1788, BP; JR to SGT, 19 Feb., 1 March 1789, St. George Tucker Papers, LC; JR to SGT, [undated], Randolph-Macon Woman's College; Bruce, *Randolph of Roanoke* 1 : 82 – 83. On Witherspoon, see Daniel Calhoun, *The Intelligence of a People* (Princeton, N.J., 1973), 152 – 55. For the use of Revolutionary heroes by late eighteenth-century parents, see Fliegelman, *Prodigals and Pilgrims,* 222 – 23, 235 – 36. Smith in

Inside the Great House, 181–86, explains that eighteenth-century uncles in the Chesapeake felt a strong responsibility to assist their nephews in educational matters.

42. JR to SGT, 25 Dec. 1788, quoted in Bruce, *Randolph of Roanoke* 1:83. See also JR to SGT, 25 Jan. 1789, 19 Oct. 1790, St. George Tucker Papers, LC; JR to Henry Rutledge, 24 Feb. 1791, Henry Rutledge Papers, Historical Society of Pennsylvania.

43. Frances Bland Tucker to SGT, [Nov. 1787]. For a complaint that parents were increasingly educating their children within their homes under their own supervision, see Walker Maury to SGT, 1 April 1783. See also Smith, *Inside the Great House,* 105. For John Coalter, see his "Autobiographical Sketch," VHS.

44. John Coalter to Michael Coalter, 27 Jan. 1789, BCT Coll.; SGT to Theodorick Randolph, 20 Feb. 1790, BP; Brugger, *Beverley Tucker,* 11–15; HSGT to SGT, 11 May, 23 May 1794, 1 Sept 1799. For a tutor's place in a gentry household, see Smith, *Inside the Great House,* 107–11.

45. SGT, "Garrison Articles to Be Observed by the Officers and Privates Stationed at Fort St. George in Wmsburg," [c. 1790]; Brugger, *Beverley Tucker,* 45; Robert L. Scribner, "Fort St. George," *Virginia Cavalcade* 5 (Autumn 1955): 21–23; HSGT to SGT, 7 Sept. 1796; see also Fanny Tucker to SGT, 23 June 1794, HSGT to SGT, 29 Aug. 1796, 11 Aug. 1799, NBT to SGT, 4 Aug. 1799, 13 Sept. 1800, 11 June 1801.

46. SGT to Theodorick Randolph, 10 July 1786, 29 Oct. 1788, 20 Feb. 1790, BP; SGT to Alexander Campbell, 7 July 1809.

47. See Sellers, *Market Revolution;* Melvyn Stokes and Stephen Conway, eds., *The Market Revolution in America: Social, Political, and Religious Expressions, 1800–1880* (Charlottesville, Va., 1996); Richard Lyman Bushman, "Markets and Composite Farms in Early America," *WMQ,* 3d ser., 55 (July 1998): 351–74; Perry Miller, *The Life of the Mind in America: From the Revolution to the Civil War* (New York, 1965), 109–10.

48. Roeber, *Faithful Magistrates and Republican Lawyers,* 213–15; Robert A. Ferguson, *Law and Letters in American Culture* (Cambridge, Mass., 1984), 12–14, 64–65; SGT to Charles Lee, 3 Sept. 1791.

49. SGT, *Blackstone's Commentaries* 1:xvi, xiv-xv. For St. George Tucker's choice of Blackstone's *Commentaries* for his law lectures, see Cover, "Tucker, *Blackstone's Commentaries,*" 1477–79; Julius S. Waterman, "Thomas Jefferson and Blackstone's *Commentaries,*" in *Essays in the History of Early American Law,* ed. David H. Flaherty (Chapel Hill, N.C., 1969), 455, 460–61, 480–81; Miller, *Life of the Mind in America,* 130–31, 139.

50. Quoted in Roeber, *Faithful Magistrates and Republican Lawyers,* 237–38.

51. Shepard, "Lawyers Look at Themselves," 4; Chapman Johnson to David Watson, 14 Aug. 1800, "Letters to David Watson," *VMHB* 29 (1921): 272; see also Wood, *Radicalism of the American Revolution,* 322–23; John Coalter to SGT, 5 Dec. 1793.

52. "Plan for Conferring Degrees on the Students of Law in the University of William & Mary," [1792?]; John Coalter to Michael Coalter, 29 March 1788, BCT Coll. See also Cullen, *Tucker and Law in Virginia,* 121–22; Robson, *Educating Republicans,* 169–70; John Coalter to James Rind, 13 May, 27 June 1791, BCT Coll.

53. Walker Maury to SGT, 31 July 1784, Richard Randolph to Frances Bland Tucker, 19 May, 4 Oct. 1786, William Nelson to SGT, 2 Feb. 1787; Dawidoff, *Education of John Ran-*

dolph, 102; Stokes, "Randolph of Roanoke," 74–75, 83–84, 150; HSGT to SGT, 13 Oct. 1798, 4 Aug. 1799, NBT to SGT, 27 Jan. 1803, John Coalter to SGT, 14 Jan. 1804; Brugger, *Beverley Tucker,* 24–28; Cullen, *Tucker and Law in Virginia,* 126; Joseph Shelton Watson to David Watson, 4 Nov. 1799, "Letters from William & Mary College," *VMHB* 29 (1921): 146. For the difficulty of St. George Tucker's regime at William and Mary, see Kate Mason Rowland, ed., "Letters to William T. Barry," *WMQ,* 1st ser., 13 (1904–5): 109; J. S. Watson to David Watson, 1 April [1801], "Letters from William & Mary," 165.

54. SGT's essay, "The Dreamer, No. 1"; Dawidoff, *Education of John Randolph,* 128–29, 143–44, 149; John Page to SGT, 4 July, 10 Aug. 1790, 15 Jan. 1792, 28 Feb. 1796, 13 July 1797.

55. [SGT], "Ode II: To Atlas," "Ode XI: To Atlas, Being the Second Part of Ode II," "Ode IX: To Liberty," *National Gazette,* 5 June, 28, 14 Aug. 1793. Tucker's odes are reprinted in Prince, *Poems of St. George Tucker,* 82–107. At the time many thought Philip Freneau wrote the Jonathan Pindar poems; see Thomas Jefferson to James Madison, 29 June 1793, in Paul L. Ford, ed., *The Works of Thomas Jefferson,* 12 vols. (New York, 1904), 6:328. In 1797 Tucker drafted a political play attacking the Federalist edifice which he hoped John Page would help get onto the stage in Philadelphia (SGT to John Page, 31 Jan. 1797, John Page Papers, Perkins Library, Duke Univ.). The play apparently was never performed and has not survived.

56. Jordan, *Political Leadership,* 21–23.

57. SGT, "Some Thoughts on the Improvement of the Police &c. in Virginia [1797]," Unnumbered Notebooks, no. 1. Rhys Isaac argues that the Revolution gained its "popular" tone right at the start of the war (*Transformation of Virginia,* 258–59).

58. Walter Jones to SGT, 5 Jan. 1793; Page quoted in Jordan, *Political Leadership,* 111; SGT, *Blackstone's Commentaries* 1:xvii-xviii. For Page's great bitterness about the growing challenges he faced at elections, see Page to SGT, 4 July 1790.

59. SGT to Joseph C. Cabell, 20 Sept., 11 Oct. 1807, BP; Edmund Brooke to Joseph C. Cabell, 16 Jan. 1809, to SGT, 26 Nov. 1809. For tensions between overseers and planters, see William Kauffman Scarbough, *The Overseer: Plantation Management in the Old South* (1965; rept. Athens, Ga., 1984), 102–37.

60. SGT, "The Constitution of Virginia," *Blackstone's Commentaries* 1:135–36.

61. SGT, "Copy of a letter to Professor Ebeling, Hamburg," 11 Dec. 1801; SGT to Theodorick Randolph, 29 Oct. 1788, 1 March 1789, BP; Maria Rind to [John Coalter], [June–Aug. 1790], BCT Coll. See also SGT to JR, 18 Aug. 1791, BP.

62. Henry Tucker Jr. to SGT, 30 April 1796, BP; Brugger, *Beverley Tucker,* 11. See also Donald Campbell to SGT, 15 Jan. 1795, Henry Tucker Jr. to SGT, 23 May 1795, Thomas Tudor Tucker to SGT, 31 Aug. 1795, Elizabeth Tucker to SGT, 15 Feb., 4 April 1796.

63. "Character of Beverley Randolph," [1797], Unnumbered Notebooks, no. 1.

64. Elizabeth Tucker to SGT, 15 Feb. 1796.

65. Henry Tucker Jr. to SGT, 23 May 1795, Elizabeth Tucker to SGT, 15 Feb. 1796.

66. For Nathaniel's belief in Swedenborg, see Leary, *Literary Career of Nathaniel Tucker,* chap. 6.

67. Archibald Campbell to SGT, 6 March 1796.

4. The Crisis of the Rising Generation

1. HSGT to SGT, 30 July 1805.

2. Quoted in Garland, *Life of Randolph* 1:61—62.

3. William Nelson Jr. to SGT, 2 Feb. 1787; Stokes, "Randolph of Roanoke," 76—77; SGT to Thomas Mann Randolph, 15 Nov. 1789.

4. John Woodson to SGT, 11 Jan. 1790, Richard Randolph to Neill Buchanan, 24 Feb. 1790.

5. Neill Buchanan to Duncan Rose, 28 April 1790, Richard Randolph to Duncan Rose, 30 April, 11, 15, 23 May, 6, 12, 25, 29 June, 4, 22 July 1790, Neill Buchanan to SGT, 9 June 1790, John Woodson to SGT, 18 Nov. 1790.

6. Richard Randolph to Duncan Rose, 9, 22 June 1790, James Brown to SGT, 14 March 1791.

7. SGT to Theodorick Randolph, 20 Feb. 1790, BP; John Woodson to SGT, 14 Nov. 1792; see also John Woodson to SGT, 28 Oct. 1791.

8. Thomas Tudor Tucker to SGT, 18 Aug. 1791; Dawidoff, *Education of John Randolph*, 97.

9. Ann Cary (Nancy) Randolph Morris to JR, 16 Jan. 1815, quoted in Bruce, *Randolph of Roanoke* 2:282—83.

10. "*Commonwealth v. Randolph,* John Marshall's Notes of Evidence" in *The Papers of John Marshall,* vol. 2, ed. Charles T. Cullen and Herbert A. Johnson (Chapel Hill, N.C., 1974), 168—69.

11. *Virginia Gazette and General Advertiser* (Richmond), 29 March 1793, quoted in Herbert Johnson's "Editorial Note," *Papers of Marshall* 2:161—69 (quote on 163). See also Bruce, *Randolph of Roanoke* 1:106—23, 2:273—85; H. J. Eckenrode, *The Randolphs: The Story of a Virginia Family* (Indianapolis, 1946), chap. 8.

12. SGT, "To the Public," dated 5 May 1793 and printed in the *Virginia Gazette,* 15 May 1793.

13. Thomas Randolph Jr. quoted in Ann Cary (Nancy) Randolph Morris to SGT, 9 Feb. 1815; Stokes, "Randolph of Roanoke," 99.

14. Garland, *Life of Randolph* 1:60—63; Stokes, "Randolph of Roanoke," 102—3.

15. Judith Randolph to SGT, 24 July 1796, 18 Oct. 1801. See also Judith Randolph to JR, 25 Sept. 1796, BP.

16. Dawidoff, *Education of John Randolph,* 104; Henry Lee to SGT, 29 June 1792; Bruce, *Randolph of Roanoke* 1:123—25; JR to SGT, 26 Jan. 1794, quoted ibid., 128—29.

17. JR to Henry M. Rutledge, 29 April 1797, Rutledge Papers, Historical Society of Pennsylvania; JR to SGT, 24 June 1797, Randolph-Macon Woman's College; Garland, *Life of Randolph* 1:70; Dawidoff, *Education of John Randolph,* 104; Bruce, *Randolph of Roanoke* 1:132.

18. Bruce, *Randolph of Roanoke* 1:90; Garland, *Life of Randolph* 2:147—48.

19. Dawidoff, *Education of John Randolph,* 81—88; JR to SGT, 2 June 1798, Randolph-Macon Woman's College; Stokes, "Randolph of Roanoke," 141; Jordan, *Political Leadership,* 159—60; Personal Property Tax Records, Charlotte County, 1800, Cumberland County,

1798, LV. For the importance of land ownership to one's personal honor, see Wyatt-Brown, *Southern Honor,* 72–74.

20. JR to Josiah Quincy, 30 Aug. 1813, John Randolph Papers, LC; see also JR to Richard Kidder Randolph, 7 Feb. 1812, ibid.

21. Stokes, "Randolph of Roanoke," 226–27, 233–34; Kulikoff, *Tobacco and Slaves,* 157–58; Craven, *Soil Exhaustion,* 73–74, 82–84; Gray, *History of Agriculture* 2:753–54; JR to James M. Garnett, 18 June 1821, John Randolph Papers, LC.

22. Garland, *Life of Randolph* 1:71; JR to SGT, 24 June 1797, Randolph-Macon Woman's College.

23. Burstein, *Inner Jefferson,* 143; Margaret Lowther Page to SGT, 16 Oct. 1809; see also Margaret Lowther Page to SGT, 29 Oct. 1808, 8 Jan. 1809, 22 March 1817, 20 June 1818, 21 Jan. 1821, John Page Jr. to SGT, 14 Aug. 1819.

24. William Munford to SGT, 22 Dec. 1805; Marion Tinling, ed., *The Correspondence of the Three William Byrds of Westover, Virginia, 1684–1776,* 2 vols. (Charlottesville, Va., 1977), 1:305n, 2:806n.

25. Judith Nelson to SGT, 4 May 1808. See also Judith Nelson to SGT, 18 June 1818, Sally Nelson to SGT, 11 Nov. 1824. On formerly wealthy Virginia women taking in boarders, see Cynthia A. Kierner, "'The Dark and Dense Cloud Perpetually Lowering over Us:' Gender and the Decline of the Gentry in Postrevolutionary Virginia," *Journal of the Early Republic* 20 (Summer 2000): 209–11.

26. Robert Gamble to SGT, 24 March, 19 April, 17 June, 9 Dec. 1803; Starnes, *Sixty Years of Branch Banking,* 16–17. See Shade, *Democratizing the Old Dominion,* chap. 1, esp. 30–33, for the economic robustness of the western Virginia counties.

27. [SGT], "A Short and Candid View of the Operations and Affects of the Establishment of the Bank of Virginia," Henry Skipwith et al. to Daniel Hylton, 9 May 1804, R. B. Stark et al. to SGT, 12 May 1804, SGT to Daniel Hylton, 15 May 1804, Philip Barraud to SGT, 19 April 1804. On the opening of the Bank of Virginia, see Starnes, *Sixty Years of Branch Banking,* 29. Tucker organized another purchase of Bank of Virginia stock for sixty-nine Williamsburg residents in 1805; see SGT to John Brockenbrough, 30 March 1805. On Tucker's holdings in the Farmer's Bank, see Richard Scott to SGT, 8 Oct., 5 Nov. 1810, 25 April, 23 May 1811, 12 March 1812, 6 April 1813, 10 Oct. 1817, 7 May 1818, William Herbert to SGT, 26 Feb. 1811, SGT to Richard Scott, 27 Feb. 1812; Starnes, *Sixty Years of Branch Banking,* 43–44. On his holdings in the Bank of the United States, see Joseph Lynch to SGT, 7 Dec. 1818. In the 1790s Tucker may have purchased some stock in the First Bank of the United States, despite his ideological opposition to Alexander Hamilton. In January 1796 his agent in Philadelphia, John Barnes, cryptically wrote Tucker: "Int[erest] due on your public stock. Treasury U.S. 13.50 less 50 cents my commiss."

28. John Randolph Tucker, "Judges Tucker of the Court of Appeals of Virginia," 797–98.

29. JR to SGT, 3 Nov. 1801, Randolph-Macon Woman's College; Thomas Tudor Tucker to SGT, 19 Dec. 1801. Tucker would express similar sentiments when Beverley left him in 1806; see NBT to SGT, 2 Feb. 1806.

30. Thomas Tudor Tucker to SGT, 19 Dec. 1801, Charles Carter to SGT, 4 June 1802, Henry Hiort to SGT, 15 June 1802, Elizabeth Tucker to SGT, 30 July 1802.

31. Shade, *Democratizing the Old Dominion,* chap. 1, esp. 24, 45–47; Frederick F. Siegel, *The Roots of Southern Distinctiveness: Tobacco and Society in Danville, Virginia, 1780–1865* (Chapel Hill, N.C., 1987), 61–91; John W. Wayland, *A History of the Shenandoah Valley of Virginia* (Strasburg, Va., 1927); Kulikoff, *Tobacco and Slaves,* 421–35.

32. HSGT to SGT, 5 Nov. 1802. See also HSGT to SGT, 16 Feb., 21 July 1803, 25 Aug., 3 Dec. 1805.

33. George Tucker, "Autobiography of George Tucker," *Bermuda Historical Quarterly* 18 (1961): 120.

34. HSGT to SGT, 5 Nov. 1802; see also HSGT to SGT, 24 Nov., 3 Dec. 1802.

35. HSGT to SGT, 7 May 1803; Shepard, "Lawyers Look at Themselves," 4. See also HSGT to SGT, 4, 24 Feb. 1803, Ellyson Currie to SGT, 5 April 1800. For another analysis of Henry's experiences in western Virginia, see Cullen, *Tucker and Law in Virginia,* 138.

36. HSGT to SGT, 15 Oct., 16 Feb. 1803.

37. HSGT to SGT, 26 May 1803. For the need to work diligently and also to scale back material ambitions, see Chapman Johnson to SGT, 16 Dec. 1802; McLean, *George Tucker,* 15, 20; Lewis, *Pursuit of Happiness,* 107–8, 151–52.

38. HSGT to SGT, 24 Feb., 24 June, 10 Oct. 1803; see also HSGT to SGT, 4 Oct. 1803.

39. HSGT to SGT, 17 June 1806; see also NBT to JR, 20 Jan. 1806, HSGT to SGT, 21 March 1812.

40. HSGT to SGT, 5 Feb. 1806. For the achievements of Henry Tucker Jr.'s sons, see Elizabeth Tucker to SGT, 7 Oct. 1790, 27 Sept. 1796, 6 April, 30 Oct. 1801, Henry Tucker Jr. to SGT, 12 Nov. 1790, 23 May 1795, 10 Jan. 1802, 13 July 1807, Frances Bruere Tucker to SGT, 8 Oct. 1793, Thomas Tudor Tucker to SGT, 30 June 1801; Tucker, *Descendants of William Tucker,* 198, 239–49; Brugger, *Beverley Tucker,* 12–13.

41. Charles Carter to SGT, 12 April 1808.

42. SGT to John Coalter, 20 July 1790 [transcript], BP. See also NBT "Autobiographical Fragment." For relatives in the Chesapeake moving to the "periphery of the individual's affectional world," see Smith, *Inside the Great House,* 228.

43. Elizabeth Tucker to SGT, 21 March 1803. For Beverley Tucker's education, see Brugger, *Beverley Tucker,* 14–32.

44. NBT to SGT, 15, 20 Sept. 1805, to JR, 18 Nov., 26 Dec. 1805, 20 Jan., 29 April, 15 May 1806.

45. NBT to JR, 19 Feb. 1806.

46. On the Southside and Charlotte Court House, see Shade, *Democratizing the Old Dominion,* 44–45, 129–32; Brugger, *Beverley Tucker,* 32–33.

47. Brugger, *Beverley Tucker,* 32.

48. NBT to JR, 19 Feb. 1806, to SGT, 22 March, 17 May, 26 Dec. 1807; Brugger, *Beverley Tucker,* 32–34. On Beverley's hopes for quick success, see NBT to SGT, 22 June 1806.

49. Brugger, *Beverley Tucker,* 24; see also ibid., 40.

50. NBT to SGT, 16 March 1811; Shepard, "Lawyers Look at Themselves," 16. On Scotch-Irish immigration into the lower piedmont, see Shade, *Democratizing the Old Dominion,* 155–56. Tucker's other law students complained about these changes; see Chapman

Johnson to SGT, 29 May 1802; see also William Wirt, *The Letters of the British Spy* (1816; rept. Chapel Hill, N.C., 1970), 206. For competition at the bar, see NBT to SGT, 13 Sept. 1812, 15 April 1814.

51. NBT to SGT, 16 Nov. 1807, 29 Jan. 1810; George Tucker quoted in McLean, *George Tucker,* 60–62; Brugger, *Beverley Tucker,* 38.

52. NBT to SGT, 28 Feb., 25 April 1807, to JR, 12 Sept. 1807; see also NBT to SGT, 16 Feb. 1807, 4 June 1808, to JR, 11 March 1808.

53. SGT to Fanny Tucker Coalter, 17 April 1807, BCT Coll.

54. NBT to JR, 10 March 1806, 28 Jan. 1806 [1807?], 12 Sept. 1807, 16 Nov. 1806 [1807?], 28 Nov., 10 Dec. 1807, 27 Jan., 20, 26 March, 30 June, 9 July, 20 Aug. 1808, 22 April, 13, 17 Sept. 1809, 17 June 1810.

55. NBT to SGT, 23 July, 21 Aug. 1807, NBT to JR, 4 Nov. 1807; Personal Property Tax Records, Charlotte County, 1809, LV; Brugger, *Beverley Tucker,* 33–34. John Randolph had earlier thought of purchasing Cawsons, the Blands' old family seat, and placing Beverley Tucker there. Predicting paternal objections, Beverley dissuaded him; see NBT to JR, 12 Feb. 1806.

56. SGT to NBT, 28 July 1807. See also Brugger, *Beverley Tucker,* 33–36.

57. NBT to SGT, 28 Feb., 21 Aug. 1807; see also NBT to SGT, 21 April, 25 Sept., 6 [16?] Oct. 1808, to JR, 4 Jan., 6 April 1808; Brugger, *Beverley Tucker,* 41.

58. NBT to JR, 19 Jan. 1808; see also NBT to JR, 21 April 1807, 4 Jan., 3, 20, 26 March, 17 April 1808, [July 1808]; Brugger, *Beverley Tucker,* 34–35; Drew Gilpin Faust, *A Sacred Circle: The Dilemma of the Intellectual in the Old South, 1840–1860* (Baltimore, 1977), 25–26.

59. NBT to SGT, 6 [16?] Oct. 1808. See also SGT to John Coalter, 4 Dec. 1808, BCT Coll.

60. HSGT to SGT, 18 Dec. 1808. For another example of conflicts within families because of changing economic realities and differing expectations, see Lewis, *Pursuit of Happiness,* 178–79. My analysis sharply differs with Lewis in one important respect on this issue: she writes, "Clearly, parents intended to give each of their children an 'independence,' an estate upon which each child could subsist in comfort. Such was the goal in the eighteenth century and so in the nineteenth century" (112). As far as the Tuckers are concerned, however, children continued to expect "independence" while their father sought to disabuse them of this traditional notion.

61. Brugger, *Beverley Tucker,* 43.

62. John Coalter to Fanny Tucker Coalter, 17 April 1806, BCT Coll.

63. On the changing expectations of marriage, see Lewis, *Pursuit of Happiness,* chap. 5, and "Republican Wife"; Jabour, *Marriage in the Early Republic,* chap. 1. On cooperative marriages, especially within Scotch-Irish clans in the late eighteenth century, see ibid., 23–25.

64. See esp. Smith, *Inside the Great House,* 293. For the development of separate private and public spheres, see among others Linda K. Kerber, "Separate Spheres, Female Worlds, Woman's Place: The Rhetoric of Women's History," *Journal of American History* 74 (1988–89); Nancy Cott, *The Bonds of Womanhood: "Women's Sphere" in New England, 1780–1835* (New Haven, 1977); Jeanne Boydston, *Home and Work: Housework, Wages, and the Ideology of Labor in the Early Republic* (New York, 1990); Carroll Smith-Rosenberg, "The Female World

of Love and Ritual: Relations between Women in Nineteenth Century America," *Signs: Journal of Women in Culture and Society* 1 (1975).

65. Jabour, *Marriage in the Early Republic;* see esp. pp. 163–70.

66. Brugger, *Beverley Tucker,* 39; Fanny Coalter Tucker to SGT, 21 Sept., 1 June 1803. See also Fanny Tucker Coalter to John Coalter, 27 Sept. 1809, SGT to Fanny Tucker Coalter, 17 Feb. 1809, BCT Coll. Coalter faced similar complaints during his first two marriages; see John Coalter to SGT, 30 Nov. 1795, Margaret Coalter to SGT, 10 Jan. 1796. On 24 April 1812 Henry complained to his father, "*I* am more a slave than ever" to the law because of the constant need to travel and attend court sessions.

67. Daniel Jordan notes in *Political Leadership* that many Old Dominion politicians of this era were farmers as well as lawyers. On the demand for Virginia wheat, see Shade, *Democratizing the Old Dominion,* 30–33.

68. Fanny Tucker Coalter to John Coalter, 7, 12 Sept. 1809, 12 Sept., 3 Oct. 1810, John Coalter to Fanny Tucker Coalter, [1802?], 4, 9, 15 April, 10 Sept. 1809, 8 Sept. 1810, [John Coalter?] to [?], April 1809, BCT Coll.; John Coalter to SGT, 1 June 1809, 23 Jan. 1810.

69. Fanny Tucker Coalter to John Coalter, 9 March 1804, BCT Coll.; Fanny Tucker Coalter to SGT, 8 May 1806. See also Fanny Tucker Coalter to SGT and Lelia Skipwith Tucker, 23 March 1809. Fanny Coalter also depended upon her mother-in-law, Frances Davenport, for assistance with cloth production; see Fanny Tucker Coalter to Frances Davenport, 28 Feb. 1803, BP. For Fanny's cloth production on the estate, see Fanny Tucker Coalter to John Coalter, 11 April 1809, BCT Coll.

70. Fanny Tucker Coalter to SGT and Lelia Skipwith Tucker, 27 Dec. 1809, NBT to SGT, 11 May 1804.

71. Lois Green Carr and Lorena S. Walsh, "Economic Diversification and Labor Organization in the Chesapeake, 1650–1820," in *Work and Labor in Early America,* ed. Stephen Innes (Chapel Hill, N.C., 1988), 176.

72. Starnes, *Sixty Years of Branch Banking in Virginia,* 14–15; Drew R. McCoy, *The Last of the Fathers: James Madison and the Republican Legacy* (Cambridge, Mass., 1989), 15–16, and "The Virginia Port Bill of 1784," *VMHB* 83 (1975): 288–303; Wiebe, *Opening of American Society,* 150.

73. John Barnes to SGT, 12 Jan. 1794. For Tucker's dealings with Richmond merchants, see James Brown to SGT, 5 Jan. 1794, Robert Burton to SGT, 15 Dec. 1800, Robert Patton to SGT, 5 March 1809; for Philadelphia merchants, see John Barnes to SGT, 15 March, 22 June 1794, 21 Nov. 1795; for dealings with Norfolk merchants, see Donald Campbell to SGT, 15 Jan. 1795, Archibald Campbell to SGT, 11 Feb. 1797, John Tabb to SGT, 1 Feb. 1810, SGT to Edward Waddy, 4 April 1817, Edward Waddy to SGT, 7, 11 April 1817. In the early 1800s Tucker started to sell and buy goods from Baltimore and New York City; for dealings with Baltimore merchants, see John P. Pleasants to SGT, 24 May 1808, 8 Aug. 1812, SGT to Joseph C. Cabell, 8 Oct. 1808, John Richeson to SGT, 9 Oct. 1816, John Pleasants & Sons to SGT, 18 Oct. 1821. Tucker also kept abreast of prices for corn and wheat in New York City; see SGT to Joseph C. Cabell, 19 May 1808, BP.

74. John Coalter to SGT, 18 May 1811, BCT Coll.

75. John Coalter to Fanny Tucker Coalter, [1807], ibid.; Personal Property Tax

Records, Augusta County, 1809, LV. The Coalters also owned two slaves between the ages of 12 to 16.

76. Fanny Tucker Coalter to John Coalter, 4 Oct. 1809, BCT Coll. For plantation mistresses, see Fox-Genovese, *Within the Plantation Household,* 1–35.

77. Fanny Tucker Coalter to John Coalter, 30 Aug. 1803, 11, 19, 26 April 1809, BCT Coll. Judith Randolph, isolated on Bizarre, wrote John Randolph about her many difficulties on the farm, adding, "How differently would your admirable mother have acted in such a situation" (Judith Randolph to JR, 3 Nov. 1809, BP).

78. Fanny Tucker Coalter to John Coalter, 18 April 1804, BCT Coll.; John Coalter to SGT, 19 April 1804. See also Fanny Tucker Coalter to JR, 18 March 1809 [transcript], John Randolph Papers, VHS; Fanny Tucker Coalter to John Coalter, 10 Oct. 1809, 30 March, 12 Sept. 1810, 20 April 1811, BCT Coll.; NBT to SGT, 16 Dec. 1802, Fanny Tucker Coalter to SGT, 16 May 1805, 18 May 1809.

79. Fanny Tucker Coalter to Frances Davenport, 23 Jan. 1803, BP; Fanny Coalter Tucker to John Coalter, 28, 30 March, 11 April 1810, BCT Coll.; see also HSGT to SGT, 22 April 1809, Fanny Tucker Coalter to SGT, 27 Dec. 1809, Polly Coalter Tucker to SGT, 10 Dec. 1809. For similar tensions in William and Elizabeth Wirt's marriage, see Jabour, *Marriage in the Early Republic,* 91.

80. Maria Rind to [John Coalter], [June–Aug. 1790], BCT Coll.

81. Fanny Tucker Coalter to Frances Davenport, 23 Jan. 1803, BP; Polly Coalter Tucker to Fanny Tucker Coalter, 15 July 1810.

82. Fanny Tucker Coalter to SGT, 18 Feb. 1804.

83. Fanny Tucker Coalter to John Coalter, 27 Sept. 1809, 3 Oct., 27 April 1810, BCT Coll.

84. Fanny Tucker Coalter to Frances Davenport, 23 Jan. 1803, BP.

85. SGT to Joseph C. Cabell, 13 Aug. 1807, ibid.

5. Disillusion and Reaction

1. Philip Norborne Nicholas to SGT, 13 Nov. 1803, Legislative Petitions, LV. This letter is also cited in Cullen, *Tucker and Law in Virginia,* 167.

2. HSGT to SGT, 14 May, 5 Nov. 1803; Cullen, *Tucker and Law in Virginia,* 164. As early as 1793 Daniel Call referred to Tucker as "the most learned judge of the [General] court" (ibid.).

3. The references to Bailey's character are from "Petition of St. George Tucker to the Honourable Speaker, and the Members of the House of Delegates, of Virginia," 26 Nov. 1803, 43-page copy in Tucker's hand in the Tucker-Coleman Collection. The quote concerning "gross partiality" is from George Tucker to SGT, 18 Dec. 1803. See also SGT to George Tucker, 28 Nov. 1803, George Tucker to SGT, 11 Dec. 1803; JR to SGT, 29 Nov. 1803, Randolph-Macon Woman's College.

4. See George Tucker to SGT, 7 Jan. 1804; Cullen, *Tucker and Law in Virginia,* chap. 9; Robert Bailey, *The Life and Adventures of Robert Bailey* (Richmond, 1822); Wyatt-Brown, *Southern Honor,* 151, 346–47.

5. Quoted in Bruce, *Randolph of Roanoke* 2:268. See also Thomas Tudor Tucker to John Page, 24 Dec. 1803, Thomas Tudor Tucker Papers, LC.

6. [SGT], "On Patriotism," "The Old Batchelor Essays," no. 9, MS copy; see also William Wirt to SGT, 18 Aug. 1811; SGT, "Of the Several Forms of Government," *Blackstone's Commentaries* 1:31−32.

7. Sellers, *Market Revolution,* 116−17. See also Wiebe, *Opening of American Society,* 39−40; Roeber, *Faithful Magistrates and Republican Lawyers,* 177−79.

8. Kulikoff, *Tobacco and Slaves,* 281−82; SGT, "Of the Trial by Jury in Virginia," *Blackstone's Commentaries* 4:64−66; SGT to John Page, 18 July 1806, John Page Papers, Duke Univ.; see also Thomas Tudor Tucker to John Page, 24 Sept. 1807, Thomas Tudor Tucker Papers, LC; Roeber, *Faithful Magistrates,* 213−14, 224−25. For Tucker's proposals for a property qualification for jurors, see SGT, "Of the Trial by Jury in Virginia," *Blackstone's Commentaries* 4:64−71. On his proposal for the state to hire teachers of religion, see [SGT], "The Old Batchelor Essays," no. 20, MS copy; SGT, "Summary of the Laws Relative to Glebes and Churches," *Blackstone's Commentaries* 2:115−18.

9. John Page to SGT, 29 June 1806; SGT to John Page, 18 July 1806, John Page Papers; see also Thomas Tudor Tucker to John Page, 21 June 1806, Thomas Tudor Tucker Papers, LC.

10. Timothy S. Huebner, "The Consolidation of State Judicial Power: Spencer Roane, Virginia Legal Culture, and the Southern Judicial Tradition," *VMHB* 102 (1994): 60.

11. See, for instance, F. Thornton Miller, *Juries and Judges versus the Law: Virginia's Provincial Legal Perspective, 1783−1828* (Charlottesville, Va., 1994), 65−73.

12. Chapman Johnson to David Watson, 18 May 1800, "Letters to David Watson," *VMHB* 29 (1921): 268−70; Cullen, *Tucker and Law in Virginia,* 134−35.

13. Huebner, "Consolidation of State Judicial Power," 52−54; see also Mays, *Edmund Pendleton,* 299−300.

14. Tucker to Wirt, quoted in Henry St. George Tucker (St. George's great-grandson), "Patrick Henry and St. George Tucker," [undated], Henry Family Papers, VHS; SGT to William Wirt, 25 Sept. 1815, in "William Wirt's *Life of Patrick Henry,*" *WMQ,* 1st ser., 22 (1914): 255.

15. William Fleming to SGT, 12 May 1809, Spencer Roane to SGT, 30 May 1809, SGT to Spencer Roane, 3 June 1809. See also SGT to William Fleming, 29 April, 10, 11 May 1809, William Fleming to SGT, 30 April, 8, 10 May 1809, SGT to Spencer Roane, 31 May 1809, Spencer Roane to SGT, 2 June 1809; William Fleming to SGT, 2 April 1811, Robert Alonzo Brock Papers, VHS; Heubner, "Consolidation of State Judicial Power," 61−62.

16. George Tucker to SGT, 27 May, 6 July 1809; see also William Wirt to SGT, 9 June 1809.

17. HSGT to SGT, 23 May 1809; JR to SGT, 5 June 1809, Randolph-Macon Woman's College. See also Thomas Tudor Tucker to SGT, 12 March 1810, NBT to SGT, 18 June 1809, Robert Saunders to SGT, Jan. 1810.

18. Fanny Tucker Coalter to SGT, 4 Oct. 1809; see also SGT to John Coalter, 22 Nov., 9 Dec. 1811, Grinnan Family Papers, VHS.

19. See esp. Jan Lewis, "'The Blessings of Domestic Society': Thomas Jefferson's Family and the Transformation of American Politics," *Jeffersonian Legacies,* ed. Peter S. Onuf (Charlottesville, Va., 1993), 109–46.

20. SGT to Fanny Tucker Coalter, 15 Jan. 1807, BCT Coll. See also SGT to Fanny Tucker Coalter, 15 May 1807, 5 Feb. 1808, ibid.

21. SGT to Joseph C. Cabell, 13 Aug. 1807, BP; HSGT to SGT, 22 April 1809; SGT to John Coalter, 14 June 1809, BCT Coll. See also SGT to John Coalter, 7 July 1809, ibid.

22. SGT to James Monroe, 26 Dec. 1810; SGT to James Monroe, 2 April 1811, *Calendar of State Papers* 10:102–7. See also SGT, "Rough Draft" to Governor Monroe, 25 Jan. 1811."

23. SGT to Joseph C. Cabell, 4 Jan. 1811. See also NBT to SGT, 10 Jan. 1811, George Tucker to SGT, 12 Jan., 15 March 1811, HSGT to SGT, 27 Feb., 3 March, 4 April 1811.

24. Jordan, *Political Leadership,* 158–61.

25. Quoted in Kenneth Shorey, ed., *Collected Letters of John Randolph of Roanoke to Dr. John Brockenbrough, 1812–1833* (New Brunswick, N.J., 1988), xvi-xvii. On the absence of any systematic theory behind Randolph's thinking, see Dawidoff, *Education of John Randolph,* 259–60.

26. Jordan, *Political Leadership,* 222–23; Norman K. Risjord, *The Old Republicans: Southern Conservatism in the Age of Jefferson* (New York, 1965), 19–20; Bruce, *Randolph of Roanoke* 1:158–78.

27. Risjord, *Old Republicans,* 25, 40–41, 42, 66; Dawidoff, *Education of John Randolph,* 173–83. See also Peter Magrath, *Yazoo: Law and Politics in the New Republic* (Providence, 1966).

28. JR to SGT, 27 Dec. 1807, Randolph-Macon Woman's College; JR to Fanny Tucker Coalter, 11 April 1807, Tucker-Coalter Papers, Perkins Library, Duke Univ.; Judith Randolph to JR, 29 Jan. 1808.

29. HSGT to SGT, 19 Feb. 1809, 7 Nov. 1807.

30. For St. George Tucker's unhappiness with his son's decision to run for office, see HSGT to SGT, 1 March 1807, 10 Feb. 1805.

31. Shade, *Democratizing the Old Dominion,* 115; Jordan, *Political Leadership;* Richard E. Ellis, *The Jeffersonian Crisis: Courts and Politics in the Young Republic* (New York, 1971), 116; Roeber, *Faithful Magistrates and Republican Lawyers,* 252, 254, 259–60; George Tucker, *The Valley of Shenandoah, or Memoirs of the Graysons,* 2 vols. (1824; rept. Chapel Hill, N.C., 1970), 1:228–29; HSGT to SGT, 27 March, 7 April 1807.

32. See esp. JR to James Monroe, 20 March 1806, quoted in Bruce, *Randolph of Roanoke* 1:333–34. See also JR to James Monroe, 17 April 1807, Monroe Papers, LC.

33. Risjord, *Old Republicans,* 75, 86–88.

34. Ibid., 90–91.

35. HSGT to SGT, 3 March, 14 Jan. 1809, 1, 3 March 1810; see also HSGT to SGT, 19 Feb. 1809, 31 May 1811, 6 Feb. 1813. For similar disgust, see Joseph C. Cabell to SGT, 2 Feb. 1813.

36. NBT to SGT, 23 May 1807.

37. Wyatt-Brown, *Southern Honor,* 38. On immigration into the Old Dominion, see Shade, *Democratizing the Old Dominion,* 24, 132–34.

38. NBT to JR, 15 April 1806, NBT to SGT, 25 April, 23 May 1807.

39. Robson, *Educating Republicans,* 170–71, 176; Brugger, *Beverley Tucker,* 16–17; NBT to JR, 12 Jan. 1807, HSGT to SGT, 14 Jan. 1809.

40. Brugger, *Beverley Tucker,* 28–29; NBT, "Garland's *Life of Randolph," Southern Quarterly Review* 4 (July 1851): 43.

41. Brugger, *Beverley Tucker,* 28–29. For John Randolph's familiarity with Burke's work, see Bruce, *Randolph of Roanoke* 2:410; see also JR to Richard Kidder Randolph, 15 Feb. 1814, John Randolph Papers, LC.

42. JR to Josiah Quincy, 1 July 1814, John Randolph Papers, LC.

43. HSGT to SGT, 1 March 1810. Henry's reference probably was to Thomas Church (1717–1756), an English divine and author of *An Analysis of the Philosophical Works of the Late Viscount Bolingbroke* (London, 1755).

44. JR to Fanny Tucker Coalter, 11 Oct. 1805, Tucker-Coalter Papers; NBT to JR, 12 Feb. 1806.

45. HSGT to SGT, 3 June 1817. For Henry St. George Tucker's land, see Samuel Hanway to SGT, 27 Sept. 1796, HSGT to SGT, 19 Feb. 1809, 9 Aug., 16 Sept. 1818; Land Tax Records, Frederick County, 1810, Winchester City, 1805, 1816, 1820, LV.

46. HSGT to SGT, 21 Aug. 1810, 3 June 1817; on the number of Henry's slaves, see Personal Property Tax Records, Winchester City, 1815, LV. See also HSGT to SGT, 19 Feb. 1809, 22 June 1811, 25 July 1820. For the divided personas of both farmer and lawyer or judge, see John Coalter to SGT, 30 July 1810; Shepard, "Lawyers Look at Themselves," 10–11; Jordan, *Political Leadership,* 51, 54, 72.

47. NBT to SGT, 27 May, 18 June 1809, May 1813, to John Coalter, 20 Dec. 1808.

48. Dunn, "Black Society in the Chesapeake," 58–59; Robert McColley, *Slavery and Jeffersonian Virginia,* 2d ed. (Urbana, Ill., 1973), 117. For the geographical spread of slavery in the 1790s, see Frey, *Water from the Rock,* 218.

49. SGT, "Reflection," Unnumbered Notebooks, no. 1, 60. For these rumors, see Larry E. Tise, *Proslavery: A History of the Defense of Slavery in America, 1701–1840* (Athens, Ga., 1987), 199–200. For a minor controversy against Tucker when he expressed his concerns publicly, see Daniel Brent to John Tyler, 17 Feb. 1798, Lawrence Brook, "Recollection of a Conversation," 17 May 1798.

50. Douglas R. Egerton, *Gabriel's Rebellion: The Virginia Slave Conspiracies of 1800 and 1802* (Chapel Hill, N.C., 1993), chap. 6; John Randolph quoted in McColley, *Slavery and Jeffersonian Virginia,* 108–9. See also George Tucker to SGT, 1 Sept., 2 Nov. 1800.

51. George Tucker, *Letter to a Member of the General Assembly of Virginia, on the Subject of the Late Conspiracy of the Slaves with a Proposal for Their Colonization* (Richmond, 1801). See also Egerton, *Gabriel's Rebellion,* 151–62; James Sidbury, *Ploughshares into Swords: Race, Rebellion, and Identity in Gabriel's Virginia, 1730–1810* (Cambridge, 1997), 130–31.

52. Egerton, *Gabriel's Rebellion,* 163–68; McColley, *Slavery and Jeffersonian Virginia,* 159–61; Helen Tunnicliff Catterall, ed., *Judicial Cases concerning American Slavery and the Negro* (Washington, D.C., 1926), 1:73; [SGT], *Reflections on the Cession of Louisiana to the United States* (Washington, D.C., 1803), in Scott, "St. George Tucker and the Development of American Culture," 258–81 (quote on 279).

53. The case *Hudgins v. Wright* (1806) reveals with particular clarity how the now-

aging Revolutionary gave up the fight; see Phillip Hamilton, "Revolutionary Principles and Family Loyalties: Slavery's Transformation in the St. George Tucker Household of Early National Virginia," *WMQ*, 3d ser., 55 (Oct. 1998): 543–44.

54. Rose, "Domestication of Domestic Slavery," 22–23. On slavery in the colonial era, see esp. Ira Berlin, *Many Thousands Gone: The First Two Centuries of Slavery in North America* (Cambridge, Mass., 1998); Morgan, *Slave Counterpoint.*

55. SGT to John Coalter, 21 Feb. 1802, Indenture concerning marriage of John Coalter to Anne Frances Tucker, 5 June 1802, Fanny Tucker Coalter to SGT, 27 Jan. 1804, Fanny Tucker Coalter to Lelia Skipwith Tucker, 11 April 1805. See also Fanny Tucker Coalter to Frances Davenport, 28 Feb. 1803, BP; Fanny Tucker Coalter to SGT, 1 June, 10 Aug. 1803.

56. Lelia Skipwith Tucker to Fanny Tucker Coalter, 12[?] Dec. 1808, BCT Coll.; Polly Coalter Tucker to SGT, March 1811. For a child speaking sentimentally about slaves inside the household, see Frances Lelia Coalter to Fanny and John Coalter, 10, 31 July 1813, BCT Coll.

57. SGT to Fanny Tucker Coalter, 6 Feb. [1804?], BCT Coll.; HSGT to SGT, 19 May 1819, NBT to SGT, 23 Feb. 1812. See also SGT to John Coalter, 21 Sept. 1808, BCT Coll.; HSGT to SGT, 16 Jan., 8 March 1820, NBT to SGT, 24 July 1814, 13 July 1817, 25 June 1825, NBT to Elizabeth Tucker Coalter, 14 Aug. 1828.

58. Brown, *Good Wives, Nasty Wenches,* 356–59 (quote on 358); Morgan, *Slave Counterpoint,* chap. 9.

59. John Randolph's Commonplace Book, [1810s?].

60. NBT to SGT, 21 April 1808, 23 Feb. 1812, Fulwar Skipwith to St. George Tucker, 12 Nov. 1817; Freehling, *Road to Disunion,* 60. See also NBT to SGT, 30 Jan. 1814.

61. [SGT], "The Old Batchelor Essays," no. 26, MS copy. See also Genovese, *Roll, Jordan, Roll,* 49–70; James Oakes, *The Ruling Race: A History of American Slaveholding* (New York, 1982), 135–36; Rose, "Domestication of Domestic Slavery"; Lewis, "Problem of Slavery," 289–90; Frey, *Water from the Rock,* 279–80. For the Tuckers' growing dependence upon their bondpeople for confirmation of their own goodness and worth, see NBT to SGT, 7 Nov. 1804, Elizabeth McCroskey to SGT, 23 Dec. 1803, 16 Jan. 1804.

62. HSGT to SGT, 17 Feb., 1 March 1804. For a different interpretation of this incident, see Mechal Sobel, *The World They Made Together: Black and White Values in Eighteenth-Century Virginia* (Princeton, N.J., 1987), 143–44.

63. Fanny Tucker Coalter to John Coalter, 12 Sept. 1809, Lelia Skipwith Tucker to Fanny Tucker Coalter, 23 March 1812, BCT Coll.; SGT to Joseph C. Cabell, 12 Feb 1808, BP. Not only did St. George separate Bob from his mother, but in 1815 he separated an elderly slave named Peter Baten from his loved ones who worked in the Williamsburg mansion; see Peter Baten to SGT, 17 June 1815; see also Ellyson Currie to SGT, 25 Aug. 1808.

64. JR to John Brockenbrough, 20 Feb. 1826, quoted in Garland, *Life of Randolph* 2:266–67; see also ibid., 222.

65. Philip Barraud to SGT, [May 1812]. See also Charles Carter to SGT, 21 Nov. 1807.

66. Charles Carter to Lelia Skipwith Tucker, 18 Jan. 1813, SGT, "Memo for Mrs. Tucker," 19 Jan. 1813.

67. See Wood, *Radicalism of the American Revolution,* 327; Steven Watts, *The Republic Reborn: War and the Making of Liberal America, 1790–1820* (Baltimore, 1987).

68. HSGT to SGT, 24 Aug., 24 June 1812; Bruce, *Randolph of Roanoke* 1:378; NBT to JR, 15 April 1806. See also JR to John Coalter, 29 March 1808, John Coalter to JR, 11 May 1808, BP; Garland, *Life of Randolph* 1:236–37; Bruce, *Randolph of Roanoke* 1:234–35.

69. SGT, "Reflections on the Policy and Necessity of Encouraging the Commerce of the Citizens of the United States of America, and of Granting Them Exclusive Privileges in Trade," *American Museum* 2 (1787): 263–76, in Scott, "St. George Tucker and the Development of American Culture," 236–57 (quote on 238–39); SGT to Joseph C. Cabell, 30 July 1807, BP. To maintain a spirit of enmity against Britain during the *Chesapeake* crisis, Tucker wrote several lines of verse to be publicly read at the 1807 Fourth of July celebrations; see Prince, *Poems of St. George Tucker,* 125.

70. Thomas Tudor Tucker to SGT, 10 April 1813.

71. *The Patriot Rous'd,* in Scott, "St. George Tucker and the Creation of American Culture," 285–319 (quote on 318–19); William Wirt to SGT, 29 Jan., 9 Aug. 1812, SGT to Mr. Green, 24 June 1812.

72. Donald R. Hickey, *The War of 1812: A Forgotten Conflict* (Urbana, Ill., 1990), chap. 1.

73. HSGT to Governor James Barbour, 6 July 1813, 14 Aug., 26 July 1814, *Calendar of Virginia State Papers* 10:245, 361; Frances Lelia Coalter to John and Fanny Tucker Coalter, 18 July 1813, BCT Coll.; HSGT to SGT, 14 Aug. 1813, 8 Sept., 3 Dec. 1814. See also HSGT to SGT, 23 Jan. 1815.

74. NBT to SGT, 3 July 1813; Brugger, *Beverley Tucker,* 45.

75. NBT to SGT, 24 Aug. 1813, 14 Sept., 18 Dec. 1814, 18 Jan. 1815, Polly Tucker to SGT, 4 Sept. 1814, NBT to John Coalter, 24 Sept., 10 Dec. 1814. On sickness at the Norfolk encampment, see Philip Barraud to SGT, 17 Jan. 1813 [1814?]; Bruce, *Randolph of Roanoke* 1:402.

76. For St. George Tucker's worries about his sons, see SGT to John Coalter, 9 Aug. [Sept.?] 1814, John Coalter to SGT, 13 Sept., [17 Sept. 1814], Thomas Tudor Tucker to SGT, 1 Oct. 1814. For the enemy raid at Corotoman, see Joseph C. Cabell to SGT, 6 May 1813, Thomas Tudor Tucker to SGT, 7 July 1813, SGT to Henry Tucker of Sandy's Parish, 2 May 1815. See also Joseph C. Cabell to SGT, 13 Feb., 20 Feb., 24 Nov. 1813; SGT to Fanny Tucker Coalter, 9 July 1813, Joseph C. Cabell to John Coalter, 24 July 1813, Joseph C. Cabell to Fanny Tucker Coalter, 31 July 1813, BCT Coll..

77. John Coalter to SGT, 2 Oct. 1814; see also HSGT to SGT, 15 May 1814, Philip Barraud to SGT, 2 Aug., 30 Aug. 1814, John Coalter to SGT, 30 Aug. 1814, John Hockaday to SGT, 29 Aug. 1814.

78. Thomas Tudor Tucker to SGT, 24 Aug., 9 Sept. 1814; see also Thomas Tudor Tucker to SGT, 28 May, 27 Sept. 1814, 21 June 1815.

79. William Wirt to SGT, 19 Jan. 1815.

80. Philip Barraud to SGT, 14 Feb. 1815.

81. SGT, *The Patriot Cool'd,* MS copy, 2, 17.

82. See Bruce, *Randolph of Roanoke* 1:376–77.

83. SGT, *The Patriot Cool'd,* MS copy, 13, 37.

84. JR to Josiah Quincy, 11 Dec. 1813, quoted in Bruce, *Randolph of Roanoke* 1:404; JR's Commonplace Book, [1814]; *Richmond Enquirer,* 1 April 1815.

85. Risjord, *Old Republicans,* 164–65, 226.

6. Twilight

1. SGT to Fanny Tucker Coalter, 24 April 1807, Fanny Tucker Coalter to John Coalter, 20 Sept., 10 Oct. 1809, 30 March, 2 Sept. 1810, BCT Coll.

2. SGT and Lelia Skipwith Tucker to Fanny Tucker Coalter, 27 Aug. 1813, ibid.

3. John Coalter to JR, 25 Sept. 1813, SGT to John Coalter, 8 Oct. 1813, ibid.; Lelia Skipwith Tucker to John Coalter, 3 Sept. 1813. On the dead becoming perfected beings, see Elizabeth Tucker to SGT, 29 April 1816.

4. SGT to Fanny Tucker Coalter, 5 Feb. 1808, BCT Coll.

5. Judith Randolph to SGT, 28 Sept. 1808, to JR, 21 Nov. 1807; Judith Randolph to Mary Randolph Harrison, [1806], quoted in Cynthia A. Kierner, "Dark and Dense Cloud," 208.

6. SGT to Joseph C. Cabell, 13 Aug. 1807, BP; SGT to Fanny Tucker Coalter, 15 Jan. 1807, BCT Coll.; see also John Coalter to JR, 11 May 1808, BP.

7. SGT to Joseph C. Cabell, 13 Aug. 1807, BP.

8. Price, *Poems of St. George Tucker,* 11–12.

9. Charles Royster, *The Fabulous History of the Dismal Swamp Company: A Story of George Washington's Times* (New York, 1999), 290, 314, 369–70, 402–5.

10. Kierner, "Dark and Dense Cloud," 205.

11. SGT to Fanny Tucker Coalter, 22 Jan. 1804, 11 June 1803, BCT Coll. For the effect of the growing influence of women upon entertainment, see Isaac, *Transformation of Virginia,* 303, 309–10. For Fanny Coalter's assertion that entertaining company helped her overcome her "extreme grief" at her husband's many absences, see Fanny Tucker Coalter to John Coalter, 1 Sept. 1811, Grinnan Family Papers, VHS.

12. SGT to Fanny Tucker Coalter, 3 Aug. 1812, BCT Coll.

13. Lelia Skipwith Tucker to Fanny Tucker Coalter, 30 May [1809?], 17 March 1809, ibid.; William Nelson Jr. to SGT, 2 March 1809. See also SGT to Fanny Tucker Coalter, 23 Feb. 1810, BCT Coll. On the importance of colonial gardens to gentility, see Bushman, *Refinement of America,* 127–31.

14. See Smith-Rosenberg, "Female World of Love and Ritual." See also Kerber, "Separate Spheres"; Cott, *Bonds of Womanhood;* Smith, *Inside the Great House,* 249–60; Degler, *At Odds,* 189–92.

15. Judith Randolph to Fanny Tucker Coalter, 25 Oct. 1807, 21 Feb. 1808, BCT Coll. See also Judith Randolph to Fanny Tucker Coalter, 3 March 1812, ibid.; Kierner, "Dark and Dense Cloud," 202–3.

16. Lelia Skipwith Tucker to Fanny Tucker Coalter, 20 Nov. 1807, April 1805, BCT Coll. On visiting as a new phenomenon in Virginia, see George Tucker, "Autobiography," 98–99.

17. See, for instance, Rebecca Innes to SGT, 3 March 1809, Harry Innes to SGT, 22 Aug. 1811.

18. On evangelicalism in the South, see John B. Boles, *The Great Revival, 1787–1815* (Lexington, Ky., 1972); Isaac, *Transformation of Virginia,* pt. 2; Lewis, *Pursuit of Happiness,* 45–68; Kierner, *Beyond the Household,* chap. 5. On the changing meaning of virtue, see Ruth H. Bloch, "The Gendered Meanings of Virtue in Revolutionary America," *Signs* 13 (1987): 37–58.

19. HSGT to SGT, 3 March 1805, Philip Barraud to SGT, 17 Dec. 1812; JR to George Hay, 23 Oct. 1808, John Randolph Papers, VHS; see also Philip Barraud to SGT, 21 Jan. 1813, and Tucker's poem "Woman" (dated 11 Sept 1819). For Elizabeth Merry, see Catherine Allgor, *Parlor Politics: In Which the Ladies of Washington Help Build a City and a Government* (Charlottesville, Va., 2000), 42–47.

20. John Page to SGT, 17 May 1807.

21. For examples, see Henry Tucker Sr. to SGT, 31 July 1774, John Page to SGT, 28 Sept. 1776, 5 April 1780, Henry Tucker Jr. to SGT, 14 April 1784, Donald Campbell to SGT, 7 March 1785. See also SGT to Theodorick Bland Jr., 3 Jan. 1781, BP.

22. Sir Peyton Skipwith to SGT, 12 Dec. 1795. See also Martha Bland to SGT, 17 March 1786, Thomas Tudor Tucker to SGT, 29 May 1786, 29 June 1794, Henry Tucker of Somerset to St. George Tucker, 30 May 1786. For the near absence of mourning for children who died before the age of two in early modern England, see Stone, *Family, Sex, Marriage,* 81, 420.

23. John Coalter to SGT, 28 June 1805, HSGT to SGT, 12 Feb. 1808, NBT to John Coalter, 3 Jan. 1810; Brugger, *Beverley Tucker,* 43–45. Naming patterns continued much as they had beforehand; Henry dutifully named his first son St. George. Boys were still preferable to girls; see Ann Cary (Nancy) Randolph to SGT, 29 June 1805.

24. Fanny Tucker Coalter to SGT and Lelia Skipwith Tucker, 17 Aug. 1809, John Coalter to SGT, 25 May 1804; Fanny Tucker Coalter to JR, 18 March 1809 [transcript], John Randolph Papers, VHS.

25. Frances Tucker to SGT, Aug. 1800.

26. Fanny Tucker Coalter to SGT, 4 Nov. 1803; Judith Randolph to JR, 12 April 1803, BP.

27. HSGT to SGT, 22 April 1809.

28. On the decline of indiscriminate hospitality, see Bushman, *Refinement of America,* chap. 8; Kierner, *Beyond the Household,* 145–47, and "Genteel Balls and Republican Parades: Gender and Early Southern Civil Rituals, 1677–1826," *VMHB* 104 (1996): 193–99; Wyatt-Brown, *Southern Honor,* 90–92, 331–39; Isaac, *Transformation of Virginia,* 302–11.

29. John Allison to SGT, 4 Jan. 1800; see also William Wirt to SGT, 25 Aug. 1811.

30. NBT to SGT, 4 Aug. 1805, HSGT to SGT, 14 July 1821; SGT to Fanny Tucker Coalter, 20 Nov. 1808, Lelia Skipwith Tucker to Elizabeth Coalter, 5 April 1822, BCT Coll.; Carl Dolmetsch, "The 'Hermit of the Mountain' Essays: Prolegomenon for a Collected Edition," in *Essays in Early Virginia Honoring Richard Beale Davis,* ed. J. A. Leo Lemay (New York, 1977).

31. See Fanny Tucker Coalter, 19 Aug. 1810, BP; NBT to SGT, 9 June 1811, HSGT to SGT, 30 July 1811.

32. SGT to JR, 14 June 1808, BP. See also JR to Fanny Tucker Coalter, 3 May 1803, BCT Coll.; SGT to JR, 21 Sept. 1808, 7 Nov. 1809, BP; JR to Fanny Tucker Coalter, 7 Nov. 1808, Tucker-Coalter Papers, Duke Univ.

33. Dawidoff, *Education of John Randolph*, 205–6. Regarding the fire at Bizarre, see Judith Randolph to SGT, 4 April 1813. When he learned of the fire, Tucker sent Judith $500.

34. JR to Harmanus Bleeker, 4 April 1814, quoted in Shorey, *Collected Letters of John Randolph*, xvii; Garland, *Life of Randolph* 2:37; JR to Josiah Quincy, 22 March 1814, John Randolph Papers, LC.

35. JR to SGT, 11 April 1814.

36. SGT to JR, 13 April 1814, JR to SGT, 14 April 1814.

37. JR to SGT, 14 April 1814.

38. JR to Josiah Quincey, 22 March 1814, John Randolph Papers, LC; JR to SGT, 14 April 1814; JR to Littleton Waller Tazewell, 8 Nov. 1814, Southern Historical Collection, Univ. of North Carolina.

39. SGT to JR, 15 April 1814, John Coalter to SGT, 7 March 1816.

40. HSGT to SGT, 4 April 1815, 22 Feb. 1816, SGT to HSGT, 10 March 1816.

41. SGT to HSGT, 10 March 1816.

42. HSGT to John Coalter, 19 March 1816, BP; HSGT to SGT, 30 April 1820. For Henry's break with Randolph, see also HSGT to SGT, 15 March, 12 April, 10 May, 10 Dec. 1816, 9 May 1819, SGT to HSGT, 19 March 1816, Thomas Tudor Tucker to SGT, 23 May 1816. For the attitudes of other family members toward Randolph, see Elizabeth Tucker to SGT, 21 June 1815, 24 April 1820. See also JR to Elizabeth Coalter, 5 Feb. 1822, John Randolph Papers, VHS.

43. NBT to SGT, 13 Dec. 1813, 16 March 1811, Judith Randolph to SGT, 3 Oct. 1807.

44. Ann Cary (Nancy) Randolph to SGT, 17 Dec. 1804.

45. NBT to SGT, 16 March, 27 Oct. 1811.

46. NBT to SGT, 16 March 1811.

47. NBT to SGT, 24 July 1814, 26 Feb. 1815; see also NBT to SGT, 25 March 1815.

48. For the Skipwiths' efforts in Louisiana, see HSGT to SGT, 27 Oct. 1799, Peyton Skipwith to SGT, 26 Dec. 1803, 6 Nov. 1804, Fulwar Skipwith to SGT, 27 Sept. 1809, 29 June 1810, 1 May 1815, 12 Nov. 1817, Evelina Skipwith to SGT, 20 April 1812, Elizabeth Skipwith to SGT, 20 Oct. 1814.

49. For Beverley's sale of land, see NBT to John Coalter, 8 Feb. 1814, 24 March, 7 May 1815, to SGT, 24 July 1814, 8 May, 24 Nov. 1815, John Coalter to SGT, 3 Jan. 1816. See also Brugger, *Beverley Tucker*, 46.

50. Polly Coalter Tucker to SGT, 3 Feb. 1811.

51. HSGT to SGT, 17 Nov. 1815; see also HSGT to SGT, 2 Jan. 1816.

52. NBT to SGT, 17 May, 11 Aug. 1816, to JR, 21 Sept. 1817; see also Polly Coalter Tucker to SGT, 13 July 1817.

53. NBT to SGT, 24 Sept. 1816; Brugger, *Beverley Tucker*, 47–49. See also NBT to SGT, 12 Dec. 1816, Polly Coalter Tucker to SGT, 21 June 1817.

54. NBT to SGT, 16 Nov. 1817; Brugger, *Beverley Tucker,* 50.

55. Brugger, *Beverley Tucker,* 51.

56. NBT to SGT, 19 Jan. 1819; see also NBT to John Coalter, 8 Jan. 1819.

57. Elizabeth Tucker to SGT, 4 July 1819.

58. [NBT], "From Missouri, Extract of a Late Letter from This Interesting Country to a Virginian," *Missouri Gazette & Public Advertiser,* 26 Jan. 1820; [NBT], "Hampden, Jun.," ibid., 16 Feb. 1820; Brugger, *Beverley Tucker,* 61.

59. Joseph C. Cabell to SGT, 10 Feb. 1820, HSGT to SGT, 8 March 1820, Robert Evans to SGT, 13 Dec. 1819.

60. See esp. *Missouri Gazette,* 7 April 1819; see also Brugger, *Beverley Tucker,* 52–57.

61. NBT to Thomas Smith, 15 May 1819.

62. *Missouri Gazette,* 28 April 1819; Brugger, *Beverley Tucker,* 77–78.

63. *Missouri Gazette,* 12, 26 May 1819.

64. Brugger, *Beverley Tucker,* 61, 70–71.

65. Polly Coalter Tucker to SGT, 23 Oct. 1819, NBT to SGT, 13 July 1817. See also NBT to SGT, 26 June 1825.

66. Judith Randolph to SGT, 22 Feb. 1816; SGT to Joseph C. Cabell, 20 Sept., 11 Oct. 1807, BP.

67. SGT to Henry Skipwith, 19 Sept. 1812, to Joseph C. Cabell, 15 Jan. 1813.

68. SGT to President James Madison, 27 Jan. 1813.

69. On early republican patriarchalism, see Kulikoff, *Tobacco and Slaves,* 166; Wood, *Radicalism of the American Revolution,* 183–84; Norton, *Liberty's Daughters,* 230–35, 243–46; Mintz and Kellogg, *Domestic Revolutions,* 54; Wall, *Fierce Communion,* 131–33. See also John Demos, "The Changing Face of Fatherhood," *Past, Present, and Personal: The Family and the Life Course in American History* (New York, 1986), 41–67.

70. SGT to Ann Cary (Nancy) Randolph Morris, 16 Aug. 1820.

71. SGT to Elizabeth Coalter, 14 Sept. 1822, BCT Coll. Tucker's children often had to defend themselves from charges of neglect; see JR to SGT, 3 Nov. 1801, 7 Dec. 1804, 10 July 1807, Randolph-Macon Woman's College; NBT to SGT, 30 Oct. 1804, 8 Feb. 1807, 28 Aug. 1808, 19 Feb. 1817, 7 Aug. 1826, HSGT to SGT, 5 Oct. 1816, 14 July 1817.

72. John Coalter to SGT, 16 Aug. 1816; SGT to John Coalter, July 1816[?], John Coalter Papers, VHS.

73. For the court's expansion, see Miller, *Juries and Judges versus the Law,* 72.

74. John Coalter to SGT, 18 May, 30 May 1811; SGT to John Coalter, 3 June 1811, BCT Coll. See also HSGT to SGT, 31 May 1811.

75. Thomas Tudor Tucker to SGT, 26 April, 27 June 1808, 9 Dec. 1811, 3 May, 26 May, 11 Sept. 1817. For other loans by the brothers, see George Tucker, "Autobiography," 126; George Tucker to SGT, 2 July 1809, SGT to Henry W. Tucker, 3 Feb. 1826, niece Elizabeth Tucker to SGT, 23 July 1826, Henry W. Tucker to SGT, 19 Oct 1824. On worries among some family members that St. George was stretching himself too thin with these gifts, see John Coalter to SGT, 19 Dec. 1815, SGT to John Coalter, 27 April 1817.

76. See Elizabeth Tucker to SGT, 6 April 1801. See also Frances Tucker to SGT, [April 1804], Elizabeth Tucker to SGT, 7 Feb., 23 Sept. 1807, 17 June 1811, 21 June 1815,

16 Nov. 1816, Thomas Tudor Tucker to SGT, May 1812, Edward Waddy to SGT, 1 June 1816, W. G. Lyford to SGT, 6 Feb. 1826. For St. George's shipments of foodstuffs and cash to the six daughters of their distant cousin Colonel Jennings of Sandy's Parish, see Edmund Waddy to SGT, 6 Feb. 1815, 15 June 1818, Elizabeth Tucker to SGT, 5 May 1818, Katherine Brownlow to SGT, 24 July 1822, Robert J. Tucker to SGT, 27 May 1822, Elizabeth Tucker to SGT, 13 May 1825, Richard Tucker Jr. to SGT, 17 April 1826.

77. This letter of Robert J. Tucker was transcribed for St. George in Thomas Tudor Tucker to SGT, 27 July 1822.

78. Richard J. Tucker to SGT, 2 Aug. 1825.

79. NBT to SGT, 10 Dec. 1809.

80. HSGT to SGT, 24 Dec. 1809. On this broader trend within Virginia of neglecting extended family ties, see Smith, *Inside the Great House,* 289–90.

81. SGT to Fanny Tucker Coalter, 10 Sept. 1813, to Elizabeth Coalter, 10 Aug. 1822, BCT Coll.; SGT to John Coalter, 3 Oct. 1813, HSGT to SGT, Jan. 1818, 23 Jan. 1821, Polly Coalter Tucker to SGT, 9 July 1819, John Coalter to SGT, 10 June 1826.

82. HSGT to SGT, 12 June 1822.

83. Henry Tucker of Sandy's Parish to SGT, 18 Nov. 1810.

84. Elizabeth Tucker to SGT, 29 April, 16 Nov 1816, Henry Tucker of Sandy's Parish to SGT, 22 Oct. 1817, Thomas Tudor Tucker to SGT, 28 Nov. 1817, 27 Aug., 28 Dec. 1818, 16 Jan., 16 April 1819.

85. Elizabeth Tucker to SGT, [Jan. 1821?], SGT to Henry Tucker of Sandy's Parish, 2 Jan. 1820 [1821]; see also Henry Tucker of Sandy's Parish to SGT, 9 Jan., 15 Feb. 1821.

86. Thomas Tudor Tucker to SGT, 10 March 1821. Tucker of Sandy's Parish returned to America in 1823 but did not again approach his Uncle St. George; see Thomas Tudor Tucker to SGT, 13 March 1823. For the troubles faced by other nephews in Bermuda, see Elizabeth Tucker to SGT, 12 Nov. 1822, 10 March 1825.

87. HSGT to SGT, 10 May 1816. On the growing burdens of public duties, see George Tucker to SGT, 12 Feb. 1820. For George's complaint that while he was in Congress, his legal practice quickly left him, see George Tucker, "Autobiography," 131.

88. HSGT to SGT, 10 March 1819, 8 Sept. 1818, 10 May 1816.

89. See St. George Coalter to St. George Tucker, 14 Oct. 1825, BP.

90. John Coalter to SGT, 19 July 1818.

91. NBT to SGT, 2 July 1825; see also Polly Coalter Tucker to SGT, 26 April 1825, NBT to SGT, 17 May 1825.

92. See, for instance, John Page Jr.'s moving letter to St. George Tucker, 9 Oct. 1827. Robert Brugger states that Beverley was indifferent to his father's death. Brugger, however, incorrectly dates the elder Tucker's death as in 1826 instead of 1827; see Brugger, *Beverley Tucker,* 71.

93. HSGT to St. George Coalter, 10 May 1828, BCT Coll. See also Brugger, *Beverley Tucker,* 71–72; John Coalter to SGT, 24 Aug. 1827.

94. NBT to Elizabeth Coalter, 19 May 1828.

Afterwards

1. Tucker, *Valley of Shenandoah* 1:224–26.
2. Ibid., 2:52–53.
3. Lelia Skipwith Tucker to Elizabeth Coalter, 3 Dec. 1827, BCT Coll.
4. Tucker, *Descendants of William Tucker,* 283–84.
5. Brugger, *Beverley Tucker,* 73–74.
6. HSGT to St. George Coalter, 10 May 1828, BCT Coll.
7. Bruce, *Randolph of Roanoke* 2:519, 49–60, 357.
8. St. George Hunter Tucker to NBT, 2 Aug. 1848, quoted in Tucker, *Nathaniel Beverley Tucker,* 448.
9. Brugger, *Beverley Tucker,* chaps. 5–6; Tucker, *Nathaniel Beverley Tucker,* chaps. 6–8.
10. Brugger, *Beverley Tucker,* 177–87; Tucker, *Nathaniel Beverley Tucker,* 453–57.
11. Brugger, *Beverley Tucker,* 176–77.
12. Tucker, *Nathaniel Beverley Tucker,* 466.

Index

Jeffersonian America

Jan Ellen Lewis and Peter S. Onuf, editors
Sally Hemings and Thomas Jefferson: History, Memory, and Civic Culture

Peter S. Onuf
Jefferson's Empire: The Language of American Nationhood

Catherine Allgor
*Parlor Politics: In Which the Ladies of Washington Help Build a
City and a Government*

Jeffrey L. Pasley
*"The Tyranny of Printers": Newspaper Politics in the Early American
Republic*

Herbert E. Sloan
Principle and Interest: Thomas Jefferson and the Problem of Debt (reprint)

James Horn, Jan Ellen Lewis, and Peter S. Onuf, editors
The Revolution of 1800: Democracy, Race, and the New Republic

Phillip Hamilton
*The Making and Unmaking of a Revolutionary Family: The Tuckers of
Virginia, 1752–1830*